DHARMENDRA

DHARMENDRA

NOT JUST A HE-MAN

A BIOGRAPHY

RAJIV VIJAYAKAR

RUPA

Published by
Rupa Publications India Pvt. Ltd 2018
7/16, Ansari Road, Daryaganj
New Delhi 110002

Sales centres:
Allahabad Bengaluru Chennai
Hyderabad Jaipur Kathmandu
Kolkata Mumbai

ISBN: 978-93-5333-298-3

First impression 2018

10 9 8 7 6 5 4 3 2 1

The moral right of the author has been asserted.

For my wife, Nishika
who I hope remains my fan as much as she is of Dharmendra
And for darling Ananya,
for simply being there during my low phases

Contents

My book on him was all pre-ordained!

Yes, some things are pre-ordained, and are simply beyond the rules and laws of science. They are beyond logic, beyond anything remotely explicable. As I sit down to write this prologue to my book, one thought echoes and re-echoes in my conscious mind: I was probably predestined to write this!

A bit of background here: My parents were raised in Mumbai city, and were as crazy about films as was possible to be in those days. My father was working for a leading bank; and my parents' only link with their roots, when he was posted in different parts of India, was Hindi cinema.

Since I was the only son, I was carted along to the theatres since the age of five, thus kicking off my exposure to and eventual love affair for films. So, by the time I was ten, with my parents then based in New Delhi, I was already a 'veteran' of a few Dharmendra films.

Once upon a time, my family and I stayed at the Hotel Clarks Shiraz, Agra, along with some relatives visiting from Mumbai. We were three kids, gambolling outside in the foyer while the grown-ups were eating in the dining room. I remember making a dash to the washroom, and banging my head on someone's midriff on the way.

All I recall now is that two strong hands helped me regain my balance. I looked up to a gentle smile, and some remark that I did not catch in my nervousness. The face was familiar—wasn't he the man who had starred in one of my favourite songs at the time: 'Saathiya Nahin Jaana Ke Jee Na Lage' from the film *Aya Sawan Jhoom Ke*?

Yes, he was! It was Dharmendra, and this was our first 'meeting' ever! I mumbled an apology and ran(!) from there. And did not meet him again until well over thirty-five years later! And how that happened is a super story in itself. As a journalist, having 'broken into' very well-established publications in my early days as a freelancer, I would often suggest subjects for interviews. This enabled me to meet the iconic stars, film-makers, music makers and technicians whose work I cherished and had enjoyed over the years.

Those were the times when my suggestions to meet and interview Dharmendra were nixed with disdain. He was passé, one editor told me. The truth was that he was acting in several big films that were unceasingly bombing at the box-office, and he was also taking on smaller, less 'respectable' action films. I read somewhere then that he was doing all of this to support his extended family of multiple relatives and to invest in a studio he was planning to build near Mumbai. And Sunny Super Sound had also just come up in Juhu, Mumbai.

Around 2006, he had started working on three decent films— Anurag Basu's *Life In A ... Metro*, Sriram Raghavan's *Johnny Gaddaar*, and Anil Sharma's *Apne*, which was his home production.

In June 2007, *Apne* (featuring his sons Sunny Deol and Bobby Deol with Dharmendra for the first-time) was set to release. A few days before that, my colleague Lisa Tsering at *India-West* (the newspaper for which I write in the United States) had mailed me, stating that Dharmendra was going to be in the US for the film's premiere. She wanted to know if I had any specific questions to be asked of him from my side when she interviewed him. But all I could think of was that the movie's PR team could have had him meet me—the Indian correspondent of *India-West* in Mumbai itself (only the top Indian publications had been called, I came to know later). After all, I had once again missed meeting Dharmendra!

A day later, Lisa mailed again. She requested me to write a 250-word introduction for her interview of Dharmendra, as she was not very aware of his pre-1970s career. I replied rather emotionally that I could not encapsulate the man within such a restricted word length. After all, his career spanned forty-seven years at the time! She replied, 'Go ahead and write what you want.'

My piece on Dharmendra's life and career, also touching on his marriage to Hema Malini, emerged well over 800 words long! I mailed it across and Lisa magnanimously did not cut a word but used it as a separate piece on the same page as her interview.

After watching *Apne*, with Dharmendra in one of his finest dramatic performances in years, my ire at the PR of the film increased. But it was useless, fruitless indignation. What a man and actor! I thought. Forty-seven years after he had started out as an actor, he could still hold a film! It is my considered belief that he deserved all the Best Actor awards that year!

And then, it happened.

It was probably early in July that my mobile phone rang at breakfast one morning. 'Unknown number,' said the screen, and I said, 'Hello'. A voice that was vaguely familiar said, 'Can I speak to R.M. Vijayakar?' (That byline of mine still holds in the US).

'Speaking,' I replied. 'Who is this?'

'Dharmendra.'

The penny dropped! I gasped, 'Dharmendra, the actor?'

There was a hearty chuckle. 'Yes!'

'What can I do for you, sir?' I asked, rather nervously, fearing that I had written something he did not like in my story, for there was no other possible reason why he could have called me, an unknown writer for him.

What came from the legend was something quite the opposite, however!

'I really loved what you wrote about me, including about my marriage to Hema! I just wanted to tell you that I have read over 5,000 interviews and articles on me in my life. *Par aap ne meri rooh ko chhoo liya* (You touched my soul)!'

'Thank you, sir!' I mumbled, overwhelmed and a little incoherent in my sudden ecstasy.

'We Deols speak what we feel from the heart!' he went on. 'I am in America for another few weeks, as I have a knee surgery scheduled, but when I come back to Mumbai, I will come and hug you! Because that's how we Deols express affection!'

'Thank you, Dharamji! It was so nice of you to call up,' I said.

'I will also give you my personal number,' he added.

As he hung up, more realization sunk in. Here was a man who had done something a huge star like him absolutely did not need to do—call up my newspaper office there, get my phone number from them, and call me up from the US at a time convenient for me in India, just to thank me!

Three months passed, and then on Diwali, he called me again! He just wanted to wish me and my family. He said that he was now in India, but not in Mumbai. As promised, he gave me his personal number. And a few months later, we finally met, and the promised hug was duly given!

But this personal saga of Dharmendra will never be complete without narrating something that was kept from me by, of all people, my wife Nishika. Throughout a self-confessed fan of Anil Kapoor and later Shah Rukh Khan, she startled me in 2011 by turning out to be a huge closet fan of this magnificent star.

I had taken Nishika along for the music launch of the Deols' new film, *Yamla Pagla Deewana*, again starring him and both his sons. As a sidelight, let me also narrate what was a huge reflection of Dharmendra's goodwill: A quarter-kilometre stretch to the Novotel Hotel in Juhu, where the event was being held, was jammed with bumper-to-bumper traffic. Mumbai readers will understand when I say that the jam began near the Hotel Juhu Centaur.

As we were already late, my wife suggested that I walk to the venue while she navigated that bumper-to-bumper crawl. When I reached the venue, there was barely room to stand and the formal function was almost over. When Nishika entered ten minutes later, Dharamji had left the stage, and I had not been able to meet him.

Then came the first surprise. When I told her that he had gone into one of the rooms adjoining the banquet hall and I was going in to see him, she asked, 'Can I come too?' Now, this was something she had never done before. When we met him and touched his feet and he hugged us both, came surprise number two: My wife requested me to click a picture of them together! He happily obliged.

At the venue itself, Dharmendra fixed up a day and time when we could take an interview for *Yamla Pagla Deewana* at his home. And so came my final and biggest surprise: Nishika told me that she wanted to come along for the interview, something she had never done when I had met stars, including Anil Kapoor and Shah Rukh Khan, in twenty-one long years!

Dharamji was immensely pleased to meet us again, and we had pictures clicked and a whopper of an interview. But to date, my wife has nothing to say when I ask her how she never revealed that she had been such a huge fan of his. After all, we must have watched more than 40–50 of his old and new movies together in theatres or on television. Trust wives to guard their innermost secrets so well!

For me, Dharamji will thus always be the reason for one of the most rewarding moments in my career as a journalist—his transatlantic phone call—and the fact that he still remembers that *India-West* article, more than a decade later. And I also understood why he is always called the 'ladies' man'!

Here is a man beyond comparison in the corridors of Hindi cinema. I guess God fabricated a new mould for making Dharmendra, and broke it after he made a wonderful human packaged as an evergreen megastar! Big names have come and gone, will come and go, but this man is, simply, forever.

PART 1

From DHARMINDER
To DHARMENDRA

Chapter One

The Man Who Saw Tomorrow

*Jhilmil sitaron ka aangan hoga / Rimjhim barasta
saawan hoga*

*H*ad his dreams remained just dreams, Dharmendra could well have been driving a tractor in the verdant fields of Punjab all through the years during which he was, instead, one of the biggest stars of Hindi cinema.

Born Dharminder Singh Deol on 8 December 1935 in Nasrali, a peaceful village in Ludhiana district, Punjab, to schoolteacher Kewal Kishan Singh and Satwant Kaur, his family had its roots in the nearby less-than-a-dot-on-the-map village of Dangon, near Pakhowal, Ludhiana.

Dharminder Singh spent his early life in the village of Sahnewal and studied at Government Senior Secondary School at Lalton Kalan in Ludhiana district, where his father was the headmaster. He later did his Intermediate (as Class Twelve was then called) from Ramgarhia College, Phagwara in 1952.

This multitude of places associated with him, as he grew into his teenage years, became the *raison d'etre* for the many differences of views about his roots. Never mind if, today, Dharminder Singh, known to the world as Dharmendra (meaning the God of religion), belongs to not just the entire country, but perhaps, to the globe. Wherever Indian cinema is watched and cherished, he is, simply, one of the biggest and longest-lasting stellar entities, belonging to what is now the biggest film industry in the world.

A Rooted Young Man

'...Dharam is a beacon of all that Punjab represents, with his purity of heart!' comments Shatrughan Sinha, one of his closest friends in the industry. 'He is so handsome and full of the Punjabi dabangpan,[1] seedhapan[2] and sanskaar.[3] Plus, he has the alhadpan,[4] masti[5] and befikri[6] that is so typical of the Punjabis. He is even today, a typical Jat, and that's his USP!'

And Sinha goes on to add, 'That is the reason why, even today, he continues to be the darling of Punjab and everyone there. He does not have to visit his roots often, but they still adore him.'

Shatrughan Sinha is right. A detailed yet slightly incoherent news report from 2002[7] about the actor's visit to Lalton Kalan states, 'Dharmendra descended on the village at around 9.30 pm and knocked at the door of a farmer. A lady came out and he asked for the residence of Ram Singh, a petition writer, in whose house Dharmendra's family had lived as a tenant. The lady (recognized him and) instantly took hold of his hand and insisted that he should enter her house.

[1]Resolute
[2]Straight and honest
[3]This term has a broad base. There cannot be an exact translation in English, but it can be used to mean tradition, culture, moral norms or values.
[4]Carefree due to innocence
[5]Naughtiness
[6]Carefree attitude
[7]Sumbly, Vimal; Bains, Loveleen, 'Dharmendra walks down memory lane', *Ludhiana Tribune*, 4 January 2002.

'Ram Singh may have had forgotten Dharmendra. But when the star walked into his house late in the night, he could not believe that the superstar was in front of him in flesh and blood. "Dharmendra was much the same person he used to be in his childhood days—always smiling," recalled Ram Singh. He and his son Randhir Singh were elated that the star remembered them even after forty years. "Who could believe that such a big man would walk into our modest house?" asked Ram.

'Within no time, news spread that Dharmendra was in the village. A village that is usually asleep by 10 p.m. came to life with people, most of them Dharmendra's acquaintances, coming out to meet him. There was a festive atmosphere like in a fair. Everyone wanted him to visit their home. He sat on a cart outside a house and people started bringing milk and jalebis. Some offered sarson ka saag and makki ki roti.

'People began pushing each other as everyone wanted to be photographed with the film star. The local photographer, Balwinder Dhillon, who had also joined the crowd, was instantly in great demand. Within no time he ran short of film rolls. Some people had to be content to only shake hands with Dharmendra, as they could not get themselves photographed with him.

'Dharmendra was moved to tears when Ram Singh gave a photograph of the film star's father to him. He also went to see the wife and daughters of his classmate Surjit Singh, who died a few years ago. Dharmendra also offered some sagan[8] to the daughters. So did he to Bittu, son of his other friend Ranjit Singh. He also cracked jokes with some village youths like Mahavir Grewal, Narender Bhakoo and Gurmit Bassi, narrating his childhood antics for which he would be reprimanded.

'Earlier on his arrival, he had driven to the shop of Raj Kumar,

---

[8]Gift in the form of cash.

a barber. When he found the shop closed, he told the security man that he was Dharmendra and wanted to see Raj Kumar. The security man could not believe his eyes, and he too embraced the star.' (Before calling the barber, we assume.)

There are two more paragraphs in this report.

'Dharmendra had come to Ludhiana along with his wife, Prakash, to attend the marriage ceremony of the nephew of Los Angeles-based Dr Ranjit Singh Grewal. After attending the marriage, he went to Sahnewal. He reached there in the dead of the night and woke up some neighbours. He also visited his ancestral home in the old market.'

Another report reads: 'Residents of this nondescript village, Dangon, the native village of Dharmendra, were overwhelmed to receive the actor on Monday afternoon.'

Dharmendra told me that the report was about his first visit to Dangon after years, and that he touched the soil of his '*jaddi jagah* (the place where his family had their roots)'. '*Hum jahaan jahaan gaye hum wahin ke kehlane lage* (We went on to belong to wherever my father was posted). Did you know that he was not allowed to be transferred from Sahnewal for 18 years?' he informed me.

Bombay Dreams

Dharmendra spoke to me about his early ambitions during our first interview meeting in 2011. Since he was a simple boy from Punjab who wanted to set out to enter the big, bad world of films, how had his family reacted?

The actor told me, 'My father wasn't happy because he was not too sure of the outcome, and of what would happen if I met with failure. My mother, however, was always supportive.' So the obvious question that comes to mind is: Why did the young Dharam have stardust in his eyes? Candidly, he said, 'I was in awe of the stars like Dilip (Kumar) saab, Raj (Kapoor) saab and even heroines like Nargis, Madhubala and Vyjayanthimala. But my ambitions were quite restricted! My big dream and my simple prayer to God was my pictures being present everywhere, just like those of my idols.'

A naive and simple Dharmendra was not at all bothered whether he earned no money, a little money, or a lot! He said: 'My goal was very simple—one flat and one Fiat (car)! When I came to Bombay—that's what Mumbai was known as then—I only had my dreams. I was an untutored villager, with no idea of acting. I wasn't even aware [that] I was good-looking until I began getting movie offers because of my good looks. When I arrived here, I was in fact shocked by the lifestyles of the stars—it was far different from what I had imagined back in Punjab!'

The Churning Point

So, what had actually stirred the pot and made the lad wish to get into films? What was, so to speak, the churning point? The answer to this was as simple as the man himself: Years ago, he had gone with his uncle for a relative's wedding to a nearby town. He was about twelve or thirteen years old at the time, studying in Class Eight, when he got to watch (the result of a promise made by the uncle as an incentive to attend the wedding) a film called *Shaheed* at the Minerva cinema in Ludhiana.

And that did it!

Suddenly, life changed for the young boy. The images from the film began to haunt him. Nothing else was of any interest. His mother continued to tell the boy fairy tales and inspirational stories; the grocer in the village continued his spell of ghost stories, but young Dharam was no longer the avid listener. He believed in the boy Ram from the film, who grew up to be a freedom fighter enacted by the famous Dilip Kumar. He felt Ram and he were brothers.

He began to spend a lot of time on his own, with thoughts of the little boy (interestingly played by one Sashi Kapur, who had nothing to do with Shashi Kapoor!) from *Shaheed*[9] for 'company'. He felt that he knew and understood him, and he certainly wanted to be like him and grow up to be—in an interesting interplay of reel and real—Dilip Kumar!

Years passed and Dharam grew into a strapping young man. He even joined an American drilling company as what he now calls 'a mechanic'. Around this time, it is said Dharam Singh lost his virginity to an older woman, and also had his first drink in the company of his American colleagues from the drilling company. In 1954, he married Prakash Kaur.

But the ambitions of becoming an actor continued to seethe within him like lava waiting to erupt from a dormant volcano. His visits to Ludhiana city to watch films became more and more frequent. Dharam found these to-and-fro journeys tedious, but everything was worth it just to watch the great actors he had come to adore and wanted to emulate.

The First Visit to Mumbai—and a 'Job' Application

In his heart, Dharmendra was living with pain because he was not able to do the one thing he wanted since the age of twelve. His mother could not bear his suffering, and with her blessings and support, he finally left for Mumbai. Facing a reality harsher than he had imagined, he could not get used to his city of dreams, and after a few blows of rejection, he opted to return.

But the desire to make it big remained within him—insatiable, inexorable, like a fierce and stubborn bidding by his destiny. The

[9]*Shaheed* was a 1948 film on India's freedom struggle directed by Ramesh Saigal, produced by Filmistan Ltd. and starring Dilip Kumar and Kamini Kaushal.

rejection had piqued him, killed his enthusiasm for the moment, but had luckily not destroyed his dream.

One incident stood out in this phase. Dharam decided to pay his idol, Dilip Kumar, a visit at his Pali Hill, Bandra home. To his surprise, he entered the superstar's bungalow without anyone asking him who he was, or stopping him. He even went up to the star's bedroom (he did not know which one it was, but randomly opened a door) without coming across anyone.

A slim youth was sleeping in there, but at the sound of the door, he woke up. It was his idol, Dilip Kumar himself! Seeing a completely unknown youth staring at him as if transfixed (Dharam could not believe he was face-to-face with his idol!), Dilip Kumar shouted loudly for a servant, and a scared Dharam dashed down the stairs and out of the house.

He realized later that, unlike in his village where all houses were open to fellow villagers 24/7, he had had no business entering someone's house without any introduction, merely because, as it had turned out, his idol seemed to live just like his own folks did back in Punjab—in an open house!

It would be almost five more years before Dharmendra would venture Mumbai-wards again, armed this time with his father's reluctant blessings and a son, Ajay (born in 1957), who seemed to have brought his father luck. He was now participating in the Filmfare-United Producers' contest for new entrants. He had filled in the form after reading an advertisement back home, been chosen as one of the finalists, and invited to Mumbai for the actual round.

As he put it, 'I had taken my mother to watch a film. My mother told me that it would be better if I could apply for a job even in the Mumbai film industry—then my father would not be so upset. I wondered how one could get a role that way! But it was probably her blessings that the first Filmfare Talent contest was held that very year and I happened to see the advertisement. And so, I *applied* for a job as an actor!'

And so, the 'sunny' phase in his fortune first began. Yes, today Ajay, the eldest of Dharmendra's sons, is coincidentally known by the name Sunny Deol!

As Dharmendra stated once, 'I loved the camera—and God heard me. Even today, I sometimes feel that I have not done anything. If you stop dreaming, you are over. The camera and I may be away from each other for a short while now and then. But it does not leave me even after almost six decades!'

Dharmendra still loves the camera—more than ever. And the camera, too, is still in love with him.

Chapter Two

The Struggle—and the Big Break

Thaam le tu mast pawan ka lehrata aanchal /
O manjhi chal

*T*oday, there is one frequently asked question: Do the contestants of various reality shows on acting, music and more, actually get platforms and end up with successful careers? Gulzar recalls a personable young man who actually won the first position in one such contest but never went anywhere, whereas Dharmendra, at second position, scored high in life. Dharmendra remembers that the young man was Suresh Puri, while three girls, Nimman, Usha and Eva, were the remaining finalists.

The story goes that Dharmendra went to the nearby (30 kilometres!) town of Maler Kotla and got his friend Jaan Mohammed, who owned the photography shop 'John & Sons' (a British era hangover perversion of his name Jaan!), to click photographs of him. He went to the post office and mailed them to *Filmfare*, after paying to register the post.

Dharam was yet again disgruntled upon not hearing anything from the contest in response. In sheer frustration, he went and cut his hair very short! Not long after, he was going back from work when he saw his friend cycling towards him with a letter for him.

That was how he received a letter from *Filmfare* asking him to go to Mumbai. He was to stay there for a week and would be looked after by the magazine—that is, they would pay for his first-class fare to Mumbai and make him stay in a five-star hotel there!

Dharmendra remembers a choking sensation in his throat after getting the news, because he suddenly began to wonder what would happen if things just failed to work out. His mother took him to a doctor, who checked him out and stated that the alarming symptom was only his anxiety! 'I was the eldest in my family, and always had a sense of responsibility,' he confessed in a recent video interview.

And here came the ironic twist: In the photographs that he had sent to the magazine, he had much longer hair. So when he alighted from the train, he was not recognized because of the change in his appearance! Gulshan Ewing of *Filmfare*, and later editor of *Star & Style*, had gone to receive him.

'It was a Sunday and I alighted at Victoria Terminus (Mumbai's rail terminal), which was opposite the Times of India House,' Dharmendra says. 'I called up the *Filmfare* office and luckily Ewing had come in. When we met, she extended her hand, *aur maine apna haath sharmaate sharmaate uss ki taraf badhaayaa* (and I shyly extended my hand too). I was from a village, and my plus point was the basic sabhyata (civility) ingrained within me. I also blushed, and this habit of blushing is not something that can be forced into you!' he smiled.

Dharam was taken to a hotel. But the air-conditioned room suffocated the actor and despite being a Punjab da puttar, he shivered in the artificial cold. It took the young Dharam a good while to make friends with the city and the sea!

When it came down to business, he was put in a bus full of young men (and women), nervously cracking their fingers and chewing on their nails. They were all contestants of the first-ever Filmfare Talent Hunt. It was on this bus that he finally was to meet his destiny! A young man named Arjun Hingorani, a dental surgeon by qualification, had accompanied a female candidate, and was struck by his looks. At that point, Dharam could have never guessed that he would one day be everlastingly grateful to this man.

The *Filmfare* phase created a mélange of memories for him. One more pleasant memory again pertained to Dilip Kumar. He was introduced to his sister Farida, who was in charge of doing make-up for the contestants. Dharam declared his adulation for her brother and she actually arranged a meeting between Dharam and his idol the next day. It was winter and Kumar gave Dharam a jacket to protect himself. It was manufactured in Paris and was obviously expensive, and Dharam preserved it for a long time as a memento.

The Dilip Kumar-Dharmendra friendship continues to this day, with the actor still an avid fan of the senior legend. It pains him now to see his idol and inspiration be so unwell and frail, and it pains him even more that Dev Anand and Raj Kapoor are no more.

It was not an easy phase for Dharmendra, whom Gulzar describes as someone who, even now, remains an innocent child at heart. Insults, heartbreaks, humiliations and setbacks are part and parcel of every human being's struggle package. For this soft-natured young man from the hinterlands of Punjab, it was, arguably, a shade more intense, a tad more unsettling and demoralizing.

So, what kept Dharamji going? Was it his mother's blessings? Or his destiny? Or his innate hunger for achieving his dreams? Without doubt, it was all three factors put together, and both he and this writer would give the greatest chunk of the credit to that wonderful lady who had seen her son dream his dream—his mother. In one of his poems, a skill he developed almost five decades later, he has also credited his success to his father's love.

Dilip Kumar, Raj Kapoor, Dev Anand, Motilal and later Uttam Kumar: these were tough icons to live up to when you wanted to—completely—alter your life's direction. And when you arrive in your city of dreams and find that things are nothing like the glamorous images you conjured up after watching their films, these flowering dreams can be suddenly beset with so many accompanying thorns.

For example, two years were spent in a single room over a garage in Mumbai's suburb of Versova. It was a nightmarish phase, and Dharmendra often went without a square meal. It was also a tough walk from his place to the studios that he would have to visit every day.

Poignantly, Dharmendra remains all too aware of how he would pass the very site in which he now resides, at Juhu, as he walked from Versova to the studios—as far as midtown Dadar. In one of our meetings that was held at Sunny Super Sound, the studio he built in a different location in Juhu, he talked about meeting with co-struggling friends right opposite what was then barren land, and dreaming of having property there!

Manoj Kumar, his bosom friend since the 1960s, whom Dharmendra always calls 'Manno' and who always addresses him as 'Dharmu', vividly recalled those days when they took the blows that life offered together, solidly backing each other's dreams and trying to buffer the setbacks they individually received.

'I don't really remember where we met first,' said Kumar. 'In those days, L.P. Rao, editor of *Filmfare*, would throw a number of parties presenting the stars of tomorrow. We met, I think, at Ranjit Studios[1] in Dadar.'

Manoj Kumar revealed, 'Dharmu mentioned to me that he had come to Mumbai much before the *Filmfare* contest. He had stayed, struggled and gone back to his village after a while. I had already worked in *Sahara*, and he said that he had seen my show-cards of the film and had wondered who this six-footer, who had some scenes

---

[1]Ranjit Studios, also known as Ranjit Movietone, produced films between 1929 and the early 1960s. It was one of the three largest studios of its time.

with Meena Kumari, was!'

Things, admitted Kumar, were far from rosy. Film-maker Ramesh Saigal, whose office was in Ranjit Studios, took their screen test at Roop Tara Studios nearby along with Suresh Puri, the other *Filmfare* contestant, and another man who went on to become a distributor in Bangalore. He was planning a two-hero film.

Of the four, he liked Dharmendra and Kumar, and told both of them to go and watch William Holden's Hollywood film *Picnic*. Both of them understood the film's story, but for safety's sake, they confirmed the plotline with a man at the tuck-shop outside the theatre! They thought the film-maker would ask them to narrate the story, but he never did.

Kumar also recalled, 'Lekhraj Bhakri, writer-producer-director and also my cousin, had his office at Ranjit Studios, and it became our adda (regular hangout). We would spend time there, sitting or lying on a charpai (cot) and sharing our problems. I had an affair on in Delhi and wanted to marry the girl, and Dharmu revealed in confidence that he was married and had a son, Ajay.'

There was a third candidate, Shashi Kapoor, well-known as a child star and as Prithviraj Kapoor's son, and Raj Kapoor's and Shammi Kapoor's brother. Kumar remembered fondly, 'But he never behaved like a star. We three would seek assignments together, with the selfless aim that it would be okay if any one of us got a break,' said Kumar.

Shahid Lateef[2] was making a film for Filmistan, and producer Seth Tolaram Jalan, too, liked both Kumar and Dharmendra—it was again a story with two heroes. Jalan offered Kumar ₹450 for the film and ₹350 to Dharmendra. Kumar turned down the film, and Jalan dismissed them both. The two of them were later sitting in a small

---

[2]Veteran writer and film-maker who made hit films like *Jhoola* (1941) and *Ziddi* (1948) and later directed Dharmendra in *Baharen Phir Bhi Aayengi* (1966).

restaurant when Kumar said that Dharmendra should have done the film as it was the former who had refused the remuneration. But the latter said that he did not want to do the film without his friend.

Kumar recalled telling him, 'What are you saying? As it is, we have little money. At least you could have made some.' And that was when Dharmendra said something that Kumar will never forget: '*Yaar, paise ki baat hai na, to mere paison mein se le lena* (If it's just about money, take what you need from whatever I get)!'

Kumar said that he had a lump in his throat. He held Dharmendra's hand and told him, 'Let's go!' They went back to Jalan and told him that they would like to do the film. Jalan told them to wait for a few days.

But a shock awaited Kumar a few days later. At Shanbhag Restaurant, their haunt outside Ranjit Studios, the actor was given a letter from Dharmendra, stating that he was returning to his town by Frontier Mail. Kumar rushed to Matunga and found that his friend had packed his bags. He fought with him, and argued endlessly, but Dharmendra was adamant. He had got a job in Dhaka Colony, New Delhi, and was afraid that nothing would happen in Mumbai. 'I will lose my job!' he told Kumar. 'And anyway, you don't have much money either!'

Kumar was equally stubborn. 'Nothing doing!' he told Dharmendra. 'Wait for two months—I will look after all your expenses!' Dharmendra relented eventually. And just days later, muhurats for the two films took place. The two friends shot for a few days for Jalan's *Picnic*, but Dharmendra contracted jaundice and suddenly lost a lot of weight.

Dharmendra's role was that of an Army officer, but unfortunately, since the actor was beginning to develop sunken cheeks and a thin, unhealthy look all over, he was removed from the film—after Jalan waited ten days for him to recover!

The second film was Ramesh Saigal's *Shola Aur Shabnam*. Kumar had unfortunately confided the story of that film in his friend, actor M. Rajan, who had also been struggling himself since the late 1950s. Rajan also happened to be the brother of producer Roshan Lal Malhotra and distributor Chaman Lal, and the latter approached Saigal for the distribution rights, provided Rajan was given the role earmarked for Kumar!

And so the two friends lost both the chances to come together in a film.

Kumar and Dharmendra starred later in *Shaadi*, where they had only one scene, in the climax, and did not have any dialogue with each other on-screen. The same was the case in *Mera Naam Joker*, even though they individually had substantial roles in it. They also came together for just one sequence in the 1995 non-starter *Maidan-E-Jung*.

Manoj Kumar also has some fun anecdotes from this period of struggle. He recalls with a smile, 'In our better days, both of us were given a first class railway pass (season ticket) from Churchgate to Goregaon, the suburb where Filmistan Studios was located. For three days, we just went back and forth on this return journey of two hours! We would also have juices and malai (cream) and stitched suits on credit.'

On one such train ride, they came across a beautiful girl who had soft wavy hair, sitting by the window with her eyes closed. Just like them, she too got down at Goregaon, and luckily they saw her again in Filmistan, where they later came to know her name—Sadhana!

Manoj Kumar and Sadhana were to later co-star in the film that established him as a big star, *Woh Kaun Thi?*, as well as in *Anita* and in Sadhana's last film, *Amaanat*; while Dharmendra worked with her in *Ishq Par Zor Nahin*. Interestingly, Sadhana got her first break in the 1959 Sindhi film, *Abana*, directed by Arjun Hingorani, who was to later give Dharmendra his first film, *Dil Bhi Tera Hum Bhi Tere*. Both were given second leads in these respective films.

For most of that struggle period, the two friends together went through low morale and loneliness—especially, since both were away from their families. 'It used to get to us,' recalls Kumar.

But one high point during that phase was Dharmendra's first interaction with Dev Anand. Dharmendra recalls, 'Dev Anand had been one of my idols. And one day, when I was standing in a queue for some audition and he was passing by, he saw me and came over. Out of the blue, he told me, "You will make it!" and that boosted my morale like nothing else could have!'

Anand had then taken him aside, chatted briefly with him, and even gave him cold water from his ice-box. Dharmendra recalls emotionally, 'I was dying to meet Dev saab, and here he was, talking to me!' And why wouldn't he? Dev Anand's keen ability to spot new acting talent was active even then! But at the time this happened, Dharmendra was the *Filmfare* contest winner. That was not the time to lose hope. And when you crave for something deeply, providence does turn benevolent.

'Arjun Hingorani came to me and signed me for *Dil Bhi Tera Hum Bhi Tere*. After that, I signed *Shola Aur Shabnam* and *Bandini*, with Ramesh Saigal and Bimal Roy respectively,' Dharmendra told me in my first interview with him. 'The other talent contest judge besides Bimal Roy was Guru Dutt, and he too was contractually bound to give me a film. Sadly, the turmoil in his life prevented that and I could never work with him.'

The way Dharmendra and Guru Dutt's banner came to be associated later is a part of both history and Dharmendra's stellar journey: Dharmendra ended up doing two films later that were directed by Dutt's younger brother, Atma Ram—his blockbuster production *Shikar* (1968) under the banner of Guru Dutt Films Combine, and the modest success *Resham Ki Dori* (1974). In 1994, the delayed film *Khule Aam*, starring him, was made by Dutt's sons Tarun Dutt and Arun Dutt.

Hingorani made films all the way to the 2003 film *Kaise Kahoon Ki Pyaar Hai* and *every* film starred the friend he had first met in that *Filmfare* bus! In turn, the eternal simpleton never forgot his debt to his mentor. 'Even today, if Arjunji enters a room, I go and touch his feet,' an emotional Dharmendra said. 'He was a patient and hard-working director who relied on my talent and gave me ample scope to improve my performances even if a number of takes were required.'

The actor recalled with gratitude that the film-maker (among the first to do cameos in his own films) would give him eight annas (which was half a rupee) if he had a rupee on him and Dharmendra needed money. The story goes that Hingorani even arranged for the actor's breakfast in those days at Merwan's, an Irani restaurant outside Mumbai's Grant Road suburban station, every morning. Legend has it that he was to get tea and two slices of bread but no butter. Of course, downtown Grant Road was five stations away from Dadar, and even farther from where Dharmendra lived at the time!

Incidentally, *Dil Bhi Tera Hum Bhi Tere* also marked the directorial debut of Hingorani (who called himself A. Hingo in the credit titles) himself, and Dharmendra had a parallel, or almost supporting, role to the then star Balraj Sahni in it. He played a cigarette vendor who often walked on stilts to sell his wares, and later falls in love with a maidservant played by Kum Kum.

But in his very first film, destiny ordained Dharmendra's link with machismo: He was shown to have a yen for boxing, and becomes a professional boxer midway through the movie! Interestingly, the credit titles of the film billed him as 'Dharmender', using the Punjabi pronunciation of his name.

For the film's premiere in December 1960, the actor walked to Andheri station from where he was staying in Versova, a distance no less than 4–5 kilometres, and took a train to downtown Charni Road, almost 20 kilometres away. He then walked the short distance to Central Talkies from there.

And the irony was that, incredibly, despite his Adonis-like good looks, he was not even recognized as the second hero of the film! 'I was scared and nervous—*woh hustle-bustle ka zamana tha* (it was a chaotic era),' he confided.

Worse still, Dharmendra did not like the film *at all*! 'I ran away as soon the interval came on. I was so depressed I wanted to leave it all and go home. I thought, "Have I come here for this?" I did not also like my own performance in it!' he admitted with a smile.

'Even today, I am never satisfied with anything I do. I never think "*Wah! Kya kaam kar diya* (What a great job I have done)." *Mere kaam pe mujhse kabhi wah nahin nikli* (I have never applauded any of my performances)!' the actor replied, when I mentioned that his performance was more than decent for a rank newcomer, who was not even a trained actor.

Films in India conventionally release on a Friday, and in the following week, the review of his debut performance, in the industry's leading publication, *Screen,* read thus:

> Newcomer Dharminder contributes a tolerably good piece of work, although in the romantic sequences as well as in the tense moments, he is not quite at home. With better guidance, he should be able to do well.

Circa 2018, this actor has now acted in more than 300 films (including cameos and roles in non-Hindi films). And so, fifty-eight years later, the above appraisal by the *Screen* critic pretty much looks like the understatement of the century!

Chapter Three

A Star was Born

*Chamka paseena banke nagina / Kaali raat beeti re kaali
raat beeti / Mehnat kee thi re mehnat kee thi*

Slowly the dark night of struggle began to give way to
the inevitable dawn of hope and success. The fact that
Dharmendra never got the instantaneous variety of fame,
which comes and goes faster than a meteor, was obvious. But then,
to repeat a cliché, a diamond shines best only if burnished ever so
slowly.

In those times, new leading men with strong persona effortlessly
stood out as there were relatively very few newcomers (there
were no training institutes or multiple talent contests to spew out
contestants by the dozen back then), and a dazzlingly good-looking
actor like him was quickly lapped up.

His name was spelt in different ways on posters, in credit titles
and even in articles. He was named Dharmender in *Dil Bhi Tera
Hum Bhi Tere*, but spelt Dharminder in the *Screen* review and even
as Dharmindera in one early film.

The 1962 films *Soorat Aur Seerat* and *Anpadh* were, therefore,
his earliest films in which the name 'Dharmendra' was correctly
used. Interestingly, the former was top star Nutan's home production

and was directed by her husband Rajnish Bahl. In the latter film, Dharmendra played a second lead, yet again to Balraj Sahni.

A full half-dozen years were to pass before Dharmendra actually became *the* Dharmendra famous today. And that actually remains a big mystery! This is because he acted in twenty films between 1960 and 1965, and of these, twelve were hits or average successes and only three were absolute flops—giving Dharmendra a massive 85 per cent success ratio! But logic rarely has a place in the environs of Indian cinema.

The actor shed some light on this once, during a chat with me. 'My films were hits, but *Phool Aur Patthar* (1966) was like the *Sholay* of those times. And my rugged character of Shaaka became iconic.'

Why did he sign some really routine films in this phase? Dharmendra was very frank about this. 'A career is not a small thing for an actor who wants to be loved and liked,' he admitted. 'It's a big step, and there is fear and insecurity that comes along with the obstacles. There is always the feeling that a great opportunity or hit should not slip away from our hands, and I would constantly pray to God about that.' Candidly, he also added that there are financial necessities for a newcomer, especially someone like him—a man from a village, with humble beginnings, who has to get somewhere.

The actor recalled, 'I bought my first car—a second-hand one— the way I had dreamt. It was a Fiat. That was very early in my career and I showed it proudly to Bimal Roy. My second dream—a flat, took a little longer—two years. I first rented one on 14th Road, Khar for ₹180 a month, a big sum in those days. I then called my parents, wife and son to Mumbai. My mother was willing, but my father was still angry, because I had shattered his dream of my becoming a professor. I told him that I had played someone with an academic touch in one of my early films, and he shouted, "*Ullu ke patthe* (you moron)! I meant a proper, real professor!" However, he did come.'

But we are skipping too far ahead. As Dharminder, the actor

worked in two films in 1961—first, the Madhubala–Shammi Kapoor starrer *Boy Friend*, in which he played the supporting role of a police inspector, and then *Shola Aur Shabnam*, which was not only his first hit, but also the first film in which Dharmendra got top billing over the other hero, M. Rajan, whom Manoj Kumar had mentioned earlier.

Shola Aur Shabnam had Dharmendra playing a young man torn between his childhood love (Tarla Mehta was the heroine) and his gratitude for a friend (M. Rajan) who had given him a lucrative job and was also in love with the heroine. A love triangle with an unusual climax, it struck empathy with the audience, with Khayyam-Kaifi Azmi's 'Jaane Kya Dhoondti Rehti Hai Yeh Ankhen Mujh Mein' and 'Jeet Hi Lenge Baazi Hum Tum' also becoming added allures.

(Interesting trivia: M. Rajan later played the villain in the 1967 Dharmendra-Mala Sinha starrer *Jab Yaad Kisi Ki Aati Hai* and also had a small role in *Professor Pyarelal* in 1981, because his career as a hero never took off.)

The superb and dominant association between Mohammed Rafi and Dharmendra began with that film's songs. Dharmendra recalled, 'Mohammed Rafi saab gave me such a soft voice and tone.' This association ended only with the rousing 'Apne Dil Mein Josh Hai' in *Mera Karam Mera Dharam* (1987), which was recorded almost eight years before the delayed film released.

An interesting trivia is that *Shola Aur Shabnam* is the film in which Dharmendra removed his shirt for the first time, though for a casual, natural scene. Another highly interesting point was its director—Ramesh Saigal. Yes, Dharmendra thus got to work, in just the third movie of his career, with the man who made the film that changed his life—*Shaheed*! And the same film-maker gave him his first hit and his first film as the principal male lead.

After that, it was a matter of time before the future He-Man worked, one by one, with almost all the stars he had idolized as a young boy back in Punjab.

The then top lyricist Rajendra Krishan's brother, producer Hargobind, produced the film *Shaadi* in 1962. This film, directed by Krishnan-Panju,[1] finally brought Manoj Kumar and Dharmendra together, even if just for a couple of post-climax frames. The story is structured in a way that Kumar and Dharmendra have no interaction with each other, and in the two or three frames that they share, they do not even exchange a single word!

The credit titles of that film were amusing: 'Starring Balraj Sahni, Saira Banu, Manoj Kumar' read the first still, and the second read, 'Indrani, Dharmindera, Sulochana'. And here's the tangy part: Dharmendra played Saira Banu's elder brother in this one, while Indrani (Mukherjee, who played Dharmendra's elder sister-in-law in *Chacha Bhatija* fifteen years later) enacted the role of his wife!

Anpadh was Dharmendra's next film—again with Balraj Sahni. Of his two releases in 1963, *Bandini* had him as the second lead to Ashok Kumar, while *Begaana* had Shailesh Kumar, never a big name, who bagged all the songs here, leaving Dharmendra with more footage and a key role only in the second half.

Still, *Anpadh* (directed and co-written by Mohan Kumar), *Bandini* (directed by Bimal Roy) and *Begaana* (directed by Sadashiv J. Row Kavi) became the first three socially relevant movies to star this actor.

Anpadh highlighted the importance of education for the fairer sex, though this is something the rich heiress (Mala Sinha) in the film realizes only when her lack of education leads to multiple issues after her marriage. Her literature-oriented husband (Dharmendra), after his initial shock, decides to take things positively and educate

---

[1]Krishnan-Panju was a famous director-duo from South India, and they have the honour of being Dharmendra's first directors from Madras, as Chennai was then called.

her, but when she almost gives a poisonous medicine (tincture of iodine) to a child instead of the prescribed tonic as she cannot read the labels, her father-in-law throws her out of the house. Angry with his father, Dharmendra leaves home in search for her, meets with an accident and dies in a hospital.

The film thus featured Dharmendra's first on-screen death, although there wasn't a 'dying' scene in particular in it!

The actor gratefully recalls that during the shoot of *Anpadh*, Mala Sinha sensed his shyness and nervousness in the first romantic sequence they shot together. She helped the young man overcome his diffidence by taking both his hands in hers and cupping them on her face!

Another interesting fact: When Mala Sinha's character is finally accepted by Dharmendra's in the film despite her illiteracy, she sings the now cult Lata Mangeshkar song: 'Aap Ki Nazaron Ne Samjha Pyaar Ke Qaabil Mujhe (You have finally considered me worthy of your love)'.

Raja Mehdi Ali Khan, the lyricist of this film, had actually penned the entire song in praise of his spiritual guru, and with his express permission, had given the song to the film—with its words magically fitting this situation!

Unconfirmed news from Putul Guha, son of the late Dulal Guha, who made many films with Dharmendra, suggests that the actor was to be offered Ashok Kumar's role, while Shashi Kapoor was to do Dharmendra's character in *Bandini*. But because Ashok Kumar's freedom fighter character of Bikash had a characteristic laughter that Bimalda wanted, he chose Ashok Kumar and gave Dharmendra the other role (after all, Bimal Roy was committed to a film with this *Filmfare* talent contest winner).

But writer-lyricist and future director-to-be Gulzar, who assisted Roy on that film, refutes this information, stating, 'I was privy to whatever was happening. This is not true. As you can see, Ashok

Kumar's character was that of an older man. How could Dharam, who was just twenty-eight when the film *released* after some delay, have played the role?'

Dharmendra's own statement tends to back Gulzar's. 'I remember restlessly waiting for the results on the day of the final test during the *Filmfare* contest. The great Bimal Roy was one of the judges, and his assistant Debu Sen (who later directed Roy's 1968 production *Do Dooni Chaar*) was very fond of me. Debu sized me up and simply said, "*Hai baat!* (There is something special in you)"while I waited. A little later, he called me inside, stating that Bimalda wanted to see me. I went in, and Bimalda said, "Come, come, Dharmendu"— the name he stubbornly called me [by], stating that he was saying Dharmender in his Bengali way—"Your *boudi* (sister-in-law) has sent maach (fish)."'

Roy, no less, was sharing his lunch with a struggler, much like Dev Anand had shared his ice-box earlier, but Dharmendra recalled that he was unable to swallow his food, as he was tense about the results! Some minutes later, Roy casually stated, '*Aur Dharmendu, tum Bandini kar rahaa hai* (And Dharmendra, you are doing *Bandini*)'!

'Now I was unable to eat because I was so happy!' laughed Dharmendra. 'There is always that moment that comes after months and years of struggle that you catch and do not want to let go! All my years of struggle coalesced into that one moment! I wanted to live it forever!'

Dharmendra had this to say about his first 'signed' film: 'Getting a role in a Bimal Roy film was not a small thing, and my other director was to be Guru Dutt, but that film, sadly, never happened. But I was starting out with the best!'

Bimal Roy's daughter, Rinki Roy Bhattacharya, has made a slightly contradictory statement, stating that her father had signed Dharmendra much earlier for ₹100 and had told him to wait. The role which he ultimately got was of the doctor in *Bandini*. The confusion can probably be explained by the fact that Roy might have had to sign him formally as a Filmfare-United Producers' contest winner.

Bhattacharya, in her book, says that Dharmendra was so enthusiastic about such a big film that for a 7 a.m. shift, he would report at around 6.30 a.m. The only other person on the sets at that hour would be the sweeper!

The actor has always raved about the film and his abbreviated role in it, wherein he walked away with the audience's sympathy even though Nutan's character went back to a dying Ashok Kumar, her ex-lover, who, as she comes to know in the end, had never betrayed her, unlike what she had always thought.

However, since *Bandini* took a while to launch, it finally became his sixth movie to release. But that short role that begins and ends in the first half of this cult film is extremely dear to the actor. And that is so for various reasons, not just the fact that it was actually the first film he would be a part of, and that it was made by the great Bimal Roy.

'See the beauty of the story!' said a still-enthused Dharmendra to me. 'I, a doctor who also visits a jail, fall deeply in love with the girl prisoner (Nutan), the Bandini, despite coming to know everything about her past, as well as the fact that she is in jail for killing the wife of her lover. She also feels for me, but does not wish to spoil my life, which is just taking off.'

The actor recalled a masterly shot where Dharmendra's and Nutan's hands touch each other unknowingly from two sides of a door, and she instantly withdraws her hand. The film was full of beautifully depicted love, the actor feels.

But would it not have been more progressive to show Nutan picking up the pieces of her life and settling into a happy union with a progressive doctor, for whom this woman's past was of no importance?

'Actually, Nabendu Ghosh, the writer, and Bimalda, would have arguments and fights every day!' the actor revealed with a laugh. 'I would be listening outside as they vehemently argued their points of view, waiting just as if Bandini was coming to my own home—or maybe not!'

Finally, two different climaxes were shot. And ultimately, Ghosh's wish prevailed and the woman went back to her former lover. However, despite the short role, Dharmendra pointed out how important his character was to the film: 'I was the symbol of hope for a happy, new start for the woman, before her past caught up with her. Remove the doctor, and the film would not have any clash of conscience or interest. The possibility of a new turn in Bandini's life added to the poignancy of this unique love story.'

Finally, the doctor resigns, as he cannot face her anymore. The shot where the sound of the hoof beats of his horse carriage are heard fading behind the high wall, as the doctor leaves the jail for the last time, shows how Bandini is wounded yet again. Then follows a scene where his mother asks him, 'Why did you resign?' And the doctor says, '*Man nahin laaga, maa* (My heart was not in it, mother)!'

'What a statement!' the actor had marvelled. 'It spoke volumes. Everyone praised my performance, and complimented me on how beautifully I had underplayed. But I never even knew the meaning of "underplaying"! Without being a method actor, I would merge into my roles, and change myself for each film by feeling the character and his emotions.'

Uncharacteristically but clinically, justifiably immodest, Dharmendra indulged in self-praise as he talked about how 'the Dharmendra of *Bandini, Pratiggya, Chupke Chupke* and *Satyakam* were all completely different!'

The other 1963 release, *Begaana*, for those times, was progressively focused on how a broad-minded and educated husband (Dharmendra) accepts his wife (Supriya Chowdhury), who had strayed before marriage, and the son she gave birth to, as his own, even asking her why she had not taken him into confidence, so that she could have spared herself all the misery.

In 1964, for the first time, Dharmendra had as many as seven releases. He had yet another film with Kum Kum, this time playing her brother-in-law, in the Devi Sharma-produced and directed *Ganga Ki Lehren*. While the film had him in a central role, it was Kishore Kumar who got all the songs and played to the gallery as his friend. The film was said to be a success at the time. It was the South Indian actress Savitri who played Dharmendra's lady-love in a tangled melodrama that, nevertheless, had some cute touches.

It would be a full six years before Kishore Kumar would go on to sing playback for his co-star for the first time—in the hit song 'Munne Ki Amma'—from the 1970 Shankar-Jaikishan film *Tum Haseen Main Jawan*. As Kishore Kumar had earlier stated (to composers Kalyanji-Anandji specifically), 'I am an actor—not a playback singer!' and would make exceptions only for his favourite person, Dev Anand. He changed his stance only in 1968!

Dharmendra also went on to essay his first negative role in the silver jubilee hit *Ayee Milan Ki Bela*, directed by Mohan Kumar of *Anpadh*. Once again, there was Saira Banu in the lead, but although Dharmendra's character also loved the heroine, it was Rajendra Kumar's character who went on to win her. The film was a huge hit, and the senior actor, then in the midst of his record-breaking jubilee run, was highly impressed by this young Jat.

And soon, when Rajendra Kumar's brother-in-law O.P. Ralhan broached the subject of *Phool Aur Patthar* with him, was it not the senior superstar who reportedly suggested Dharmendra's name for the role that was to really put him on the fast track? Dharmendra says that he is unaware of anything like this. 'As far as I know, I was doing well and suited the role,' he said pragmatically.

But, with *Ayee Milan Ki Bela*, Dharmendra again became realistically proud of his achievement. He said, 'People loved me even as a bad guy in *Ayee Milan Ki Bela*. Women sighed during my entry on screen—I have heard that with my own ears! People did not mind that *maine ladki ko uthaake bhagaaya*. I received great fan mail. One person said that the clash between Rajendra Kumar and me was like the one in the Hollywood classic *Duel In The Sun*! Naseem Banuji, Saira Banu's mother, even said that I looked like an American in the film!'

AVM Productions' Madras melodrama (this was a well-known term coined for their films then) *Pooja Ke Phool* saw Dharmendra do his second film with Mala Sinha. Yet another lesser-known Hindi cinema heroine, again from Bengal, Sandhya Roy, was also in a parallel lead.

Very interestingly, the same year saw AVM (with the banner's chief A.V. Meiyappan's sons M. Murugan, M. Kumaran and M. Saravanan as producers) release yet another melodrama with a happy ending in *Main Bhi Ladki Hun*. And this time, there was a small social message as well—that one's inner beauty matters more than the complexion of the skin.

Chronologically, this was the beginning of yet another successful team—Dharmendra and Meena Kumari. And the relationship was to soon grow beyond just being professional.

Aap Ki Parchhaiyan was a hit too, this time produced and directed by Mohan Kumar. Once again, though in a lesser role, Bengal's top actress Supriya Chowdhury was back as Dharmendra's heroine after *Begaana*. Like with most social films of the early '60s, this was a tear jerker as well!

Mera Qasoor Kya Hai, too, continued in the same vein. Again, showing Dharmendra's perennial and natural yen for generating loyalists, the film was made by the same team as *Shaadi*—producer Hargobind and directors Krishnan-Panju. This was Dharmendra's first film with Nanda (cast here in a double role), that top star who made signing films with—and thus encouraging—new heroes a regular habit.

Last, but by no means the least and probably the most special, was *Haqeeqat*, the drama on the Indo-China war. And among all these films, this time Dharmendra's performance was indeed special, in an ensemble cast led by Balraj Sahni, Vijay Anand and Jayant (better known to today's readers as Amjad Khan's father) with a one-film old Sanjay Khan.

Mention the film and Dharmendra turns nostalgic. 'It is the mother of all war films,' he states emotionally. 'I still have fond memories of shooting war scenes in Ladakh. Sometimes, we even went without food. I think Chetan Anand directed an evergreen film. My role of Captain Bahadur Singh is one of my best performances till date.' General Jayanto Nath Chowdhury, Chief of Army Staff of the Indian Army from 1962 to 1966, no less, described his performance as 'realistic and convincing'.

Considered even now the ultimate war drama in Indian cinema, this film had Dharmendra playing the pivotal role of the man who gives his life to save his battalion. And his rugged physique came into perfect play for a superhero soldier's character, upon whose screen death we got to hear the immortal Mohammed Rafi-Kaifi Azmi-Madan Mohan masterpiece, 'Kar Chale Hum Fida Jaan-O-Tann Saathiyon'. Decades later, in 2004, Dharmendra's son, Bobby Deol, was to play one of the leads in a film called *Ab Tumhare Hawaale Watan Saathiyo*, named after the second line of this song.

By then, Dharmendra was easily the most consistently successful new star on the move. Manoj Kumar had just broken through with *Woh Kaun Thi?*, Shashi Kapoor was struggling, and new heroes like Jeetendra and Sanjay Khan had just appeared on the scene. Joy Mukerji and Biswajeet were doing reasonably well, and Sanjeev Kumar and Feroz Khan were still juggling between their B-grade leads and A-grade supporting or minor roles.

In this clear field, the actor starred in four more successful (to varying extents) melodramas—*Purnima* (his second film with

Meena Kumari), *Neela Akash* (his third with Mala Sinha), *Kajal* (Meena again, but not in a romantic role with her) and *Akashdeep* (his second film with Nanda). The only film that did not work, *Chand Aur Suraj* with Tanuja, and with Ashok Kumar and Nirupa Roy leading the cast, was the beginning of one of his most treasured associations—that with film-maker Dulal Guha, which went on till 1987.

And so we enter 1966, the year that Dharmendra made it to superstardom. The actor was now poised to cash in on his uniquely perfect amalgamation of brawn and the gentleness so transparent in his personality.

Chapter Four

1966 Gives Birth to a Superstar!

*Apne dil mein josh hai / Apna khoon garam hai / Karam
hi dharam hai / Karam hi dharam hai*

The floodgates finally opened for a torrent of films
that suddenly placed Dharmendra right at the forefront,
among the big heroes of that era—Dilip Kumar, Dev
Anand, Raj Kapoor, Shammi Kapoor, Rajendra Kumar, Sunil Dutt
and Raaj Kumar. This was also the last-burst-of-glory phase for
Pradeep Kumar, while Manoj Kumar, Shashi Kapoor and Jeetendra
had already earned their first hits.

And Dharmendra came up with eight big films in Hindi. Apart
from his first Bengali film, *Paari*, also being a hit.

For any newcomer, all this could have been too heady. Success
could have been too intoxicating—destructively so. It could have
turned Dharmendra's head, made him arrogant, and ultimately
stymied his growth as a human being, actor, star and icon. Lesser
icons across the board—actors, composers, singers and film-
makers—have amputated their careers with the short-lived but
intoxicating elixir of sheer arrogance bred by immense success.

Jeetendra, Dharmendra's co-star in almost a dozen films from
Dharam-Veer to so many forgettable potboilers of the 1990s,

spoke with amusement tinged with admiration when he recalled how Dharmendra and he would have drinks together after their location shoots. 'Unlike most people who become aggressive, rude and generally unpleasant after some pegs, Dharam became a better person with every drink—mellower and more affectionate!'

I have mentioned this seemingly irrelevant observation by a close colleague here, only to show that the actor, now a superstar (even if that term in filmdom was to be first used almost half a decade later for Rajesh Khanna), actually changed for the better after big-time stardom, which was a potent sublimation of his dreams and must have been like nasha (intoxication) for him.

If anything, the actor in him improved, the star remained not only professional but became an ace team player, and the man remained grounded as if he was still the determined yet simple and shy boy from the hinterlands of Punjab. As Asha Parekh said, 'Dharam never lost the real man within—the simple peasant from Punjab.'

Dharmendra seemed to follow to the hilt a song Anand Bakshi was to write for him in the late '80s—'Apne Dil Mein Josh Hai/ Apna Khoon Garam Hai/Karam Hi Dharam Hai/Karam Hi Dharam Hai (There is zeal in my heart, my blood is racing and my credo of life is work, work and work)!' The josh (spirited enthusiasm), the garam khoon (hot-blooded fervour), the karam (deeds of duty) and dharam (credo of life) merged into an exhilarating and galvanizing ride into the future.

You could well have replaced *Karam Hi Dharam Hai* with the words *Karam hi DHARAM hai*! Since from that period on Dharam would mean nothing but Karam.

Dharmendra was well past the 'Flat and Fiat' stage. He had earned the love of both viewers and industry associates, and so there was no way the blitzkrieg could slow down now. The rollercoaster had begun, and Dharmendra not only had to enjoy the ride but try and make sure that he did not lose everything he had earned through his hard work, as the momentum accelerated. The 1966–75 decade thus was the golden period of this megastar's acting career.

The Big One: *Phool Aur Patthar* (1966)

Phool Aur Patthar, as pointed by the actor, was the *Sholay* of its time. Everything just fell into place due to the sheer force and extent of its impact. The actor takes some credit for the sequence in which he removes his shirt, not to show machismo, but to cover the frail and poor woman (Leela Chitnis, the former singing superstar actress of the '30s) his character Shakka had adopted as his mother.

Modestly, Dharmendra admitted, 'Film-makers would listen to my suggestions frequently. I thought this gesture would be a nice emotional touch.'

However, most of the current generation chose instead to recall the sequence in which Meena Kumari, rescued by Dharmendra and a guest in his house, pretends to be asleep as her host-cum-benefactor comes in drunk and bare-chested. Kumari realizes that he is inebriated, and fears the worst when he enters her room. But he only leans over her to check whether she is asleep, and gently covers her with a blanket.

What people could not have foreseen, however, was that this very sequence, over time, would come to be considered the foremost symbol of masculinity and virility in Hindi cinema. With just one scene, Dharmendra became the He-Man of the Hindi screen. He was at once the protector of women and the innocent son to them.

When Salman Khan removed his shirt in his films over two decades later, he was, therefore, said to be merely following in Dharmendra's footsteps. It was *Garam Dharam* (literally translated as 'Hot Dharam') who would always remain the trailblazer!

And as they say, destiny is supreme. Dharmendra made this

grade despite the fact that Sunil Dutt had been Ralhan's first choice for that rough and tough role. And midway through the film, Ralhan and Dharmendra had had temporary but serious differences, to the extent that the actor had almost thought of quitting the film because of what he considered as Ralhan's arrogance. He had even told his mother in that weak moment that he felt like quitting the industry.

In this context, it is of passing interest to note that in the late 1970s, Ralhan had been signed to direct the 70 mm *Samson and Delilah* with Dharmendra and Hema Malini. But the film did not even take off.

Phool Aur Patthar became Dharmendra's first movie to be the biggest hit in any year. What's more, the film earned the Best Actor female and male nominations for Meena Kumari and Dharmendra—his first as a leading man, from *Filmfare*, the same magazine that had mentored his debut. For the record, he had also been nominated as Best Supporting Actor earlier for *Ayee Milan Ki Bela*.

Some more Filmfare nominations followed in later years (for *Mera Gaon Mera Desh* in 1971, *Yaadon Ki Baaraat* in 1973, *Resham Ki Dori* in 1974, and *Naukar Biwi Ka* in 1983), but Dharmendra finally won a Filmfare Award only in 1990, and that was for being the producer of the Best Film—his maiden official production *Ghayal*! (Dharmendra had ghost-produced or financed many films before it.)

Ironically, the first acting award he won from the magazine was in 1997—the Lifetime Achievement Award, which was the first of many such trophies from other organizations.

Interestingly, for trivia hunters, *Phool Aur Patthar* had no lip-sync song for the actor, though Asha Bhosle's hits 'Sheeshe Se Pee' and 'Zindagi Se Pyar Karna Seekh Le' featured Shashikala (who loves Shakka in the film) and Dharmendra.

Aaye Din Bahaar Ke (1966)

Among the rest, *Aye Din Bahaar Ke* (released on Christmas Eve), Dharmendra's second film with producer J. Om Prakash (best known today as Hrithik Roshan's maternal grandfather), was another blockbuster. Omji, as he was known, had already produced the 1964 *Ayee Milan Ki Bela* with the actor. It was directed by Raghunath Jhalani, who had also been an assistant to Bimal Roy.

This was Dharmendra's first film with Asha Parekh as well as with composers Laxmikant-Pyarelal (L-P), who went on to compose for around sixty of his films—more than one-fifth of his A-list lead roles, including his home productions *Satyakam*, *Pratiggya* and *Yateem* (which starred not him but his son Sunny Deol).

One song enacted by Dharmendra in this 1966 hit, where he castigates the unfaithful girl he had loved, and actually wishes bad things for her in his rage, is considered iconic even today—'Mere Dushman Tu Meri Dosti Ko Tarse/Mujhe Gham Dene Wale Tu Khushi Ko Tarse' (My foe, may you pine for my friendship, and crave for happiness after giving me so much sorrow). When Anand Bakshi wrote this remarkable song (incidentally, Bakshi went on to be associated with Dharmendra in about the same number of films as L-P did), he went by the intensity of the emotions in the situation, and the song was masterfully rendered by Mohammed Rafi.

However, composer Pyarelal attributes most of the credit for the song's impact on-screen to the actor himself. 'Dharamji's expressions were incredible—natural without being over-the-top in the slightest way,' he observed. 'They were so very natural that he took our song to fabulous heights—*andar gussa bhara hua maloom padta hai* (You can actually sense the anger pent up inside him)!'

Asha Parekh, for a good many years, remained a favorite co-star of Dharmendra's. Every film of theirs as a romantic pair was to become at least a hit (*Aaya Sawan Jhoom Ke, Samadhi*), if not a blockbuster (*Shikar, Mera Gaon Mera Desh*). The pair later did more films, but never teamed up romantically in those (*Dharm Aur Qanoon, Hathyar, Batwara* and even their cameos in the Punjabi film *Kankan De Ohle*). The culmination came, oddly enough, minus Dharmendra, with Parekh playing Sunny Deol's mother in the 1984 *Manzil Manzil*.

There was an easy camaraderie between them, as if they were buddies. Parekh laughed when she recalled working with him for the first time, 'He had won the Filmfare United Producers' contest and worked with so many of my colleagues, but we did not come together for a long time. When we did, he was so shy, and I was a little hesitant to get close, as I had heard that he often drank. I had told Omji that I would not shoot with him whenever he was drunk, and to his credit, Dharam never drank when shooting with me.'

Amusingly, it was J. Om Prakash who was seriously concerned about the initial lack of rapport between his lead pair! He told Parekh, 'How will you shoot romantic scenes with him? No, no, you have to talk with him and break the ice. He's shy!' Slowly, Parekh and her reel hero became friends. 'I came to realize that he was indeed a nice person,' she said with a broad smile.

An example of their camaraderie is the very amusing incident which took place while shooting the popular song 'Mera Mehboob Hai Bemisaal' in Darjeeling, where Asha pushes him into a lake and takes away all his clothes. Parekh recollected that the water was bitterly cold even in the daytime and her hero truly froze in the water (in which he had to remain for a good while!) and had to be pulled out shivering. The unit hands rubbed a lot of brandy on him and suggested that he should drink some as well.

'And he looked at me for permission to have the brandy!' laughed the actress.

Dil Ne Phir Yaad Kiya (1966)

This film was to be originally directed by the legendary writer, lyricist and film-maker Pyarelal Santoshi (current whizkid—and Dharmendra's protégé—Rajkumar Santoshi's famous father). He had directed the hit *Dil Hi To Hai* for the same producers. However, due to creative differences, Santoshi exited and the film was directed by C.L. Rawal, brother of its producer B.L. Rawal. The film introduced the third brother G.L. Rawal as lyricist and Sonik-Omi as composers, and the music was a highlight.

This film, like most movies of that time, had an interesting plot: Dharmendra and Rehman's characters are friends who are ready to even sacrifice their lives for each other, but are unaware of each other's love interests. Dharmendra's girl Ashoo, essayed by Nutan, lives in a village. After she dies in an accident, and Dharmendra is devastated, Rehman comes to know that his fiancée Shabnam is the spitting image of the dead girl. The film is about the complications that arise when Rehman requests Shabnam to impersonate Ashoo (by pretending that she survived!).

The film rode on its emotional script and hit music—making it a winner at the box-office.

Baharen Phir Bhi Aayengi and *Mohabbat Zindagi Hai* (1966)

The third important film for Dharmendra that year was his only movie under Guru Dutt's banner, ironically after the film-maker's death and, more importantly, as his on-screen replacement.

Guru Dutt and Bimal Roy were among the main sponsors and judges of the *Filmfare* talent contest. From the plethora of newcomers, they had narrowed down the candidates to six, including Dharmendra. These were the names that were actually summoned for the finals.

And on the day of the finals, to be held at Central Studios in downtown Mumbai, Roy had taken ill, and Dutt was suddenly called to attend a court case. And so it happened that Dutt's friend and writer Abrar Alvi was left to conduct the test with instructions to check the contestants' faces, profiles and dialogue delivery from the film-maker.[1] At the contest—barring Dharmendra, who had a crew cut as mentioned earlier with hair just an inch high, everyone had long hair, modelled broadly on Dev Anand's style.

When Dutt returned, Alvi told him about this standout boy, adding that his dialogue delivery was insipid and almost without any modulation. This specialized view was but natural as Alvi was the chief dialogue-writer and modulator at Guru Dutt Films.

What turned the tables in favour of this boy were Alvi's next words, when Dutt asked him who was he like in terms of acting style. And Alvi, who had recognized the boy's originality, stated, 'Nobody! He is himself, has no pretensions, no set notions. The boy seems an original and it might be possible to mould him and develop his personality.'

Filmfare published the newcomer's photograph and Dutt was supposed to give him a break as well. But this did not happen, while Roy gave him a small but significant role in *Bandini*. It was after Dutt died, leaving *Baharen Phir Bhi Aayengi* incomplete as its producer as well as actor, and some other superstitious stars in the industry refused to take up his role, that Alvi decided to cash in on the goodwill he had earned.

Always a sentimental man, Dharmendra had earlier met Alvi by chance when the writer had gone to meet Meena Kumari in Madras. The actor had expressed how moved he was that Alvi had been gentle and kind with him over the screen test, telling him that he would willingly do any role for him. Alvi had even asked Dharmendra

---

[1] Saran, Sathya, *Ten Years with Guru Dutt: Abrar Alvi's Journey*, Penguin India, 2011.

how much he would charge, because by that time, he was already doing well for himself. But the actor had replied, 'If you think that I am right for the role, I will accept anything you pay me, from one rupee to one lakh!'

When the film was stuck for a replacement to Dutt, Alvi shrewdly cashed in on the conversation and wrote him a letter. At that time, Dharmendra was shooting for the Punjabi film *Ek Chaddar Maili Si* with Geeta Bali (which was never completed). Alvi told him that unless he took up the role, the company that had helped discover him would die, the camera would be sold and nothing would remain.

Dharmendra simply said, 'The film will be made,' and gave his dates immediately!

As it happened, the film was a flop (Dutt too was said to have mentally written off the film in his lifetime), but Dharmendra chalked up another film with Mala Sinha and Tanuja.

Ironically, the only other film of his that did not do well that year was *Mohabbat Zindagi Hai* with an interesting storyline that we will discuss later in this chapter. Common to both these flops was O.P. Nayyar's popular music: These were to be his only films with the actor.

Nayyar ended up giving Dharmendra three of his most memorable numbers: Rafi's 'Aap Ke Haseen Rukh Pe Aaj Naya Noor Hai' and Mahendra Kapoor's 'Badal Jaaye Agar Maali' (brilliantly penned respectively by Anjaan and Kaifi Azmi) in the former film and Rafi's 'Na Jaane Kyon Hamare Dil Ko Tumne Dil Nahin Samjha' (S.H. Bihari) in the latter.

The Bengal Influence—*Paari, Devar, Anupama* and *Mamta*

Dharmendra always had a huge regard for Bengalis, and a strange compatibility with them that was also mutual. The list was really long—Bimal Roy, Hrishikesh Mukherjee, Dulal Guha, Nabendu

Ghosh and a slew of other film-makers, writers and more.

At no phase in his career was this as prominent as it was in 1966. Four of his nine films had something to do with Bengal—*Paari, Devar, Mamta* and *Anupama*. And all were successful.

Paari was based on a story by the famous Bengali writer Jarasandha and starred Dharmendra with Pranoti Bhattacharya (née Ghosh), Abhi Bhattacharya and Dilip Kumar in a special cameo. Yes, Dharmendra finally realized a wish that he may not have even dreamt of—he worked with his idol and the *point d'appui* of his acting inclinations Dilip Kumar.

Paari was directed by Jagannath Chatterjee from Bengal and produced by Dharmendra's good friend and colleague Abhi Bhattacharya's wife, Pranoti, also his leading lady in the film.

A Mumbai producer, R.J. Vazirani, remade that film almost on a frame-to-frame basis as *Anokha Milan* (1972), but the move boomeranged. The film was rejected in a later starry era, in which Dharmendra as the hapless prisoner in Andaman, and also a victim of circumstances, was not accepted by audiences.

Childhood friends turning star-crossed lovers had become a recurring leitmotif in his films—*Shola Aur Shabnam, Devar* and *Paari* being examples. Discussing further how so many of his earlier films also had common character artistes like Bhattacharya, another Bengali in Tarun Bose, Mohan Choti, Shashikala, Deven Verma, Raj Mehra, Brahm Bharadwaj and even the senior leading man Balraj Sahni, Dharmendra had told me, 'In those days, these things were liked and appreciated. People would like to watch the same things, faces and combinations again and again.'

The 1966 hit, *Devar*, was the beginning of his long professional association with Sharmila Tagore. The two played childhood lovers. Due to the machinations of Dharmendra's stepbrother Deven Verma, the former marries Shashikala, whom Verma was supposed to wed, and Tagore weds Verma, who likes her and has thus engineered the switch. Of course, Verma is unaware that they were childhood sweethearts, and at that point even Tagore and Dharmendra do not realize that.

Just after Dharmendra becomes Tagore's devar (brother-in-law), a childhood song she would sing, 'Duniya Mein Aisa Kahaan Sab Ka Naseeb Hai/Koi Koi Apne Piya Ke Qareeb Hai' (Few people in this world are so lucky that they remain close to their sweethearts all their lives) makes him aware of this fact. And he is shattered.

At a party, he sings another song to make her aware of who he is—'Aaya Hai Mujhe Phir Yaad Woh Zaalim Guzara Zamaana Bachpan Ka/Haaye Re Akele Chhod Ke Jaana Aur Na Aana Bachpan Ka' (I remember again those times when we were children/Alas! that childhood has gone forever, leaving me lonely). Tagore realizes who he is, but in the finest tradition of Indian culture, accepts this 'separation' as part of life, happy that he will always be her beloved devar.

In the climax, when Dharmendra comes to know how Verma tricked all of them, they have an altercation and Verma is accidentally shot dead. During the trial that follows, an initially furious Tagore realizes that her childhood friend is actually blameless, and as the sole eyewitness to the accident, absolves him of the charge of murder.

This emotional family drama that resonated with the audience had a Bengali connect too: It was based on the Bengali short story *Naa* (No) by the Padma Bhushan and much-honoured Bengali author Tarasankar Bandopadhyay, the title signifying Tagore's character's last statement—that he was not her husband's murderer. The Mohan Segal-directed family melodrama was grandly supported by a fantastic score by composer Roshan and lyricist Anand Bakshi, with the classic Mukesh litany, 'Baharon Ne Mera Chaman Loot Kar' leading the list.

Sharmila Tagore recalled, 'When *Devar* was being made, we— Dharam, Deven Verma and I—were all newcomers. I was too busy focusing on myself as I had to make my career—*Devar* was among my first five or six films and my first serious role. But all three of us hit it off and became thick friends, enjoying the shooting, which was mostly happening at Mohan Studios, with a lot of work done at night.'

The bonhomie between them was to result in a thriller that did quite well five years later—*Yakeen*, which was produced by Verma (who also played a role), and starred Dharmendra in a double role with Tagore. The 1969 espionage drama was directed by Brij, and Verma got Hrishikesh Mukherjee to edit the film.

This brings us to Mukherjee, who went on to declare Dharmendra his all-time favourite actor. Hrishida (as Mukherjee was addressed by his associates) mischievously cast the *Devar* quartet of Dharmendra, Tagore, Shashikala and Deven Verma in a completely different way in his masterpiece *Anupama*, which also, like *Aaye Din Bahaar Ke* and *Devar*, enjoyed a silver jubilee run that year. This time Verma was supposed to marry Tagore, but Dharmendra finally marries her.

Dharmendra again 'underplayed' his role in the film. And yet again, he had a Bengali director in Mukherjee, who had been associated with Bimal Roy and had been his film editor as well. The story of an innocent girl targeted by her father because her mother died after giving birth to her saw Dharmendra essay a sensitive writer, who is inspired by the waif-like introverted girl to write a book on her. At this point, we must mention the extremely interesting fact that even in *Mohabbat Zindagi Hai*, the heroine's father keeps her away as his wife had died during her birth, but after that the story had a completely different trajectory!

As Mukherjee had told me way back in 1990, 'Many of my stories had real-life inspirations. I had seen *Anupama* happen to a cousin of mine!' The story idea was developed by him along with Bimal Dutta and D.N. Mukherjee. In fact, Hrishida was so close to this story that when he built his bungalow in Mumbai, he named it 'Anupama.'

And so we have good reason to believe that *Anupama* and his all-time favourite, *Satyakam*, which came three years later and was Dharmendra's home production, were both Mukherjee's favourites among his own films. Point is, they were not only Dharmendra's films, but also starred Sharmila Tagore.

'You are right,' said Tagore, when I mentioned another ace up Hrishida's sleeve—*Chupke Chupke*, easily the best of all his comedies— and the coincidence that both the actors had been in all three films! 'But look at how different the three films were,' said Tagore, subtly but effectively underscoring the fact that she and her co-star also played completely different characters in these three films.

We all know that Mukherjee employed stars to connect with the audiences, as his content was always different from formulaic film-making, but his scripts ensured that they all played ordinary, real life-like characters in realistic situations. And for this, the prime requisite was that the actors needed talent to deliver, to rise above their larger-than-life or stereotyped images and branding (like Dharmendra, who became an action hero, and even Rajesh Khanna and Amitabh Bachchan, with their respective popular avatars later) and let Mukherjee mould them to the requirements of his characters.

Rounding off that year was *Mamta*, based on Nihar Ranjan Gupta's Bengali story *Uttar Falguni*. Directed by yet another Bengali, Asit Sen (who had also made the Bengali original), it was essentially made in Calcutta (as Kolkata was then called) with the biggest Bengali star at the time, Suchitra Sen, playing the protagonist.

The film told the story of a woman (Sen) who ensured that her daughter from a relationship (Sen again) had a respectable and better life than her. Dharmendra (he was billed here as 'Dharmindar'!), in a way, played second fiddle to Ashok Kumar and came up with another low-key sensitive portrayal.

Stardom had finally gripped Dharmendra with a firm and lasting handshake.

Chapter Five

The Lull before the Storm

Aaj mausam beimaan hai bada / Beimaan hai aaj mausam / Aanewala koi toofan hai

A divine power always seemed to be working for Dharmendra. After 1966, a year that had made him strike truly big, there was an all-out disappointing year with four flops in 1967! Fortunately for him, *Aaye Din Bahaar Ke* had been released in the Christmas week of 1966 and had most of its silver jubilee-plus run in 1967.

In '67, to begin with, there was *Ghar Ka Chirag*, a children's film, which had Dharmendra in a special appearance. *Chandan Ka Palna* and *Majhli Didi* were his newest films with Meena Kumari, and both bombed. The latter was Dharmendra's second film with director Hrishikesh Mukherjee (and composer Hemant Kumar) after *Anupama*. Then there was the convoluted *Dulhan Ek Raat Ki*, loosely based on Thomas Hardy's *Tess of the D'Urbervilles* (with Nutan) and *Jab Yaad Kisiki Aati Hai* (again with Mala Sinha, this time in a double role).

Like *Ghar Ka Chirag*, all these movies were overcooked melodramas that were summarily rejected by the audience. Many songs from *Chandan Ka Palna* and *Dulhan Ek Raat Ki* were popular, but they could not save the films, including Madan Mohan's Rafi gem, 'Ek Haseen Shaam Ko Dil Mera Kho Gaya' from the latter movie. But this was just the lull before the storm.

My Name's Not Bond, It's Sunil!

The biggest hit of 1968 was *Ankhen*, and writer, producer and director Ramanand Sagar, known for his social films, stepped into espionage terrain with this wonderful musical blockbuster, co-starring Mala Sinha again. Dharmendra played a kind of a private spy, named Sunil Mehra.

By a tangy coincidence, this annual topper film was Dharmendra's second outing with the then top-ranking composer Ravi after the 1966 numero uno hit *Phool Aur Patthar*. It had his favourite singer Mohammed Rafi in the playback roster, but again had no song lip-syncing by him.

Songs *filmed* on him, like Lata Mangeshkar's 'Milti Hai Zindagi Mein Mohabbat Kabhi Kabhi' and 'Gairon Pe Karam Apnon Pe Sitam' for Mala Sinha, along with Rafi's 'Jis Mulq Ki Sarhad Ko Koi Chhoo Nahin Sakta' were all the rage in those times.

Ankhen was planned soon after *Sangam* (1964), and so Sagar had apprehensions about casting Dharmendra, since he was not yet a star at that time. With a business angle in mind, he cast top star Mala Sinha as the heroine. Sinha was also one of the two top heroines (alongside Nanda) who were always open to work with newcomers.

As (Dharmendra's and) Sagar's luck would have it, 1966 saw *Phool Aur Patthar* roar into the blockbuster zone, and Sagar decided to mount the film on a higher scale and confirm Dharmendra as the leading man. As we have said before, the divine power (Dharmendra is known to be an Arya Samaj follower and their doctrine is about worshipping a single supreme power) seemed to be holding

Dharmendra's hand firmly, guiding him towards bigger and bigger glories.

The film, despite its grand scale, was the biggest hit (it got the highest return on investment, the sole criterion then for quantifying a film's business level as flop, success, hit or blockbuster) of that year. And piquantly, Dharmendra's first heroine Kum Kum was his sister in the film—an index of his growth as a star.

Until then, just four Hindi films had been shot abroad, and among them, *Sangam* had been the only superhit. India's first 70 mm film *Around the World* had capsized in the previous year, and *Night In London* and *An Evening In Paris* had done only decent business. *Ankhen* became the second money-spinner, and in that year, Dharmendra also notched up another golden jubilee (a run of fifty continuous weeks at the theatres) named *Shikar*.

The Guru Dutt Connection Finally Clicks

Guru Dutt's brother Atma Ram produced and directed *Shikar*, the jungle adventure-cum-murder mystery in which Dharmendra played the intrepid manager of a forest estate who helps Kiran (Asha Parekh), suspected of killing his womanizer friend, prove her innocence.

Clearly, the canvas of Dharmendra's roles was growing. And this was a film made under Guru Dutt's banner by his brother. As if to make up for their flop *Baharen Phir Bhi Aayengi*, and reward Dharmendra with a nice gift from one of his mentors, the film, also scripted by Abrar Alvi like their earlier misadventure, emerged as a huge musical hit.

Asha Parekh was the leading lady, and this time, the man who played the cop and won the Filmfare Best Supporting Actor Award—Sanjeev Kumar—would strike a friendship along the way with Dharmendra as well, enough to be signed on as the second lead in Dharmendra's first home production, *Satyakam*. Dharmendra was to do *Dost* with him as well, later, but the film finally fell in the lap of another of the actor's closest industry friends—Shatrughan Sinha.

Future co-star Leena Chandavarkar was to recall that her brother Anil was on the *Shikar* unit's team and this was a sort of first connection for her with Dharmendra, whose fan she had always been—the Guru Dutt family and the Chandavarkars were related. When *Shikar* was being made, the actress was eking out her own struggles in the film world.

There were three more films that Dharmendra released that year, and all consolidated his strong future bond with composers Laxmikant-Pyarelal after their first collaboration in *Aaye Din Bahaar Ke—Mere Hamdam Mere Dost, Izzat* and *Baharon Ki Manzil*. Of these, the last one did not do well, and had no song lip-synched by the star, with all its four songs sung by Lata Mangeshkar. But the music of each of these films was a hit, especially of the first two movies, and helped the films' openings and performances—because in those days the soundtrack albums were always released weeks or months before the motion picture hit the screens, and also ensured repeat audiences.

Izzat was based on a story by Dulal Guha, but was directed by noted film-maker T. Prakash Rao (of *Sasural* fame) from the South. And why was that? Putul Guha, son of the late film-maker, shed light on the curious phenomenon of a story penned by one of Dharmendra's closest director friends but given to someone else to direct. 'My father had liked a story lying with producers A.K. Nadiadwala and R.C. Kumar, *Dil Maange Moti*, which he took from them but could finally never make. In those days, it was more about relationships than money, so my father offered them his own story in return, rather than paying money. He was busy with two films, *Jyoti* and *Dharti Kahe Pukar Ke*, and because they wanted to make the film immediately, they signed Rao.'

Today, *Izzat* is recalled as Tamil superstar and politician Jayalalithaa's only Hindi movie as a heroine. It was also Dharmendra's first instance of playing a double role, and had him play half-brothers, one an Adivasi and the other a wealthy heir.

The story was reminiscent of Salim-Javed's 1978 blockbuster *Trishul*, with the illegitimate son swearing revenge on his father, who had dumped his mother, but for the fact that in this one the legitimate son also had his father's tendencies and was also played by Dharmendra.

'Kya Miliye Aise Logon Se' was a hard-hitting Sahir Ludhianvi song on the fake prestige of rich men who exploit and betray others, while the all-hit score also had another all-time Dharmendra gem, 'Yeh Dil Tum Bin Kahin Lagta Nahin', featuring him (as the Adivasi) with the other heroine, Tanuja.

Guha elaborated, 'The revenge was more along the lines of a *Satyakam* rather than a *Trishul*, wherein he realizes that he has a brother who is fair-complexioned but looks like him. However, that brother too showed a gray streak.'

Despite the Mohammed Rafi-dominated music being a rage, the film did only average business. Guha attributes the reason to the main hero Dharmendra and Jayalalithaa looking unprepossessing. 'It was a lesson worth learning for film-makers, but a few have not done so even today—and that is, never to make a good-looking star look ugly on screen!' he said.

Mere Humdum Mere Dost, however, became the third consecutive hit for the Dharmendra-Sharmila Tagore pair after *Devar* and *Anupama*. Its all-hit seven-song musical score helped the show become memorable. The story was quite routinely melodramatic again, but it was liked by the audiences.

The two films that did not fare well were *Baharon Ki Manzil*, which, as it turned out, was the last Dharmendra-Meena Kumari film, and *Baazi*, which co-starred Waheeda Rehman and was produced by Tony Walker, brother to comedian Johnny Walker. Both were essentially suspense dramas, but while the latter was a murder mystery, the former had deeper elements. Once again, with Dharmendra playing a psychiatrist and a deputy superintendent of police respectively, he had no songs to 'sing' in either film.

Baharon Ki Manzil had two interesting points, one being that Dharmendra's name in the film was Dr Rajesh Khanna. Secondly, yet again a Dharmendra film had its heroine in a dual role (after Nanda in *Mera Qusoor Kya Hai*, Nutan in *Dil Ne Phir Yaad Kiya*, Suchitra Sen in *Mamta* and Mala Sinha in *Jab Yaad Kisi Ki Aati Hai*).

Ending the 1960s with a Bang

And then it was time for Dharmendra to essay a double role again in his friend Deven Verma's debut as producer, the spy drama, *Yakeen*, released just a year after *Izzat*. *Yakeen*, which did above-average business, was about a scientist kidnapped by enemy powers and replaced by a lookalike, and the drama that ensues between the impostor and the scientist's loved one (Sharmila Tagore), cook and dog. Once again, hit songs (by Shankar-Jaikishan) added to the allure and thus to the business of the film. In a way, the second role was Dharmendra's first all-negative role.

The story goes that the only difference between the two Dharmendras was in the colour of the eyes—the imposter had blue eyes, for which the actor had to wear contact lenses. This irritated Dharmendra during shooting and he was once even terse with Javed Akhtar, who was then assisting director Brij and was in charge of giving the dialogue sheets to the actors!

When Akhtar made a mistake once and gave Dharmendra a wrong sheet of lines, he rebuked him sharply. A short while later, the ever-grounded star summoned him to his make-up room, explained why he had been 'rude' (because the lenses had made him irritable!)

and apologized to the humble assistant. To date, Akhtar has never forgotten this shining example of a celebrity's down-to-earth nature.

(It is interesting here to know that the only Dharmendra double-role film that worked big-time was his 1975 home production, *Pratiggya*, where, in a cameo, he played the father of the hero who looked exactly like him. The 'two' Dharmendras never came face-to-face on screen.)

A later home production also with a father-and-son double role, *Samadhi* (1972) and then *Ghazab* (1982), in which he played dissimilar twin brothers, were also average successes. The rest of his double-role dramas flopped. It was clear that audiences did not want any dilution in their fan following for the actor—not even from a lookalike in a second role. Two Dharmendras for the price of one were, probably, not so exciting!

Aya Sawan Jhoom Ke in 1969 reprised the entire core team of *Aaye Din Bahaar Ke*—producer J. Om Prakash, director Raghunath Jhalani, co-star Asha Parekh, writers Sachin Bhaumick and Sarshar Sailani, composers Laxmikant-Pyarelal, lyricist Anand Bakshi and some key technicians. Despite the music being even more popular than that of their 1966 collaboration, the film was a hit, but fell short of the previous film's box-office performance. However, it was a hat-trick of hits for Dharmendra and Asha Parekh.

Aadmi Aur Insaan was Dharmendra's only association with Yash Chopra, and was slightly delayed due to Saira Banu's illness (a situation that, as the entire industry knows, spurred the making of the hit quickie *Ittefaq*) and finally underperformed vis-à-vis its investment. And in this saga of corruption, the script cleverly blended material corruption with the rotting of a human being, explaining the subtle difference between Aadmi (man as in the biological species Homo Sapiens) and Insaan (the meaning extended to be a good human being at heart).

Once again, in a Dharmendra film, another actor, Feroz Khan, walked away with the Filmfare Best Supporting Actor Award.

Pyar Hi Pyar did average business and was Dharmendra's only film with Vyjayanthimala and the actor's first with director-on-a-roll Bhappi Sonie. The veteran actress said about her youngest-ever hero: 'Dharam was really nice, did not speak much because he was shy, and was very charming. He was shy, I guess, because I was already an established actress when he had started out as an actor. It was very easy working with him, and I was told he agreed to do the film *only* because he knew I would be his leading lady and he had wanted to work with me.' By the time the film was ready, Vyjayanthimala had got married and had already decided to wean off films.

The young hero, she remembered, even wanted to know about a specific step in their only duet, 'Tu Meri Main Tera', and she had helped him out with that. 'Then we had an interesting song in the film that was nicely thought out—"Main Kahin Kavi Na Ban Jaaoon/ Tere Pyar Mein Ae Kavita." It was filmed on the set of a lift and we had to express love in a subtle manner,' the actress said.

One more interesting tidbit here: Hrishikesh Mukherjee had already become the go-to film editor whenever a film's footage was either excessive or confusing. He came in to edit *Pyar Hi Pyar* and had also edited the 1968 *Mere Humdum Mere Dost*, and, as mentioned earlier, *Yakeen*. So, for trivia-lovers, Hrishida was involved in five of the Dharmendra-Sharmila Tagore films—in *Anupama* and *Satyakam* as director, *Mere Hamdam Mere Dost* and *Yakeen* as film editor, and *Chupke Chupke* as both producer and director!

Later, he was to also be the scissor-hands on his *Phagun* (1973) and *Yakeen*'s director Brij's delayed but overshot saga *Professor Pyarelal* in 1981. Surely, so many films, apart from Dharmendra working under Mukherjee so often, could not be a coincidence?

Dharmendra does not exactly recall, however, how Hrishida came into all these '60s films as editor. 'I may have put in a word,' he admitted. 'But Hrishida was loved by the entire industry, and he would readily edit such films that were totally removed from the kind of stories that he himself liked to make.'

But we have reason to conclude that there was more to it (from the actor's side) than meets the eye! Their bond was respectful (from Dharmendra), deeply affectionate (from Hrishida) and very strong, and Dharmendra's instant reply when I had posed this query to him was, 'My God! You have gone so deep into my career!'

Bengal is Back

And this brings us to the two, so-to-speak, 'Bengali' Hindi films of Dharmendra that year as well—both of which were commercial flops but critically acclaimed: *Khamoshi* and *Satyakam*.

Khamoshi was produced by composer Hemant Kumar. Its script and lyrics writer Gulzar recalled, 'This film was my first association with Dharam as a screenwriter. It was a remake of Asit Sen's Bengali film *Deep Jale Jaye*. The cameo that Dharmendra did had been done in the original film by Asit Sen himself. But in that film, the character remains in the shadows and is never revealed, so only his silhouette is seen. But Dharmendra was a big star already. So in this film starring Rajesh Khanna in the lead, which was launched before the release of his breakthroughs in *Aradhana* and *Do Raaste*, it was necessary that Dharmendra be shown. And so my song "Tum Pukar Lo" was filmed on him.'

For Gulzar the lyricist, however, this was not a first with Dharmendra. In the 1963 film *Purnima*, the hit songs, 'Tumhen Zindagi Ke Ujaale Mubarak' and the duet 'Humsafar Mere Humsafar', were penned by him for the actor.

That brings us to the most important film (from the actor's point of view) of that year—Dharmendra's home production *Satyakam*. Officially produced by his brother-in-law S.J.S. Punchhe, it remains its director Hrishikesh Mukherjee's own favourite among the forty-three films he directed between 1957 and 1996.

The story narrated the travails of Satyapriya ('lover of truth') Acharya, a complete idealist who is thus a total misfit in the pre-Independence and neo-Independence Indian society. So pure is he that before he dies, he also imbibes his wife (Sharmila Tagore) and her son (who was born out of her being sexually exploited by a rich man and is adopted by Satyapriya as his own child—a second such example after *Begaana* on screen!) with the same values.

Based on a Bengali story by renowned writer Narayan Sanyal, Dharmendra's performance in *Satyakam* is considered among the best in his career, even if he was just being himself—soft, caring and gentle. And 'underplay' again became the catchword for another role essayed by Dharmendra.

The Bengali connection in *Khamoshi* (Asit Sen, Hemant Kumar, story-writer Ashutosh Mukherjee) had been prominent again, and so was it with *Satyakam*, as the screenplay also was by Bimal Dutta. Co-stars Ashok Kumar, Sharmila Tagore, and key character actor Robi Ghosh were all Bengalis.

However, as was with a fairly comparable case of Salman Khan in *Tubelight*, the goody-goody-gumdrops character did not work with the masses. They probably sensed, even in 1969, that so much idealism within the system was not just foolish but detrimental for survival within a corrupt system.

Of course, *Satyakam* was set in the times of the idealistic fervour of neo-Independence, but cynicism had already crept in, and showing how minds were already corrupted in the 1947 to '50s phase made it all too real—uncomfortably so. Maybe the film would have worked a bit with a serious actor who was not a star, or with a lesser one. And this was truly ironic, considering the very goal of the story.

The leisured pace and excessive length of the film (it was 18 reels, which translates into 175 minutes!) and the fact that that the tough softie did not so much as raise his voice (except in a passing argument with his friend Narendra, played by Sanjeev Kumar) added to the film's non-appeal.

Mukherjee also went on to break convention by including all three songs (brilliantly written by Kaifi Azmi and composed by Laxmikant-Pyarelal) in the first half, leaving the second half even drier.

Dharmendra was definitely disillusioned by the fate of this ambitious adventure (in terms of content and his image). But there was a silver lining—the film won the National Award for Best Hindi film (₹5,000 for producer Punchhe and a medal for Mukherjee) and, once again, there was a Filmfare Award for someone else—dialogue writer Rajinder Singh Bedi. How depressed Dharmendra was by the film's non-performance became really clear some five years later, when he played another idealist, as we shall see in the '70s.

And perhaps this audience's rejection of *Satyakam* is a partly, if not wholly, rational explanation of why Dharmendra went towards mainstream commercial films with a vengeance in the next two decades.

Chapter Six

Dharmendra in the 1970s: Part I

*Ek haseen shaam ko / Dil mera kho gaya / Pehle apna hua
karta tha / Ab kisi ka ho gaya*

The stage was set. Contrary to popular perception, there was quite a distinct phase in which Dharmendra *was* the absolute numero uno—from 1969 (in fact) to 1977. During that phase, he belonged to everyone who had ever watched Hindi cinema.

History tells us that Rajesh Khanna was conferred the title of being 'The Phenomenon', India's first superstar in the wake of his performance (in all senses of the term including the box-office) between late 1969 and 1971, during which he had only two flops. There was hysteria, but not consistency after that, and all through that same hyped phase, Dharmendra remained the biggest Hindi film star, the numero uno as per the trade.

We have already talked about how he had scored in 1969. In 1970, he had three massive hits—opening his account with Hema Malini, he had *Sharafat* and *Tum Haseen Main Jawan*. There was a massive hit in *Jeevan Mrityu* (which completed an incredible 100 weeks' run in matinee shows!), and the successful *Kab? Kyoon? Aur Kahan?* as well.

The year 1971 saw the giant *Mera Gaon Mera Desh* and the superhit *Naya Zamana*, besides the successful *Guddi* and *Rakhwala*. Following it, 1972 saw blockbusters *Raja Jani* and *Seeta Aur Geeta* besides more successes. And 1973 was a bumper year with four superhits in *Loafer*, *Kahani Kismat Ki*, *Jugnu* and *Yaadon Ki Baaraat* leading his list of nine releases, of which only two (one in a prolonged special appearance) were flops.

Then came the time when the Amitabh Bachchan phenomenon happened, and still, it was Dharmendra who recommended his name to Ramesh Sippy after Shatrughan Sinha turned down *Sholay*. The year 1974 had seen *Dost* and 1975 saw, besides *Sholay*, his iconic films *Pratiggya* and *Chupke Chupke*.

It was only in 1977, when Amitabh Bachchan's *Amar Akbar Anthony* outclassed the box-office collections of the same film-maker Manmohan Desai's two Dharmendra-starring hits *Dharam-Veer* and *Chacha Bhatija* that the Jat hero settled in a clear second position.

This was also the time when Vinod Khanna was being touted as the next rival to Bachchan, but his track-record could not match up even to that of top heroes Shashi Kapoor, Rishi Kapoor, Sanjeev Kumar and Jeetendra, leave alone match Dharmendra's superior-to-them-all box-office power.

There was a clear-cut situation at the time: Dharmendra was now the action hero. He was doing non-crime dramas only as a change, and the good ones among them also succeeded. The base line was that he was loved no matter what he did. And most, if not all, of these action or crime dramas could not have been even envisaged minus this macho man with the soft heart and soul.

And the '70s saw one more phenomenon: It began Dharmendra's most famous on- and off-screen romantic association with Hema Malini.

The Hema Malini Phase Begins:

Asit Sen's *Sharafat* was the first Dharam-Hema film to hit the screen. Mahesh Kaul, who had directed Hema Malini in her debut film *Sapnon Ka Saudagar*, had written this story of a courtesan (Hema Malini), the unwitting daughter of a rich man who has adopted a young man (Dharmendra) as his own and brought him up.

As the film proceeds, the courtesan and the young man, who is a lecturer in a nearby college, develop a sweet relationship—she tells him to educate her like he would any other student, and falls in love with him even before he reciprocates. Her father, who has refused to accept her mother and her in society, is now contesting a Lok Sabha election and when the young man comes to know by chance that his benefactor is the courtesan's real parent, he too is caught in the dilemma of gratitude versus truth. The film's title was satirical: *Sharafat*, which means decency or respectability, as the film exposed the hypocritical social mores of the rich and the influential.

Bandini's scriptwriter Nabendu Ghosh penned a much more positive and progressive screenplay here, and, once again, Laxmiknat-Pyarelal's music was a highlight, with trenchantly incisive songs by Anand Bakshi—with all the lyrics lambasting the spurious sanctimony of the custodians of society.

However, the other Dharam-Hema film, *Tum Haseen Main Jawan*, was a typical potboiler with an involved family story and the angle of a baby whose parentage was not known. The heroine (Hema Malini) was accused of being the baby's unwed mother. Bhappi Sonie's formulaic story had every ingredient of a commercial film of those times—a cabaret song by Helen (this one was on sneezing!), comedy, a villain, a chase, a lost-and-found element and more.

The film performed very well at the box-office. The Kishore Kumar song, 'Munne Ki Amma/Yeh To Bataa' was a hit and with this, the two co-stars of *Ganga Ki Lehren*—Kumar and Dharmendra—

began a long association as singer and actor that also extended to his home productions *Samadhi, Dillagi* and *Sitamgar*. Of course, Kishore had also sung in *Satyakam* earlier, but for supporting artistes in an ensemble song, 'Zindagi Hai Kya', in which Mukesh had been Dharmendra's voice.

Variety as Spice

Jeevan Mrityu, as mentioned earlier, also scored high at the box-office. It was a skilled adaptation (along with modernization and Indianization) by Dr Vishwanath Rai (credited with the story) and Govind Moonis (screenplay) of the classic 1884 Alexandre Dumas novel *The Count of Monte Cristo*.

Again, Dharmendra gave one of his better performances under a Bengali director: This time, it was Satyen Bose. The Mohammed Rafi-Lata Mangeshkar duet, 'Jhilmil Sitaron Ka Aangan Hoga / Rimjhim Barasta Saawan Hoga' (Our home will be either lit up by stars, or there will be the gentle patter of rain) spoke about an idyllic romantic nook of a couple in love and was a chartbuster.

(A year later, the film's Malayalam dubbed version, *Jeevitha Samaram*, was released with Yesudas and S. Janaki singing the dubbed songs. This was the first time Yesudas sang for the actor. Later, he was to sing for him in the Hindi films *Chhoti Si Baat* and *Swami*, in both of which Dharmendra had only cameos.)

Farida Jalal had an interesting but unconfirmed nugget to share about this film. She had made her debut in *Taqdeer* (1967) produced by Tarachand Barjatya of Rajshri Productions, the same banner that made *Jeevan Mrityu* as well. In a mock-complaining way, she told me, 'I was considered for the role played by Raakhee (who was the female lead). But since I played Dharam's heroine Meena Kumari's daughter from Rehman in *Baharon Ki Manzil*, he persuaded the Barjatyas not to cast me! In a way, I missed my major break as a heroine because of him! But nevertheless, Dharam is a complete darling.'

Piquantly, Tarachand's son Rajat Kumar Barjatya, who was around when his father made the film, denies that Jalal was ever considered, but the weight of credibility does seem to go towards the actress, who could not have cooked up such a story from her imagination and had already been signed as the second lead in Rajesh Khanna's *Aradhana*!

Another success that year was Dharmendra's second film with mentor Arjun Hingorani, *Kab? Kyoon? Aur Kahan?*, co-starring Babita. Kalyanji-Anandji were once again in charge of the music and gave some popular songs like 'Dil to Dil Hai' and 'Pyar Se Dil Bhar De'. The success of this film made Hingorani opt for the '3-K' formula for the titles of most of his future films, all of which starred Dharmendra.

Not all films with this formula succeeded, though—in fact, only the next film *Kahani Kismat Ki* (1973) was a superhit. *Khel Khilari Ka* (1977) just broke even, *Kaatilon Ke Kaatil* (1981) was a success, and the rest, *Karishma Kudrat Kaa* (1985) and *Kaun Kare Kurbanie* (1991) were flops.

Hingorani, a qualified dentist, was, perhaps, one of the oldest followers of numerology in films, as the above titles prove. His most ambitious venture, *Sultanat* (1986), which co-starred Dharmendra and son Sunny Deol and also introduced both Shashi Kapoor's son Karan Kapoor (we wonder if his 2-K name had something to do with it!) and Juhi Chawla, was a disaster, and so was his last movie, *Kaise Kahoon Ke Pyaar Hai* (2003), where he tried out the 3-K formula with two words added!

But if the film with Babita did well, Dharmendra's only outing with her more famous aunt, Sadhana (most people wrongly think the two actresses are cousins) was a box-office failure. The pair would have looked even better had Sadhana, by then, not developed a hormonal problem that wreaked havoc with her looks and curtailed her career.

Once again directed by Ramesh Saigal, it also starred Biswajeet in a grey role and had some fantastic music from S.D. Burman and Anand Bakshi, which included a chain of Lata Mangeshkar gems, Rafi's 'Mehbooba Teri Tasveer' and Rafi-Lata's 'Yeh Dil Diwana Hai'.

Two more films of Dharmendra were rejected that year—*Man Ki Ankhen*, directed by Raghunath Jhalani with Waheeda Rehman (this team was truly jinxed for all time!) and Raj Kapoor's *Mera Naam Joker*. The latter film, now considered a classic, had Dharmendra featuring in the second part of the three-chapter story (of 25 reels, with two intermissions!) as a circus owner.

This was the chapter in which Raj Kapoor was paired with Russian actress and ballet dancer Ksiena Rabiankina (name as billed in the film's credits). In fact, the opening sequence of the circus performance, after which the story unfolds in flashback, featured Dharmendra, shown in the beginning of the film with grey hair.

Raj Kapoor's son Rishi Kapoor, who was cast as Raj Kapoor's adolescent avatar in the film, remembered first meeting Dharmendra around 1967 or 1968, shortly after the film took off. He said, 'I saw this tough, very handsome Punjabi actor the whole country was swooning over, going ga-ga over. He was the embodiment of youth and was a big star for someone his age. And I will never forget the generosity and great gesture he showed to my father: After all, in this film, he did not have the main role. Of course, he was the hero of his part of the film.'

Kapoor remembered Dharmendra telling him, 'I used to stand outside RK Studios as a struggler, wondering when I would ever get a chance to get into the premises! And now, I actually got the chance to work with Raj Kapoor himself, not just as a co-actor but under his direction as well!' Kapoor also recalled that Dharmendra took a much lower fee than what he commanded back then for a film. And Dharmendra had said that he had once requested Raj Kapoor to give him the opportunity of working with him!

The Dharmendra–Rajesh Khanna 'Battle'

In 1971 came what is, in a way, Dharmendra's most interesting role, in Hrishikesh Mukherjee's *Guddi*, which launched Jaya Bhaduri aka Jaya Bachchan's acting career. Guddi was a film-struck girl, a rabid fan of Dharmendra the (real) actor, and so Dharmendra played himself, that too in the male lead, in this Hrishikesh Mukherjee delight. There are dozens of examples of actors playing themselves in cameos (including by Dharmendra himself), but lead roles were not seen at all, though there was an occasional example or two much later.

Story, screenplay, dialogue and lyrics writer Gulzar recalls, '*Guddi* was an already-published short story of mine. In my original story, the girl's name was Guddo and she was crazy about Dilip Kumar. Hrishida asked me to develop it, saying that he needed someone who was a top hero from the current generation on screen.'

The writer-director explained, 'There were only two options then for that kind of stardom: Rajesh Khanna and Dharmendra. We chose Dharam unanimously, both because of his personality and enduring stardom (Rajesh Khanna had just made it big) as well as the fact that he was Hrishida's favourite as well as a friend of mine. Actually, Hrishida wanted me to direct *Guddi* as well, but I was tied up with *Mere Apne*, my directorial debut. So that's how I finally missed directing Dharam in a leading role, other than in his cameo in my *Kinara*. And the world knows that my *Devdas* with him in the title-role remained incomplete.'

Here is where *Guddi* co-producer (with Mukherjee), N.C. Sippy's son Raj N. Sippy, executive producer of this film and many others, and Gulzar's assistant director in many films including his own co-productions *Mere Apne, Koshish* and *Achanak*, partly contradicts his mentor. Sippy asked: 'Can you ever imagine Rajesh Khanna, despite all his talent, in Dharamji's place in *Guddi*? As far as my father and I knew, there was no second option to Dharmendra. After all, there is not much difference between the real man and the star we showed in the film.' He added that his father never once questioned Mukherjee on his choice of subjects, cast or technicians, but was certain that the veteran director could never have thought of anyone else.

Within the film, Dharmendra is taken into confidence by the star-struck girl's family and helps disillusion the teenager by showing how her real hero is just a regular man and not a superhuman object of adoration and love, as she knows him from his movie avatars.

The second film that played a crucial part in Dharmendra's career was *Mera Gaon Mera Desh*, directed by Raj Khosla. It was an epic dacoit saga inspired by the revolutionary credo of Mahatma Gandhi, 'If I have to choose between cowardice and violence, I will choose violence.'

The plot was interesting: An ex-army Major catches a petty thief Ajit (Dharmendra) and hands him over to the police, and he is sentenced to six months in jail. After completing his sentence, Ajit approaches the Major for employment and is asked to help out on his farm. Soon, he comes to know of a dacoit (Jabbar Singh, played by Vinod Khanna) and decides to take him on. Gandhiji's dictum comes in as the entire village is terrified of Jabbar and it is Ajit who persuades them to unite against the dacoits and exterminate them.

The phenomenally popular songs, led by 'Maar Diya Jaaye/Ki Chhod Diya Jaaye/Bol Tere Saath Kya Sulook Kiya Jaaye', where the dacoit's girl (played by Laxmi Chhaya) asks the captive Ajit to tell her whether he should be freed or killed for his moves against her chief, led the endemically popular score by Laxmikant-Pyarelal and Anand Bakshi.

It is also a part of music-lore that the popular Dharmendra-Asha Parekh duet 'Kuch Kehta Hai Yeh Sawan' was cleverly reprised by R.D. Burman and Anand Bakshi in *Dacait*, the 1987 dacoit drama starring Sunny Deol, as 'Kis Karan Naiyya Doli', though it did not reach anywhere near the popularity of this chartbuster.

But more importantly, there were truly interesting parallels between this Khosla epic and the 1975 *Sholay* that is even today Indian cinema's biggest and most-watched film. Watch the two films back-to-back, and we wonder at how Salim-Javed, in their interviews, always credited two foreign films as inspirations for their blockbuster but did not so much as mention that Raj Khosla opus.

Besides common members like Dharmendra, Lata Mangeshkar, art director Ram Yedekar and lyricist Anand Bakshi, we have other piquant commonalities. Both films had a village cowering before a ruthless gang of dacoits led by a wholly amoral leader. And this villain, Jabbar Singh (Vinod Khanna's character) and Gabbar Singh (that of Amjad Khan) had names that were too similar to be coincidences.

Secondly, in both films we had a coin tossed—by Dharmendra in the former and by Amitabh Bachchan in the latter, to make crucial decisions. Thirdly, in the earlier film Dharmendra was a petty thief, and in the second, bigger movie, both heroes were small-time thieves as well.

Finally, the man who reforms them is also amazingly similar: In *Mera Gaon Mera Desh*, it was the ex-army Major, played by Jayant, who had lost a leg in a war, and in *Sholay*, it was an ex-policeman, Sanjeev Kumar, whose arms had been cut off by the dacoit when he employs these two men to catch him alive. The clincher was that Dharmendra stoutly confirmed the inspirations that *Mera Gaon Mera Desh* provided for *Sholay*!

The film was a close second to *Haathi Mere Saathi* in 1971's sweepstakes, which had the advantage of being a children's film with animals, released during summer vacations, apart from the hysteria around its hero Rajesh Khanna.

Dharmendra's *Rakhwala*, again with Vinod Khanna as the second lead and villain, was a South confection that fared modestly. But another major hit was the social *Naya Zamana*, with which Pramod

Chakravorty made a departure from his crime thrillers and formula films to fashion a hard-hitting social drama about the clash between the haves and the have-nots. The third consecutive box-office hit with Hema Malini, it was based on a powerful story by novelist Gulshan Nanda.

The hard-hitting Bakshi-written 'Duniya O Duniya Tera Jawaab Nahin/Teri Jafaaon Ka Bas Koi Hisaab Nahin' (O world, there is no limit to the injustices you mete out) perhaps completed the trilogy of angst-ridden solo songs filmed on Dharmendra, after 'Mere Dushman Tu Meri Dosti Ko Tarse' (*Aaye Din Bahaar Ke*) and 'Kya Miliye Aise Logon Se' (*Izzat*). For the record, it was the first substantial song sung for him by Kishore Kumar, and was composed by S.D. Burman, who studded this hit film with a score to match.

Zoom Lanes

The year 1972 was another fruitful year for the actor, and perhaps it was in this twelve-month period that Dharmendra finally got a decisive edge over Rajesh Khanna, for the second half was studded with superhits and hits for Dharam and a chain of flops for the latter.

We have already discussed *Paari* from the 1960s. Its Hindi remake, *Anokha Milan*, released and sank that year. *Lalkar*, the war drama with intertwined romantic triangles (Rajendra Kumar and Dharmendra with Mala Sinha, and Sinha and Kum Kum with Dharmendra) was the other flop the actor had, thanks to its expensive cost. In those days, when computer graphics were unheard of, Ramanand Sagar got many miniatures and costly sets made so that explosions and other technical aspects required to depict a war could be shown.

An *Ankhen*-inspired Sagar, with the successful Rajendra Kumar-Mala Sinha-Kum Kum film *Geet* (1970) just behind him, decided to merge the cast of both films. He wove in an interesting story: Two brothers, one in the Army and one in the Air Force, unknowingly falling in love with the same girl, with a gypsy girl falling in love with Dharmendra as well. The film was set in the aftermath of World War II, when Japan was invading India.

The last nail on this film's coffin, presumably, came from the fact that Rajendra Kumar (now on a decisive fade-out run) won the heroine again (like in *Ayee Milan Ki Bela*) over the supremely popular Dharmendra, who even 'died' in the film's climax!

Samadhi, which was produced by Dharmendra's relative Bhagwant Singh with G.L. Khanna, as mentioned earlier, was a double-role dacoit drama with the actor as father (this was his last romantic liaison on screen with Asha Parekh) and son (opposite Jaya Bhaduri). Prakash Mehra had tried to sell the same producers (and, therefore, Dharmendra) the idea for Salim-Javed's *Zanjeer*, which was rejected. He was assigned to direct this film, which did good business, with hit songs composed by R.D. Burman.

The film had the absurd angle of the younger Dharmendra not recognizing the resemblance to his father in a beard (complete with an identical voice!), and even sillier, the foster father not realizing the truth though he had seen the father who, when younger, was his son's spitting image! But then, that was how Hindi cinema functioned at that time, with liberal cinematic licences in logic! Dharmendra said about this with a laugh, 'People loved actors like me and did not bother about these things!'

R.D. Burman composed the music for two more films for Dharmendra that year, all packed with hit songs—*Do Chor* and *Seeta Aur Geeta*. The former was produced by Raj Khosla, who gave his chief assistant Padmanabh an independent film. Tanuja was the heroine in this caper movie, where Dharmendra, again a petty but notorious thief, is accused of four thefts that have been actually carried out for a specific reason by another 'thief', Tanuja.

The film paid an open tribute to its illustrious Dharmendra-Raj

Khosla predecessor—when Dharmendra is accused of one of the robberies, his alibi is: 'I was watching *Mera Gaon Mera Desh* at the time the robbery took place!'

Seeta Aur Geeta was the first of the two films Ramesh Sippy did with Hema Malini, Sanjeev Kumar and several common cast and crew members, besides Dharmendra. The biggest hit of 1972, it had Dharmendra as a street-smart performer along with the firebrand Hema Malini (Geeta). Geeta's character falls in love with the urbane doctor (Sanjeev Kumar). And Dharmendra's character, used to Geeta's volatile temperament, meets and falls for the milder twin Seeta.

Seeta Aur Geeta was the first of the smart spin-offs of *Ram Aur Shyam*, the Dilip Kumar double-role film released in 1967. Of course, the central idea was much older and had hailed from the West, but it was the racy script, co-authored by Salim-Javed and Satish Bhatnagar, which won the day. The combination of the script, direction and the superb performances by all three leading artistes led to a film with immense repeat value, with Hema Malini, on a rapid upswing, being the flavour of the season.

Another 'inspired' film was Mohan Segal's *Raja Jani*, which was reworked from the classic *Pygmalion*, complete with commercial elements like dangerous and very 'Hindi filmi' villains!

Again a humongous hit, the film was also an end-1972 release like *Seeta Aur Geeta*, and ran almost halfway through 1973. With this film, the Dharam-Hema team bagged an unprecedented five superhits out of five releases. This record was to be further enhanced in the years to come.

Boom Year

The year 1973 was a bonanza for Dharam. It saw him in nine films, one of them a prolonged special appearance (*Phagun*), and only this and the ambitious Vijay Anand movie *Blackmail* flopped. This Vijay Anand-directed thriller, however, encouraged the ace director to make two more films with Dharmendra in *Ram Balram* and *Rajput*, which released in the '80s. There was one more film announced, the multi-starer *Ek Do Teen Char*, which never happened.

Blackmail, starring Raakhee with Shatrughan Sinha, is now best remembered for Kalyanji-Anandji's magnificent music score, topped by the two songs filmed on Dharmendra, 'Pal Pal Dil Ke Paas' (which the actor has now taken as the title for his grandson Karan Deol's forthcoming debut) and 'Mile Mile Do Badan', a duet by Lata Mangeshkar and Kishore Kumar.

Both the songs are examples of fabulous filming, or 'picturization' as it is traditionally but ungrammatically called in Hindi film parlance. In the latter song, the hero and heroine get engulfed in passion while in hiding from the villains chasing them. The song was conceived by Anand and masterfully written by Rajendra Krishan, with the rousing tune punctuated by eerie music bars and the sounds of the barking canines.

Among the hits, *Yaadon Ki Baaraat* was a lost-and-found-cum-revenge drama, wherein the villain (Ajit) caused three brothers to separate after he murdered their parents and they escaped. The signature family song, 'Yaadon Ki Baaraat Nikli Hai Aaj Dil Ke Dware' was the identifying number that would ultimately bring the three siblings together when they grew up. Tariq (playing the role of a singer in a hotel) sings this song every day in a vain effort to find his brothers in the audience, and the day comes when his friend Vijay Arora hears and joins in the song—he is the sibling, and they meet at last!

Dharmendra, as the eldest of the three, is there on a criminal mission, and when he hears the song, he can neither reveal himself nor join in the singing. Dharmendra, at his natural best, despite a clumsy wig, makes a subtle but whopping impact as he stands there, shedding helpless tears, but finally sends Tariq a note through a waiter.

Interestingly, this hit music-fest of R.D. Burman had no song lip-synched by Dharmendra and no heroine in the romantic lead with him. And even more interestingly, Nasir Hussain, the King Midas film-maker and dialogue writer for the film also noted that Salim-Javed had sold *Zanjeer* to Prakash Mehra and this 'mix of *Zanjeer* and *Waqt*' to him simultaneously.

Both films were being made simultaneously, though the Prakash Mehra film released much earlier, in 1973. But both scripts were potent enough to make Salim-Javed what they were in the 1970s and 1980s—hit-machines and market leaders who were to raise the status of writers for many years.

Nevertheless, we wonder what would have happened had Dharmendra accepted the role of Amitabh Bachchan in *Zanjeer*. Would *Yaadon Ki Baaraat* have not been made? If made, which other hero would have played his role?

Two more items here for trivia-lovers. Aamir Khan (Hussain's nephew) played the baby Tariq (again Hussain's nephew!), and Padmini Kolhapure and her sister Shivangi Kolhapure (Shraddha Kapoor's mother) sang the title song's female version along with Lata Mangeshkar. For all three, it was their debut film.

Aamir Khan remains a great fan of Dharmendra even today. Kolhapure, who also sang in *The Burning Train* (1980) and acted as a child artiste in the 1977 film, *Dream Girl* (with Shivangi singing for her!), also teamed up with Govinda in *Dadagiri* (1987) in which Dharmendra headed the cast.

Kahani Kismat Ki, literally 'a story of fate', was the only superhit film Dharmendra's mentor Arjun Hingorani made with him. The typically convoluted crime drama had Kalyanji-Anandji chartbusters 'Rafta Rafta Dekho Aankh Meri Ladi Hai' and 'Duniya Mujh Ko Kehti Hai Ki Peene Chhod De' to boost the repeat audience quotient.

It was the actor's second film with Rekha that year, and the first was *Keemat*—the second Bond-like spy drama director Ravee Nagaich attempted after *Farz* with Jeetendra six years earlier. In a way, you could even call it part of an intended franchise (something unknown then to mainstream Hindi cinema) as the hero's name was again Gopal, Agent 116 as in *Farz*. The film did modestly well.

Another film that did modestly well was *Jheel Ke Us Paar* in 1973, Bhappi Sonie's third and last outing with the actor. Based on one of popular novelist Gulshan Nanda's bestsellers, the film actually had Yogeeta Bali in a grey role with Mumtaz as the leading lady.

A third success was again Dharmendra's last film with producer Hargobind, *Jwar Bhata*, co-starring Saira Banu, this time romantically, unlike in *Shaadi*. A family melodrama, it was mainly noteworthy for the frothy 'social' chartbuster by Kishore Kumar for Dharmendra, 'Dal Roti Khaao Prabhu Ke Gun Gaao'.

Leena Chandavarkar said, 'There were two films starring Dharamji that I could not accommodate out of date issues. One was *Jheel Ke Us Paar*, and the other was *Resham Ki Dori* (which released in 1974). But *Jwar Bhata* was a case in which I was signed but had to drop out due to some reasons.'

This leaves two major hits—*Jugnu* and *Loafer*. Pramod Chakravorty's follow-up to *Naya Zamana* was not another social drama but a crime caper that had all the ingredients of a blockbuster—which it did become! Hema Malini and Dharmendra thus notched up the sixth jubilee hit in a row, but what stood out in the couple's first golden jubilee was the way the emotional, patriotic, lost-and-found and crime angles were blended into the Gulshan Nanda story scripted by Sachin Bhaumick.

Ehsan Rizvi (billed here as 'Ahsan' Rizvi, who began in the '40s as a lyricist and writer) wrote the famous one-liner, '*Baap ke naam ka sahara kamzor log lete hain* (Only the weak take their father's name as a prop)' that caught on.

The other film, *Loafer*, was arguably South biggie A. Bhimsingh's slickest Hindi film ever and his most successful outing with Dharmendra. Co-starring Mumtaz, the crime drama was studded with a hit music score by Laxmikant-Pyarelal, and the sole song filmed on Dharmendra, 'Aaj Mausam Bada Beimaan Hai', ranks among the actor's foremost chartbusters of all time and is popular to this day. It was used in its entirety and in its original form in the 2001 crossover Hindi comedy *Monsoon Wedding*, in a very situational way!

Dharmendra, as a school kid, kills a classmate in a fit of rage, and on the run from the law, is given shelter by a criminal. From here on, he becomes an ace thief and falls in love with another (Mumtaz). The title was a shade misleading, but the film was one of the year's top ten grossing movies. Dharmendra's 'repeat quotient' with producers was again clear from this film—R.C. Kumar had been one of the producers of *Izzat*.

A Mixed Bag—and Only Two Heroines

Apart from a cameo in Mehmood's *Kunwara Baap* (in which he played himself), Dharmendra acted in five films in 1974, two with Hema Malini that were hits, and the remaining three with Saira Banu, of which two were flops and one did average business.

The film that did average business was the Atma Ram-directed *Resham Ki Dori*, on a brother (Dharmendra)-sister (Kumud Chhugani) relationship. Shankar-Jaikishan composed the hit 'Chamka Pasina Banke Nagina' in this melodrama.

International Crook was produced and directed by Pacchhi, who had last made India's first 70 mm film, *Around the World*. Co-starring Saira Banu, with Feroz Khan also in the cast (the trio was repeated after *Aadmi Aur Insaan*), this one too was announced originally in 70 mm, despite the calamitous fate of Pacchhi's last film. However, it was finally released in a regular 35 mm format, but was still a write-off. The third film with Saira Banu was Ramesh Lakhanpal's *Pocket Maar*. It came and sank without a trace. The only memory that is alive today is the popular Mohammed Rafi song 'Banda Parvar Main Kahaan', filmed on this man for all seasons.

But in that year, Dharmendra scored in two hits—both with Hema Malini: *Dost* and *Patthar Aur Payal*.

The latter was a dacoit drama, again with Vinod Khanna as the dacoit. Directed by Harmesh Malhotra, it was most notable as dialogues writer Rahi Masoom Reza's first hit: The writer was to peak as the dialogue writer of B.R. Chopra's mega-serial *Mahabharat*, incidentally, but do very few films with the actor later. As a dacoit who falls in love and wants to lead a straight life but is not allowed to do so, Dharmendra acted quite well.

However, what was of infinitely greater interest was the fact that Dharam-Hema, as a rapidly growing top screen pair, once again had two hits in a single year, just as in the years 1970 and 1972. The other, bigger hit was Premji's *Dost*, directed by Dulal Guha again. With these two films, the two got their seventh and eighth consecutive hits and jubilees!

Dost, scripted by Sachin Bhaumick with Shafeeq Ansari penning the 'dialogues', saw Dharmendra as a hardcore idealist who suffers the buffets offered by life and 'un-ideal' people. Hema Malini was his lady-love, and Shatrughan Sinha the criminal-friend whom he helps when the latter lands in serious trouble.

Clearly, the latter role was author-backed and Shatrughan Sinha dwarfed Dharmendra with his performance by putting everything into the role. (Sanjeev Kumar was considered for the role, but Hema Malini's mother Jaya Chakravarthy had objections as he was in love with her daughter).

The movie had an interesting starting-point. Rajesh Khanna was the new superstar, and Dulal Guha had just directed *Dushman* (a blockbuster, and Guha's second hit after *Dharti Kahe Pukar Ke*) with Khanna.

After *Dharti Kahe Pukar Ke*, Dharmendra had always wanted to work with Guha, and he was fairly incensed that the role of a rustic truck-driver had been given to Khanna rather than to him! Guha and Sachin Bhaumick had another story with them, but Dharmendra felt that he had burnt his fingers with the role of an idealist in *Satyakam* and he did not want to do something similar. Yet, he reluctantly agreed.

And so, after completing the film, the actor was even more convinced that here would be another flop to his name. Dharmendra's family and friends watched the film's copy and felt likewise. At the time of release, Dharmendra was not traceable in Mumbai, and so, as a compulsion, a small premiere was held! He was shooting in Kashmir.

After the Friday release, on Monday, someone in Kashmir informed Dharmendra that the film was a massive hit and was running housefull shows even there. And so he went to watch the film amidst the public and was thrilled. He told the producer of the film he was shooting for that he wanted to catch the early morning flight to Mumbai.

At around nine in the morning, Guha's son Putul Guha, then a young man of seventeen, opened the door to a frantic ringing of the bell. 'I saw Dharamji standing outside, and clearly, he had not slept the entire night!' recalled Putul. 'He asked for my father, dashed into my grandmother's room and began praising him. When my father came to meet him, he completely prostrated before him, and started weeping and said that his family did not know anything about cinema! My father comforted him and fed him a good breakfast.'

Putul went on, 'After regaining his composure, Dharmendra then called up producer Premji to apologize and later phoned his own family—they also had called him in Kashmir and were told he was not there! As it happened, his brother Kanwar Ajit Singh (Abhay Deol's late father) had picked up his phone, and Dharmendra said something in Punjabi to him and summoned him to our home. When he arrived, he commanded Kanwar to greet my father respectfully. Kanwar then handed over fifty thousand rupees to my father.'

No, this was not a reward, but a signing amount, for that's how *Pratiggya* was signed!

Dharmendra's brother had narrated a one-line story to Guha and his brother: A truck driver comes to know that his mother is on the death-bed, and before she dies, she reveals that he is the son of a brave police officer, whose family was murdered by a dacoit. And so Dharmendra entered 1975 with two more hits with Hema Malini.

Chapter Seven

Dharmendra in the 1970s: Part II

*Rafta rafta dekho aankh meri ladi hai / Aankh jisse ladi hai
woh paas mere khadi hai*

The year 1975 was to see Dharmendra in his career's biggest hit, *Sholay*. Correction: This was *the* career-biggest hit for everyone in the cast and crew, because it remains till date the greatest hit, the most watched film and the unmatched titan among Hindi movies in all-time history. Possibly, the footfalls in the forty-three years since its release in movie-halls alone must have crossed those of a couple or more other mega hits put together!

And…the biggest star in its mammoth ensemble cast then was Dharmendra! He played Veeru, the iconic petty criminal, who along with Jai, was hired to apprehend the unmentionably evil dacoit Gabbar Singh, portrayed by Amjad Khan. And when Shatrughan Sinha turned down the role of Veeru's crony Jai, it was Dharmendra who had recommended the promising and upcoming actor Amitabh Bachchan for it.

Ironically, this was to be Dharam's second and last film with Sippy, who made many of his subsequent films with Bachchan.

Co-writer Salim Khan narrated the simple but interesting tale of how this 70 mm all-time blockbuster was born, which was also the first Indian film ever to be filmed with stereophonic sound. He recalled, 'Producer V.K. Sobti, Jeetendra's brother-in-law, wanted us to write a film starring Jeetendra and Shatrughan Sinha. We gave him a brief synopsis, but he somehow did not like the plot. We even went to Baldev Pushkarna, who, instead, made another film, *Chacha Bhatija*, with us. Meanwhile, G.P. Sippy wanted to work with us again after *Andaz* and *Seeta Aur Geeta* and we gave him the subject of *Majboor* that producer Premji made in 1974. But Sippy saab said that the film had a small canvas and he wanted to make a big movie. When we narrated the same subject we had taken to Sobti, he jumped and said, "This is it!"'

As Anupama Chopra's book on the making of the film tells us, by this time, there was a huge turbulence in Dharmendra's life—his passionate love for leading lady Hema Malini. The fact that he was already married naturally stressed him out, and he began to consume alcohol even in the daytime. One day, he consumed so much that he decided to punish himself and walked from his hotel to the sets at Ramnagaram in the dead of night.

Next morning, the unit panicked because their hero was nowhere to be found, until a unit hand discovered him sleeping 'like a baby' in one of the make-up rooms on location! Dharmendra, it is well-known, became a more affectionate human being after drinking, and despite his propensity towards alcohol, never caused anything more than minor delays in the shoot. In fact, thanks to his attraction to his leading lady, he would find excuses to be on sets even when he was not needed—because Hema Malini was shooting!

Somewhere, the Salim-Javed script's initial demonstration of Veeru's ardent and sometimes mischievous serenading of Hema Malini's Basanti seemed to find an echo of sorts in what was going on in real life.

Two Milestone Performances

In this significant year in his career, Dharmendra had a total of six releases. The others were *Pratiggya* (his home production—third after *Satyakam* and *Samadhi*), *Chupke Chupke, Ek Mahal Ho Sapnon Ka*, and two delayed movies, *Chaitali* and *International Crook*.

The first two, probably even more than *Sholay* for fans of the actor within him, were milestones in Dharmendra's career. Dharmendra always mentioned three or four films when asked by scribes to mention his best or most favourite movies. To this list, Dharmendra has added *Pratiggya* of late. Maybe he watched it again recently and rediscovered his own empathy for and experiences from it!

Possibly, the success of *Yamla Pagla Deewana* (the title of his 2011 home production was inspired by the cult Rafi chartbuster from *Pratiggya*) may have started influencing him slowly. Maybe something else…many things else!…might have shaped this new perspective. We cannot ask an icon what prompted a new addition to his favourites that was always definitive for him yet understated.

As mentioned earlier, *Pratiggya* was based on an interesting story by Dharmendra's brother Kanwar Ajit Singh, who also produced the film officially with Bikramjit Singh, Dharmendra's brother-in-law. Nabendu Ghosh, the screenplay writer, and the Laxmikant-Pyarelal-Anand Bakshi team were given the responsibilities for the music of this silver jubilee Dulal Guha hit.

A festival of Dharmendra's on-screen and behind-the-screen favourites, the film starred Hema Malini, had good friend Abhi Bhattacharya in a key role, the new-found amigo Birbal, other Dharmendra film regulars by then like Sapru and Nazir Hussein, the hot new name Imtiaz Khan—fresh off *Yaadon Ki Baaraat's* success and brother to Amjad Khan—and veteran Ajit.

In common with *Sholay*, which released on August 15 vis-à-vis this film on June 23, besides Anand Bakshi and Lata Mangeshkar, there was character artiste Leela Misra who, while she played the crucial role of Hema Malini's mausi (maternal aunt) in the Sippy epic, was Dharmendra's foster mother here and kickstarts the film's story by revealing the truth about his birth and what happened to his real parents.

Both *Pratiggya* and *Sholay* were set in villages, and showed scared villagers cowering before dakus (dacoits or brigands), completing a trilogy of sorts in this genre for Dharmendra after *Mera Gaon Mera Desh*.

And what is super-interesting about this trilogy is that while veteran Jayant was in a key but positive role in the Raj Khosla 1971 blockbuster, his elder son Imtiaz Khan was in a negative role in *Pratiggya* as was his younger son Amjad Khan in *Sholay*.

Interestingly again, in *Pratiggya*, Dharmendra played the father of the hero in another such dual role after *Samadhi*. Obviously, since the senior Dharmendra was seen briefly before being eliminated by the dacoits, the father and son never came face-to-face here. It is when the hero comes to know what happened to his family that he takes a vow (*Pratiggya*) to avenge his family's massacre—his younger sister had also been killed.

In *Sholay* too, the thakur's family is massacred and he vows revenge by hiring Jai and Veeru: Thus revenge became another meeting-point for the two 1975 hits. Now for one more meeting-point: Even in *Pratiggya*, Dharmendra had committed a crime—though only once.

The interesting plot moves to a village where the police want to set up a small force and the dacoits oppose this by eliminating them. And it is here that the hero pretends to be a policeman and sets up a police station, bringing him face to face with his target.

A highlight of this film was its rustic and melodious music score. Recalled Putul Guha, 'Dad had thought of a mad, effervescent romantic song and Anand Bakshi and Laxmikant-Pyarelal had come up with "Main Jat Yamla Pagla Deewana". What my father and the producer were wondering was who will do the choreography, since Dharamji was no dancer and would often need to improvise steps that were shown to him.'

Guha went on, 'And dad chose the most improbable dance director—the classically trained Kathak and Bharatanatyam exponent Gopi Krishna! And Dharamji just copied him! Today, we all consider Dharamji's steps as iconic, which are much imitated by others. This song, I think, was the first in which he truly danced all by himself. And only my father could have thought of such a situation and executed it!'

Chupke Chupke, on the other hand, was the ultimate test for Dharmendra's abilities as an actor par excellence. No one else, arguably not even Sanjeev Kumar, could have portrayed Professor Parimal Tripathi, the botany professor who masquerades as an English-hating, pure Hindi zealot Pyare Mohan, with the panache he showed!

A simple prank on a proud old man became the foundation of one of Hindi cinema's biggest laugh riots, and to Dharmendra and his foil, the redoubtable Om Prakash, went the lion's share of the credit for the gag-fest the film became. Old friend and Hrishida's associate Gulzar came in to pen the dialogues and co-author the script, based on a Bengali short story, *Chhadobeshi*, by Upendranath Gangopadhyaya.

Among Hrishikesh Mukherjee's famous trilogy of hit comedies—*Golmaal* and *Khubsoorat* being the other two—*Chupke Chupke* effortlessly towers, and we do not mean just in terms of business. Proof of this also prevails in the fact that while *Golmaal* has been reworked twice in part and *Khubsoorat* actually remade, no one has dared to dream of touching this film: Who, after all, can dream of matching, let alone surpassing, Dharmendra (and Om Prakash) and the splendid script and lines?

But what went on behind-the-scenes was also very interesting. On a special 2010 episode of the game show *Kaun Banega Crorepati* hosted by Amitabh Bachchan, Dharmendra had come in as a guest, and audiences got the nostalgic pleasure of watching Veeru and Jai (or Professor Parimal and Professor Sukumar from *Chupke Chupke*) reminiscing about their memorable work together.

On this show, Dharmendra reversed the show's usual order of things by asking the first question: '*Amit, hamare kaun se aise director the jinse hum dono ghabra jaate the, darte the—jaise kisi schoolmaster ya headmaster se* (Who was that director of whom we were both scared, much in the same way a student would be afraid of a schoolteacher or a principal)?' And Bachchan had replied that they would both tremble in front of 'Hrishida'!

At the same time, Dharmendra and Bachchan have also said elsewhere that Mukherjee was like family to them and that they would have willingly worked for him anytime without even asking for the story or script—something they had actually put into practice as well!

In turn, while Dharmendra was shown to be the prankster in the film, the impish side to the director also emerged in his way of treating big stars. There is this popular story about how he punished Dharmendra for being late for a shoot by canning a scene without him, then shooting and putting in an insert of the star dashing out from a place that had a 'Toilet' signboard next to it (this scene is towards the end of *Chupke Chupke*).

Apart from Dharmendra's famous chameleonic blend into any character, it is also surmised that Mukherjee must have also loved the mischievous idea of making Dharmendra speak pure Hindi. According to Jai Arjun Singh's book on the director, the actor used to pronounce the word *parichay* (introduction) as *preechay* (in the Punjabi fashion of swallowing syllables) and Mukherjee 'got back to him' with this role.[1]

Actor Asrani also recalled, 'Hrishida was not a director, he was a headmaster.' The actor, who was first noticed in Mukherjee's *Guddi* (also starring Dharmendra), said, 'Hrishida would tell all his artistes, big and small, how and what to speak, and how and what *not* to speak.'

The film-maker never shared details of scenes until the very last moment and was known to have instructed his assistant directors to do the same. About the making of the film, Asrani remembered, 'I was on the set wearing a suit. Hrishida was playing chess. Then Dharmendra came in, wearing a driver's uniform, and asked me in surprise, "*Main tera driver banaa hoon* (Am I playing the role of your driver)?" In those days, there would be budgetary restrictions and we used to get clothes from old films. I generally did not get to wear suits in films and now that I was wearing one, Dharmendra was scared and asked, "What is going on? What is the scene? How did you get a suit and I get the driver's dress?"'

Mukherjee had roared, 'Dharam! What are you asking Asrani? About the scene, right? Arey, if you had any sense for story, would you have been a hero?' Bachchan too faced the director's ire when he expressed surprise at Asrani's character wearing a suit. Mukherjee yelled, 'Amit! What are you asking Asrani? About the story, or the scene? Dharam! Tell him what I told you. You guys, if you had the sense for the story, you wouldn't be playing heroes in films! Get to work!'

The film was a bumper hit and ran, like *Pratiggya*, for over twenty-five weeks. Today, over four decades down, like many timeless films, it does not look even a bit dated, its humour still completely fresh and relevant. A unique achievement of the film was that during a February 1980 solar eclipse, the government broadcast

---

[1]Singh, Jai Arjun, *The World of Hrishikesh Mukherjee: The Filmmaker Everyone Loves*, Penguin, 2015.

the film on Doordarshan, the official TV channel (and the only one then) to encourage people to stay inside and not venture out and look at the eclipse with naked eyes, which might have led to ocular damage!

We leave this film with a mega-compliment for Dharam. On a blog that compares *Chupke Chupke* with *Chhadmabeshi*, the Bengali film based on the same story and released earlier, the blogger compares Uttam Kumar, the Bengali titan who played the role of the botany professor, with Dharmendra and says, 'Kumar is great. I can't refute that. But, there is something about Dharmendra! He is heartbreakingly handsome and stupendously funny. His act is effortless. His eye wrinkles are cute. In short, if drivers are like this, then God should make more of them!'

The blogger goes on, 'Dharmendra's nasal twang makes the comedy even more rib-tickling. His sudden squint, stammer and tricks triple the fun quotient. Uttam Kumar is great, I repeat, but Dharmendra is just so much better.' Most responses to this blog endorse the fact that our very own, natural and instinctive mega-talent completely scored over one of India's greatest actors, Uttam Kumar, this one time! And just to mention it, Uttam Kumar acted as a character artiste in Dharam's 1987 film *Mera Karam Mera Dharam*.

The Lows in a Good Year

A significant film in terms of Dharmendra but a total washout at the box-office was *Chaitali*, also directed by Hrishikesh Mukherjee in 1975 and produced by Manobina Bimal Roy, the widow of the legendary film-maker. Again, it was, like so many Dharmendra films, a 'Bengali'-heavy movie, but it had an interesting history.

It was launched by Roy himself in 1964 as *Sahara*, just after *Bandini*, with Sharmila Tagore opposite Dharmendra and music by Roshan, then on a strong ascent. It was to be Roy's first film in colour. But after a week's shooting, Roy fell ill and never returned to the studios again as he was diagnosed with cancer.

The film, reshot in the 1970s by Roy's good friend, Mukherjee, as *Chaitali*, was apathetically dismissed by Roy's daughter Rinki Roy Bhattacharya when this writer met her in the 1990s. Her claim was that Mukherjee had ruined a beautiful subject. The new film saw Saira Banu replace the busy Hrishida favourite, Sharmila Tagore, and Laxmikant-Pyarelal in place of the late Roshan.

In the hysteria of the commercial era that 1975 was, and the gloom of the just-declared Emergency, with an overcommitted Hrishida at the helm, *Chaitali* was a spent force, with, once again, a 'soft' Dharmendra having zilch connect with the audience. Even a song as beautifully semi-classical as 'Dharti Ambar Neend Se Jaage', sung by Manna Dey for the actor with Lata Mangeshkar, remained more or less in obscurity until the YouTube era. The two remaining Lata solos becoming popular on the 8 a.m. Radio Ceylon 'farmaishi' (listeners' requests) programme but could not make a popular enough impact to pull in the crowds.

That leaves us with two more films, which in the broader picture were pretty inconsequential: The Kalidas potboiler *Saazish* (with Saira Banu again) and *Ek Mahal Ho Sapno Ka*, filmed by Devendra Goel, starring Sharmila Tagore and Leena Chandavarkar. The core of the latter's plot had a small but remarkable similarity to *Lamhe*— Dharmendra as a poet falls in love with a girl (Chandavarkar) who is the stepdaughter of his lost love (Sharmila Tagore). This film was claimed to be an average success.

Only Hema

In 1976, Dharmendra had a low year. His only releases were Ramanand Sagar's crime thriller on drugs, *Charas*, and South wizard Devar's *Maa*. Devar was known for his films with assorted animals playing integral parts in the stories alongside the stars.

Maa was an emotional story with a message that can be instantly identified by animal-lovers today—about animals not being taken captive for human amusement, like in circuses. It showed Dharmendra as a heartless supplier of animals who does not heed his mother's warnings until she is killed by the furious mother of a baby elephant he has captured for a circus. However, for whatever reason, the film did not work at the box-office and set the dubious record of becoming Dharmendra's and Hema Malini's first flop together, after eleven hits in a row! The infallibility of this pair was smashed.

And their 11th hit, released earlier that year, was *Charas*, in which Dharmendra battled a drug cartel that also indulged in flesh trade. Once again, writer, producer and director Ramanand Sagar put in a personal touch to the story of the hero—his sister (played by Aruna Irani) was one of the victims of the gang. The film was superbly lensed by Sagar's cinematographer son Prem Sagar in exotic foreign locations like Rome, Malta and Egypt.

The Dharam-Hema hit duet, the breezy 'Aaja Teri Yaad Aayi' (by Mohammed Rafi and Lata Mangeshkar with a background vocals prelude sung by lyricist Anand Bakshi) is loved to this day and has the distinction of being the first-ever duet filmed on the numero uno star pair abroad. Another Lata solo, 'Raja Na Jaa Dil Tod Ke' was also filmed in exotic Malta locations by the sea.

Due to its high cost of production, many then believed that this silver jubilee film was, at the most, an average success, if not a loser (flop) in terms of return on investment. However, its actual status as a hit took forty-one long years to be certified—in the most unusual and unpleasant way: In 2017, the descendants of Sagar were asked to shell out a big sum as penalty for a false declaration by the late film-maker's accountants to the Income-Tax Department in 1977 that they had suffered losses.

The money received from the distributor had been allegedly

reduced to almost one-fourth in the initial tax submission, supposedly to cover up the losses the film-maker suffered with his earlier two films after a chain of hits—*Lalkar* starring Dharmendra and *Jalte Badan*, which was also like *Charas* on the topic of narcotics. All this proved beyond doubt that *Charas* had definitely been quite a profitable enterprise.

In 1976, the lead pair actually starred in three films in joint cameos—actor Biswajeet's production *Kahtey Hain Mujhko Raja*, the Pramod Chakravorty (their director in *Naya Zamana* and *Jugnu*) film *Barood* and the quirky Basu Chaterjee hit *Chhoti Si Baat*, where they sang the first part of the popular song 'Jaaneman Jaaneman Tere Do Nayan'.

Two Superhits with Manmohan Desai

In 1977, Hema Malini made a cameo appearance in another Dharmendra-Arjun Hingorani film, *Khel Khilari Ka*, while Dharmendra had a cameo in the Jeetendra-Hema Malini film *Kinara*. Both these films failed at the box-office, but *Swami*, produced by Hema Malini's mother Jaya Chakravarthy and starring Shabana Azmi, Vikram and Girish Karnad, was a hit.

The Dharmendra-Hema Malini cameo in this film, like in their cameo song in *Chhoti Si Baat* in 1976, was restricted to the song, 'Aaj Ki Raat', sung by Yesudas and Asha Bhosle, interestingly the same two singers who had sung in the earlier film.

In that year, Garam Dharam, as he was now overwhelmingly called, had three more lead roles, and the least memorable after *Khel Khilari Ka* was, ironically, in Hema Malini's other (and bigger) home production, *Dream Girl*, officially produced by her mother jointly with I.K. Bahl, her then secretary.

In this film, Hema Malini steals money to run an orphanage, under different aliases. Dharmendra played a flirt who dreams of meeting his dream girl for marriage, as he has seen a painting of hers. And then he meets her. This time, the actress cashed in on the PR title she had been given when she had started out a decade back—'Dream Girl'.

The only other interesting aspects of this average success pertained to its music. One, Laxmikant-Pyarelal and Anand Bakshi composed the all-timer title track, 'Kisi Shaayar Ki Ghazal, Dream Girl' sung by Kishore Kumar for Dharmendra. Two, Hema Malini actually sang the song 'Hua Kya Agar Tu Zara Bewafa Hai', with Kishore.

But it was in this year that the actor also starred in a memorable double-bill with Manmohan Desai—in *Chacha Bhatija* and *Dharam-Veer*. Desai, that year, had the unprecedented and even-now unmatched distinction of directing four films(!)—and they were all among the five biggest hits of the year! The former film was unique in the sense that for the first time, Salim-Javed, as the numero uno writers then, scripted a film for a story written by Desai's permanent writer, Prayag Raj.

Interestingly, *Chacha Bhatija*, a classic lost-and-found Desai staple, was Dharmendra's only film with Randhir Kapoor, and was loved for its zany humour. But although it was a superhit, it was the least successful of Desai's movies that year. It released just two weeks after the more celebrated *Dharam-Veer*.

Dharam-Veer, again, remains one of Dharam's most-loved characters. As someone once said, 'Only Dharam could have convincingly carried off a He-Man wearing skirts.' Playing a prince who is brought up as a commoner, Dharam, placed in a weird timeframe and location fusion, was made to dress like a Roman gladiator! The all-macho male who wooed the arrogant princess (Zeenat Aman) and tamed her with songs like 'O Meri Mehbooba Tujhe Jaana Hai To Jaa' (O sweetheart, leave me if you want) and 'Arey Maine Tujhko Chaha Yeh Hai Meri Meherbaani' (I have done you a favour by desiring you) found an instant echo in his fans.

In those days, 50-week runs, or golden jubilee films as they were called, were common, and Dharam was no stranger to them (*Phool Aur Patthar, Ankhen, Shikar, Aaya Sawan Jhoom Ke, Mera Gaon Mera Desh, Jugnu, Yaadon Ki Baaraat,* apart from *Jeevan Mrityu* and *Sholay,* which ran for 100 and 250 weeks respectively). And this sensational hit reached that milestone too, ranking next in that year only to *Amar Akbar Anthony* in its success quotient.

An interesting part of this film was a sequence where Dharmendra as a kid wields an axe as an ironsmith's adopted son. The sequence featured Bobby Deol, all of nine years old when the scene was shot, playing Dharam the kid, and it moves smoothly into the next frame to the introduction of the adult Dharam, also the character's name in the film, in the same sequence. Of course, the axe was a fake one!

The years 1978 and 1979 emerged as dull for our superhero. The Bachchan blitzkrieg was in full fettle in these two years, and to be fair, Dharmendra had not been very careful about the kind of films he had signed. Even his home production, *Dillagi* (directed by an overworked Basu Chatterjee, cashing in on his recent successes and signing films by the dozen) sank. This, despite the fact that it was a light (but slow and boring) romantic comedy laced with some good melodies by Rajesh Roshan. Dharmendra's get-up in parts of the film even looked like a washed out version of how he looked in *Chupke Chupke.*

Clearly, the Bengali flavour seemed to have run its course in this tired and tiring romance based on a story by Bimal Kar. And *Phandebaaz* and *Azaad* were also helmed by Bengalis.

Phandebaaz, directed by Samir Ganguly, was a typical double-role potboiler for Dharmendra that did not catch the audience's fancy. *Azaad* (Hema Malini with Pramod Chakravorty again at the helm) was a tepid success with a stereotyped plot. And the biggest disaster of that year and a setback for Dharam was the Indo-American co-production, the heist film *Shalimar* directed by Krishna Shah.

The premise was interesting, a do-or-die treasure hunt, and so was the lead cast (Zeenat Aman, Shammi Kapoor, and overseas actors John Saxon, Sylvia Miles and Rex Harrison, no less). The Hindi-English bilingual was filmed in 70 mm with 6-track stereophonic sound and had a zingy music score by R.D. Burman. But it was not just the huge budget that undid the film—it just did not resonate with the audiences, even outside India.

In 1979 came the interestingly plotted film that was a tepid success, Dulal Guha's *Dil Ka Heera* (A diamond at heart). Dharmendra played a widower, an honest customs officer, who falls in love with an air hostess (Hema Malini). Concerned about the smuggling taking place under their noses, he soon comes to know that it is this woman who is actually doing it.

The only other film Dharam had in this last year of the decade was Mohan Segal's engaging jungle drama *Kartavya*, co-starring Rekha. Made on a lavish scale in Cinemascope, the new favourite widescreen medium that was far cheaper and complicated than the 70 mm format (the prints could be projected on a regular 35 mm screen with a regular 35 mm projector), it did good but not great business. The film was a remake of the hit 1973 Kannada film *Gandhada Gudi*.

The peak decade of Dharmendra's career had come to an end. A turbulent phase was set to begin.

Chapter Eight

Going Right, Going Wrong: The 1980s

Ek rastaa do raahi / Ek chor ek sipahi

The 1980s is considered, with some justification, as the most controversial decade of Hindi cinema. In the movies, it was quite a confused phase. Thanks to the aftermath of *Sholay* and the other multi-starrer films, including the mega-success of Dharmendra's *Dharam-Veer*, such movies had come into vogue.

From the stars' point of view, such films were made for absolute convenience. Big films with big heroes meant more value for ticket money for the audience. But in a milieu wherein films were never shot in single schedules like they are today, and there were at least ten top male stars coexisting—actors signing 10–15 films together and shooting for most of them simultaneously—it made sense to do multi-hero films where work on one film was much less, because a three-hour film's footage was divided between two, three or even more leading men.

Sadly, the inevitable consequence of this was that movies were designed as business proposals rather than as substantial cinema. For every multi-starrer film that justified the presence of big stars, there were at least twenty such proposals that were made—and almost double that number if we also consider the films that were announced, launched and later aborted as scripts could not be 'balanced' for every star!

Yes, ego issues (not really applicable to our Jat from Punjab) also made most such scripts lopsided, as heroes demanded equal screen-time, equal songs, dramatic sequences, fight sequences and heroines! These would be then allotted on the basis of their statuses!

As budgets spiralled (egos also decided remuneration!), 'safe' content (that is, elements considered good business, like catering to the least common denominator in the matter of skin show, fights and so on) ensured that the scripts further deteriorated, as return on investment became the most important factor. After all, there would be a minimum of two top heroines as well.

This lengthy introduction to the scene as we enter into the 1980s is just to show that Dharmendra, as one of the foremost stars in the multi-starrer set-ups, also became a victim of this trend. The wonder of wonders here was that merely on the strength of his charisma, popularity with both audiences and the industry, and his inherent golden nature, Dharmendra continued to do such films right until the '90s. Beyond a doubt, this proved that his films, even if not 'hits' (the definition of a hit is that it earns at least double the money invested) were making profits for investors.

The year 1980 saw four Dharmendra releases—*Ali Baba Aur Chalis Chor*, *The Burning Train*, *Ram Balram* and *Chunaoti*. The first film was an Indo-Russian co-production and Eagle Films, F.C. Mehra's banner, was the Indian production counterpart. Sovin Films, a government-run body similar to the National Film Development Corporation in India, was the Russian co-producer.

Released in 70 mm and Cinemascope with Stereophonic Sound, the film expanded the Alibaba fable from *Arabian Nights* into a lengthier story that did quite well in India, but was termed an average success only because of its huge budget. In Russia, however, the film, which had a Hindi and Russian mixed cast, was a big hit. And most of the supporting actors were Russians.

Said director Umesh Mehra, who along with Russian film-maker Latif Faiziev directed the film(s): 'The original Alibaba is shown as a seventeen-year-old. But in our cinema then, it did not matter what the hero's age was—on screen, he was always twenty! In those times, for such a big project, there were only three or four possible superstars, and Dharam was the most convincing for the action drama. Of course Hemaji was in as well, and Zeenat Aman played Fatima.' Aman, yet again, was not romantically teamed with Dharmendra after *Yaadon Ki Baaraat*, though they had done *Dharam-Veer* together.

In recall mode, Mehra said nostalgically, 'My first film, *Hamaare Tumhaare*, which released a year earlier, and this film started almost simultaneously, as dates had to be coordinated.' He also said, 'Dharam was quite apprehensive. The Russians were all positive about him, but though Dharam had done *Sholay* and was filming *The Burning Train* also in 70 mm, he was a bit apprehensive about how the film would turn out. "Will it happen *jaise* Hollywood *mein honda hai* (how it happens in Hollywood)?" was his constant question to me.'

The action sequences, Mehra said, showed how the actor loved that genre. 'There was one simple shot in the Russian outdoors. He had to get on his knee and shoot arrows with his bow. I kept telling him not to get distracted while giving the shot, come what may, but I did not confide in him that during that scene, two trained horses would come close behind and then crash to the ground, right on the sand. He did not so much as bat an eyelid, and after that, he got confidence in me. "I am relaxed now!" he had said with a smile. "You can do it!"'

Mehra adds an interesting piece of trivia, 'The industry knows that Dharamji does not like the camera to show a particular side and angle of his face, though we all look different and better from some specific angles. I remember him being very particular with my cinematographers, Indian veteran Peter Pereira and Russia's Leonid Travitsky.'

The Burning Train, again in 70 mm and Cinemascope, was a disaster at the box-office despite the ensemble cast and some good music by R.D. Burman, who had also composed for *Alibaba...* (along with Russian composer Vladimir Milov). This movie was inspired from the 1975 Japanese disaster movie *The Bullet Train*, opened well at 100 per cent, but could not sustain the momentum, the high budgets adding to the loss quotient. As with *Lalkar*, the miniatures were expensive propositions, but the people were not enamoured by them. Hema Malini was Dharmendra's co-star again.

Ram Balram, the third film, was planned in 70 mm but finally released only in Cinemascope. This was just as well, because though the film did decently at the box-office, it was considered a failure in terms of the return on investment. After *Sholay* (and *Chupke Chupke*), Dharmendra and Amitabh Bachchan had come together once again, with a genius like Vijay Anand at the helm, and Zeenat Aman and Rekha as leading ladies. The music by Laxmikant-Pyarelal was again popular, but then, we were still in an era when the songs and their parent film could have different destinies. Anand, however, was in declining mode, and the film suffered.

The final film, *Chunaoti*, was a Curry Western showcasing Feroz Khan in yet another cowboy kind of drama after *Khotey Sikkey* and *Kaala Sona* in the 1970s. The film opened with Dharmendra as farmer-turned-dacoit Shakti Singh in an extended special appearance, in which he even saves Khan in the climax. However, *Chunaoti* too was a no-no at the box-office. Incidentally, Dharmendra began his 1980s innings with this film, followed a week later by *The Burning Train*.

In 1981, Dharmendra acted in *Aas Paas, Krodhi, Kaatilon Ke Kaatil* and *Professor Pyarelal*, and played himself in a cameo in the song 'John Jani Janardhan' in Manmohan Desai's *Naseeb*. In an interesting tweak to logic, so typical of Desai, the star-studded event shown in *Naseeb* was the jubilee of the Dharmendra-Manmohan Desai mega hit *Dharam-Veer*, yet Dharmendra walked in with Simi Garewal and there was no trace of Zeenat Aman, Jeetendra or Neetu Singh in the cavalcade of star cameos! However, Dharmendra did have a lengthier appearance in this Amitabh Bachchan song vis-à-vis the rest of the heavyweights.

Aas Paas was directed by J. Om Prakash, who had produced three hits with Dharam in the 1960s. Very interestingly, Hrithik Roshan can be seen as a kid in the duet 'Sheher Mein Charcha Hai' as the naughty messenger of a love note between the couple. His father Rakesh Roshan, who also was a part of the star-roster in the *Naseeb* song, was to co-star with Dharmendra the following year in *Teesri Aankh*.

Above all, *Aas Paas* is memorable because this was also the last complete song ever recorded by Mohammed Rafi, Dharmendra's favourite and most identified singer.

Legend has it that as Rafi was leaving the recording studio, the composer duo Laxmikant-Pyarelal called him back to sing the four lines, 'Tere Aane Ki Aas Hai Dost/Shaam Phir Kyoon Udaas Hai Dost/Mehki Huyi Fizaa Yeh Kehti Hai/Tu Kahin Aas Paas Hai Dost' (I yearn for your arrival, then why is the evening so sad? The fragrance in the air tells me that you are somewhere close). These lines, filmed as the last frames of the tragic romance on a desolated Dharmendra and minus lip-synch, summed up his deep emotions as his beloved is no more. Rafi was never to return to the studios after this either.

About the Dharam-Rafi association, which had begun with *Shola Aur Shabnam* way back in 1961, it is also well-known that he wanted to use the original Rafi song 'Main Jat Yamla Pagla Deewanaa' half a century later in his 2011 film *Yamla Pagla Deewana*, but the clash of interests (the new film had music on a different label to the original) led to Sonu Nigam re-recording the song.

Krodhi was as good as a Dharmendra home production. Recalled writer and director Subhash Ghai, 'Word had spread that I was a good writer-director even while *Kalicharan* was being made. I had this subject with me since 1972, but had dreamt of making it with Amitabh Bachchan. However, Dharmendra invited me, and told me that he wanted to produce a film under his home banner of Vijayta Films. "Do you have a story?" he [had] asked. He heard *Krodhi* on his terrace and was very excited. His face glowed, and he said, "I will produce it!"'

A while later, Dharmendra called Ghai and said that he was signing him as a writer-director. However, the film would now be made under the banner of Ranjit Films for his brother-in-law, producer Ranjit Virk. Virk had made the successful 1974 Amitabh Bachchan thriller *Benaam*, in which, very few are aware, Dharmendra was to originally do a negative cameo.

Dharmendra told Ghai, 'Ranjit is a very good producer. Don't worry, I will be responsible for everything.' Ghai understood there were family obligations, and in good faith, developed the script with Dharmendra's long-time associate Nabendu Ghosh.

However, Ghai, candid and compassionate, recalled, 'Ranjit was happy to hear the subject but wanted to make it as a project. He went on bringing one star after another. Shashi Kapoor was okay, but we needlessly got in Hema Maliniji and Moushumi Chatterjee. The worst aspect was that Ranjit was a nice and naïve man, and he wanted to make the biggest film in 70 mm!'

Even today, Ghai maintains that *Krodhi*, as originally written, was the best script of his life. There was action, but the philosophy behind was so big that he was convinced the film would work big-time even if he could achieve 60 per cent of what he had envisioned. But he was helpless—Dharmendra, then busy with some twenty films, could only spare hours or a couple of days at intervals.

'We finally had nine stars—Dharam, Shashi, Hema, Zeenat,

Moushumi, Pran, Premnath, Sachin and Ranjeeta!' said Ghai. 'To justify some, we had to include a song. The final material was four hours and thirty minutes long!'

Ghai asserts that Dharmendra too knew that they were going wrong. 'It took ten days for me to edit the film to some kind of coherence, and I suggested some reshooting, but Ranjit put his foot down—he could not afford it and did not want to do so. Dharmendra knew what I was going through, and he would come to me and weep. But the damage was done. We still released it and hoped for the best, but it was the saddest day for me to know that the film had flopped.'

This was Ghai's first flop as a director after four successful films in a row, and happily, he would have to 'wait' a full decade before his next flop, nine films later! But as he puts it, Dharmendra willingly agreed to work with him almost three decades later in a Punjabi movie, which we will come to later.

Kaatilon Ke Kaatil was to 1981 what *Alibaba...* was to 1980: Dharmendra's only success. While his first director Arjun Hingorani was to make still more films with him, this was the last success. Zeenat Aman, as his heroine, and Rishi Kapoor and Tina Munim were the co-stars in Hingorani's latest *KKK* potboiler. A clone (a Taiwanese actor named Bruce Le!) as Bruce Lee and a 'creature' named Reecha (born out of a woman and a wild bear!) essayed by Shamsuddin were the novel gimmicks in this out-and-out entertainer.

And if *Kaatilon...* was a film with his first director, the remaining action drama, *Professor Pyarelal*, was Dharmendra's return to his first film's presenter, T.M. Bihari.

The plot had its interesting elements, with Manmohan Desai-like twists: A cop's son (Dharmendra) becomes a criminal, and another criminal's son, unknowingly his friend, is an honest man (Vinod Mehra). Moreover, Dharmendra's character actually wants to kill Mehra's father to avenge his father's death, which was actually an accident. And Mehra's father has no clue that his wife and son are alive. Starring Zeenat Aman again, the delayed Brij-directed thriller was a failure. It would also seem that the film was overshot and, yet again, Hrishikesh Mukherjee was brought in to edit the footage.

However, both films had hit music by Kalyanji-Anandji, and the popular Dharmendra songs included 'Main Woh Chanda Nahin' and 'Sar-e-Bazaar Karenge Pyar' from the former film and 'Tere Siva Na Kisika Banoonga' and 'Gaaye Jaa Gaaye Jaa' (filmed in part on him) from the latter.

The year 1982 played out similarly for Dharmendra, and only one success, *Ghazab*, stood out in a higher quantum of releases—the multi-starrer films *Rajput, Teesri Aankh, Badle Ki Aag* and *Samraat* and the solo hero movies *Main Intequam Loonga* and *Baghavat*. There was also *Do Dishayen* (produced by Hema Malini's aunt R. Renuka) which did not even get a nationwide release. The interesting part about these eight films that accounted for the only releases the actor had this year was that every film had music by Laxmikant-Pyarelal, but they musically made a mark only in *Rajput* and *Ghazab*.

Hema Malini, on the other hand, had four more flops with Dharmendra—*Rajput, Baghavat, Samraat* and *Do Dishayen*, each with a director of repute: Vijay Anand, Ramanand Sagar, Mohan Segal and Dulal Guha respectively.

The saving grace was *Ghazab*, directed by C.P. Dixit and produced by N.N. Sippy. A remake of the Tamil film *Kalyanaraman*, the film saw Dharmendra playing both a mentally challenged brother and a normal one. The former is ruthlessly murdered, and the second brother takes his ghost's help in avenging his death and also saving the family estate from the villains.

Easily Dharmendra's most acclaimed double role, it actually had the 'two Dharmendras' singing a duet on screen, 'Aage Se Dekho Peeche Se Dekho', sung by Kishore Kumar and Amit Kumar. Amit Kumar was the voice of the backward Munna, and Rekha was the leading lady in the film.

The jinx of the 1980s continued into 1983. *Razia Sultan* (a film launched in 1974!) and *Qayamat* were disasters. Only *Naukar Biwi Ka* did average business. A golden lining, however, was that Dharmendra's presentation and (unofficially) production, *Betaab*, became a superhit. After *Bobby*, in which Raj Kapoor had launched Rishi Kapoor, and *Love Story*, with which Rajendra Kumar introduced his son Kumar Gaurav to the world, this was the latest true-blue designer break given to a son by a star father.

To take them in sequence, *Razia Sultan* remains, ironically for Dharmendra's stature and track-record, one of the biggest crashes in film history and the prime Hindi disaster of the '80s as a decade! Written and directed by Kamal Amrohi, it once again showed that Dharmendra in a weak and disfigured light was anathema to the ticket-buying audience.

Worse, the film was not only delayed and in the making for almost a decade, but also was outdated in its execution. The length too was ridiculous—23 reels, translating into almost 260 minutes.

A star like Dharmendra as the ill-fated slave Yakut, Hema Malini in the title-role of the regal first female 'Sultana' of Delhi, Razia Sultan(a), who falls for her slave, and Parveen Babi were no compensations. The music by Khayyam, though melodious, had restricted popular appeal and added to the 'liabilities' of the film in terms of popular appeal. And from Dharmendra's perspective, Kabban Mirza's totally incongruous voice singing dull songs like 'Tera Hijr Mera Naseeb Hai' and 'Ayee Zanjeer Ki Jhankar' was completely unacceptable.

At the other extreme was Raj N. Sippy's *Qayamat*, a thriller with a star-studded ensemble of Shatrughan Sinha, Jaya Prada, Poonam Dhillon and Smita Patil. A rehash of the 1962 Hollywood film *Cape Fear*, the film was inexplicably remade later in Telugu as *Nippulanti Manishi*. It starred Dharmendra as Shatrughan Sinha's mentor in early years, who turns to crime while Sinha becomes an inspector, and arrests him. Now Dharmendra's character swears vengeance on his ex-friend, his wife and his sister.

Recalled director Sippy, 'Dharmendra was shown full of fury and the lines he says to Shatrughan appalled Dharam's mother, because *her son* was saying them on-screen. This was when Dharmendra's character tells Shatrughan's: "*Rape kya cheez hai main tumhein sikhaaoonga* (I will teach you what rape is)!" and his mother came out in the interval, shocked. Dharam explained to her that this was a part of the script and that she should judge all this after the film was over. He told her that if she felt so, she could slap him at the end of the film.'

The successful film, *Naukar Biwi Ka*, directed by Rajkumar Kohli, was a remake of the hit Pakistani Punjabi movie *Naukar Wohti Da*. A complicated cocktail of crime and comedy, it had Anita Raj in the central role despite the presence of the senior actress who was also a Rajkumar Kohli favourite, Reena Roy.

But the biggest cheer for Dharmendra that year was in the way the audience accepted his son Sunny Deol with arms wide open in *Betaab*. The Deols also chose Rahul Rawail to direct the film like Rajendra Kumar did, but they had smooth sailing with the director. The stellar cast was led by Shammi Kapoor, Prem Chopra and a bright and relatively new supporting actor, Annu Kapoor.

Betaab was a tight romantic script written by Javed Akhtar—his first independent work after parting with Salim Khan. The all-popular music score by R.D. Burman and Anand Bakshi had five songs, each rendered by Shabbir Kumar, the reigning Mohammed Rafi clone by then, three of which were duets with Lata Mangeshkar.

There was another interesting sidelight: The young Sunny Deol in the film was portrayed by someone else who went on to be a Rafi-esque voice—Sonu Nigam, who was destined to sing the title song of the Deols' 2011 home production *Yamla Pagla Deewana*.

The film, officially produced by Dharmendra's brother Bikram Singh Deol, was a clever mix of the *Bobby* formula of lovebirds from families belonging to contrasting social statuses, with the other time-tested formula of childhood friends becoming sweethearts after growing up. Into this confection, Akhtar's script also brought in the clever icing of the taming of the shrew leitmotif.

The other bright discovery was heroine Amrita Singh, who was the leading lady. Gushed Singh, 'Whatever I say for Dharamji will never be enough to show my gratitude for what he has done for me. I am Amrita Singh, the actor, only because of him. He picked me up at the age of sixteen, after screen-testing a hundred girls, and gave me a launch film that is, to date, a milestone in Hindi romantic movies. It is thirty-five years since *Betaab* released, and my epic journey is all thanks to our dashingly handsome Punjab *da puttar* Dharminderji!'

And Singh's professional association with that family continued for a long while after that. Dharmendra was to even co-star as her romantic lead in many films.

Sadly, Dharmendra lacked even a single success in 1984 in Hindi films. However, his old associate Pramod Chakravorty made *Jagir*, an ensemble cast film, as a bilingual, and the Bengali version *Teen Murti* became a hit! The other films, Rajkumar Kohli's behemoths *Jeene Nahin Doonga* and *Raaj Tilak*, Raj N. Sippy's *Baazi* and Joshi's *Dharam Aur Qanoon* were complete losers at the box-office. Dharmendra even made a cameo appearance in Sunny Deol's second film, *Sunny*, directed by Raj Khosla, but that too also sank without a trace.

The rejection of films that were 'proposals' rather than well-conceived movies was glaringly evident now. Each of these films, especially *Raaj Tilak*, had a massive star-cast, and in this single year, Dharmendra's male co-stars included Shatrughan Sinha, Raj Babbar, Mithun Chakraborty (twice), Raaj Kumar, Sunil Dutt, Rajesh Khanna, Raj Kiran, Vikram, Kamal Haasan and Vinod Mehra (again twice).

The one success a year story followed even in 1985, when *Ghulami*, Dharmendra's first film with debutant director J.P. Dutta, was a success. However, his next *KKK* film with Arjun Hingorani, *Karishmaa Kudrat Kaa* and his Raj N. Sippy-directed home production, *Sitamgar*, bombed.

Sippy said, 'His brother-in-law, Bikramjit, came to me because Dharam paaji wanted me to direct their next, so there was no question of turning him down. He had given me the freedom to choose the subject.' However, the complex and slightly dark (like *Qayamat*) revenge drama was not accepted.

Ghulami, however, was Dharmendra's first biopic—a trendy genre today! Remembered Dutta, 'I had walked to his bungalow, and as luck would have it, he was at home. I started narrating the story at 12.30 p.m. and came out at 6.15 p.m.! He was swept off by my script and could not believe that I had sat in Rajasthan when writing the film!'

Dharmendra's central character was based on a man called Ranjit Singh Chaudhary, and Dutta had spent over a week with him. 'In the film,' recalled the writer-director, 'I killed Dharam [his character] in the end, because I felt that his purpose to society ended with his arrest, but the real Ranjit was very much alive.'

The 'purpose to society' Dutta mentioned is the courageous fight against the feudal and caste system rampant in Rajasthan's interiors. Ranjit was the rebel, the man who decided to fight the tyrannical landowners who demanded that he pay back the 'loan' his father owed them, or forfeit his land. This after he runs away from home as a young boy, and returns on the day his father dies. Dutta seamlessly wove in a love triangle (Reena Roy, Smita Patil) into the narrative, with a cast that included Mithun Chakraborty, Naseeruddin Shah and Anita Raj.

The year 1986 proved a forgettable year for the actor. He had only two lead role releases, *Main Balwaan* and *Sultanat*, both with

Mukul S. Anand at the helm, and the latter starred him with Sunny Deol. Good friend Shashi Kapoor's son Karan Kapoor made his debut in *Sultanat* too, and the film was again produced by Arjun Hingorani. There were three forgettable cameos, in *Saveray Waali Gaadi* (absurdly, he rescues the young lead pair of Sunny Deol and Poonam Dhillon in the climax, but is shown not related to his son), *Mohabbat Ki Kasam* and *Begaana*—the second film he worked in with this title.

In 1987 came a temporary respite in the actor's career, though the kind of films he starred in did not change. His first film with Anil Sharma, *Hukumat*, had a golden jubilee run and Garam Dharam, yet again after *Phool Aur Patthar, Ankhen, Seeta Aur Geeta* and *Sholay*, starred in this biggest hit of the year.

Loha, Insaniyat Ke Dushmun and *Aag Hi Aag* were also hits, while *Watan Ke Rakhwale, Dadagiri* and *Insaaf Kaun Karega* did average business. The flops were *Insaf Ki Pukar, Mera Karam Mera Dharam, Mard Ki Zabaan* (in an extended cameo) and *Jaan Hatheli Pe*.

And that makes a whopping seven successes in a single year—an all-time record possibly for any hero, including our man, that too, out of a tally of eleven releases.

However, 1988 was again full of behemoths that tumbled under their own starry and budgetary weights at the box-office: *Zalzala, Khatron Ke Khiladi, Ganga Tere Desh Mein, Mardon Wali Baat, Sone Pe Suhaaga, Mahaveera* and *Paap Ko Jalaa Kar Raakh Kar Doonga*.

And 1989 was no better, though Anil Sharma's *Elaan-E-Jung* (again a solo hero film) sort of broke even, with its anti-terrorist wannabe-*Hukumat* flavour, while *Vardi* and *Ilaaka*, which had Dharmendra in cameo appearances, did average business. *Kasam Suhaag Ki* (a solo lead), *Shehzaade* (in a double role yet again), *Sikka, Nafrat Ki Aandhi, Batwara, Hathyar* and *Sachai Ki Taaqat* all collapsed.

Of all these movies, *Hathyar* (like *Batwara*, it was directed by J.P. Dutta) boasted of a good role for the actor, who gave one of his finest performances in the 1980s in this gangland drama. His character, said Dutta again, was modelled on noted gangster Karim Lala, who was said to be Mumbai's first don. Though Sanjay Dutt played the central character of sorts, Dharmendra could also be said to have played, as in *Ghulami* by the same director, yet another dramatized version of a real person.

'Dharam underplayed a very violent don. My film was praised as a movie way ahead of its time,' exulted Dutta. 'Yes, I never made a solo hero film with him. But which film of ours justified a solo hero?'

Rishi Kapoor also noted, 'In *Hathyar*, we played brothers. As an actor, he was very effective whenever he was given a good role, and J.P. (Dutta) handled him well. It was a film I enjoyed as an actor too.' And Dutta agrees that it could be called Dharmendra's second biopic.

But one film, not starring but presented by Dharmendra, also directed by Dutta in 1989, did have a solo hero—*Yateem*, again his home production starring Sunny Deol. Though appreciated for its music score by Laxmikant-Pyarelal and its performances, the film also failed at the box-office. The storyline was very interesting, but maybe a tad bold for those times for an A-grade big-budgeted film— an adopted son falling in love with the daughter of the house, and the young stepmother also lusting after him.

Chapter Nine

1990–2003: Too Many Films, Too Little Glory

Mujhe dard-e-dil ka pataa na tha /
Mujhe aap kis liye mil gaye

This was such a retrograde fourteen years (almost like the vanwaas in the epic Ramayana) in Dharmendra's track record that it would make logical sense to home in first on his very few successful films and worthwhile roles rather than get into the complete 'filmi' riff-raff that abounded as his films in this period.

Making his debut officially as producer, Dharmendra produced the blockbuster *Ghayal*, which in a way heralded a rewarding phase two in Sunny Deol's career. The decade also saw Dharmendra launch younger son Bobby Deol in *Barsaat* (1995), which did average business, and he also presented both of them together at the far end of the decade in the 1999 film, *Dillagi*. The last film, however, did not do well at the box-office, though it marked Sunny Deol's debut as director.

As an actor, Dharmendra featured in 1990 in *Naaka Bandi*, a crime caper, which did average business. *Tehelka* (1992) fared decently too. *Kshatriya* (1993) worked in a few centres. Then in 1998, Salman Khan cast him in his home production *Pyaar Kiya To Darna Kya*, a jubilee hit directed, written and co-produced by Sohail Khan.

However, among the multitude of flops, Dharmendra did get a few worthwhile set-ups. A major assignment was *Kal Ki Awaz* (1992), a prestigious project produced and directed jointly by B.R. Chopra and Ravi Chopra. Raj Babbar, Amrita Singh, newcomer Rohit and Mala Sinha's daughter Pratibha (playing Dharmendra's daughter) formed the rest of the cast.

Humlaa (1992), produced by Madan Mohla (*Sharafat, Raja Jani, Samraat*) and directed by N. Chandra, was another potentially good story gone wrong, as was *Aazmayish* (1995), produced by old associate Mohan Kumar but directed by actor Sachin, who had co-starred with Dharmendra in *Sholay, Dil Ka Heera* and *Krodhi*.

In theory, a sequel (in those days, virtually an unknown genre in Hindi cinema) to the 1967 classic *Jewel Thief* was a good idea. But though original heroes Ashok Kumar and Dev Anand were in the cast as the same characters in the 1996 *Return of Jewel Thief*, director Ashok Tyagi made a cocktail that was far from appetizing.

Dharmendra's addition to its cast added little value, therefore, as the film was also made at a time when Kumar and Anand were well past their primes, the three heroines (Shilpa Shirodkar, Madhoo and Anu Agarwal) had no clout and Jatin-Lalit's music, though good in itself, simply lacked the excellence and popular appeal of the earlier film's songs.

Art director Desh Mukherjee, who had directed the 1977 flop *Imaan Dharam*, had been entrusted with the 70 mm film *Aatank* in the late 1970s or early 1980s, an Indianized rehash of the Hollywood film *Jaws*. However, the producers ran out of funds, the film got stalled, and was finally completed by some other producer as well as director as a regular (not 70 mm, that is) film that was somehow

released as late as in 1996. It was to be the last of the Dharmendra-
Hema Malini films as leading stars.

Another film that was interesting when launched but lost its
lustre because of the delay in its making was Harmesh Malhotra's
Paappi Devataa, with Jeetendra and Madhuri Dixit, and Jaya Prada
as Dharmendra's lady-love. This one, too, came out in 1996 to an
indifferent release.

In 1997, Dharmendra enacted the triple roles of Brahma, Vishnu
and Mahesh in the caper *Jeo Shaan Se* directed by Talat Jani, but the
B-grade ambience and content made the film sink minus a whimper.

And in 1999, Dharmendra hit the rock-bottom in the messiest
phase of his career with the B-grade stunt film *Munnibai*. His first
film with that uncrowned czar of B-grade cinema, Kanti Shah,
came in 1997—*Loha*. This was the second film he did with this
title after the 1987 Raj N. Sippy hit. Still, this one at least starred
Mithun Chakraborty and a then-fairly popular Ramya Krishnan with
Govinda and Manisha Koirala in special appearances.

With Shah's *Munnibai* (1999), however, Dharmendra entered
the B-grade set-up in a full-fledged way with unknown co-actors
Sapna and Durgesh Nandini. A similar cadre of male and female
actors abounded in his films (including Sapna again) by Shah and
other B-grade directors until 2003. Shah directed him, in quick
succession, again in *Meri Jung Ki Elaan, Jallad No. 1* (both in 2000)
and *Jagira*.

Sample the other titles this Golden Boy of the '60s and '70s
worked in: *Sultaan, Dacait* (Sunny Deol had done a critically
acclaimed but unsuccessful film of that name with Rahul Rawail
in 1987), *Bhai Thakur, Saugandh Gita Ki, Reshma Aur Sultan* and
TADA, besides a film named *Border Kashmir* in a guest appearance.

It was postulated that Dharmendra had to keep doing such
'downmarket' cinema mainly because he was supporting a huge
extended family of relatives from Punjab, and also because he

was planning to build a state-of-the-art studio (after building his Mumbai set-up Sunny Super Sound) in Khandala. The A-grade offers had dried up due to a change in trend from the '80s action to the dominating romantic musicals of the '90s, and Dharmendra had to sign what was offered.

This is where Rajkumar Santoshi, the writer-director discovered by Dharmendra in *Ghayal*, turned passionate and vehement. 'As a fan, which I was of Dharamji from much before *Ghayal* happened, I feel that he, whatever his compulsions, diluted his charisma and deceived lots of fans like me by doing C-grade films, like those of Kanti Shah.'

In a rare burst of candour, Santoshi stated: 'Let me be clear and frank. There is a saying in Hindi—*sher bhooka marega lekin ghaas nahin khaayega* (a lion will die of hunger rather than eat grass). Another saying is that *Haathi ghode se ooncha hota hai*, because even a resting elephant is taller than a horse.' The director went on, 'All this hurts me because I am his fan as well. What happened to his status after all the work he did? Such films were a major setback, undoing what he had achieved in over twenty-five years. Dharamji could have been in a different league. His fans are ever ready to forgive, but all this has made a deep impact on his career graph and that is very sad. He should have maintained his professional dignity.'

About the reasons for doing such films, the director said: 'That, for me, is not an excuse. If you have constructed a studio by ruining your track-record, what use is that? The problem with Dharamji is that he is not a clever person, and he is too emotional. He is often surrounded by sycophants. He was exploited into doing proposals rather than proper films. Good directors always did good work with him!'

In this wayward phase, sons Sunny Deol and Bobby Deol were following a respectable track, though not with uniform success. And Dharmendra thus had passing trysts with respectable cinema when he presented the successful Sunny Deol production *Indian*, directed by N. Maharajan of the South, in 2001, and *23 March 1931—Shaheed*, which featured Bobby Deol as Bhagat Singh and Sunny as Chandrashekhar Azad, in 2002.

Dharam's discovery, Amrita Singh, after quitting films following her marriage to Saif Ali Khan and motherhood, returned to work in the second film—but as Bhagat Singh's mother. In the glut of Bhagat Singh films released that year (including the other biggie directed by Rajkumar Santoshi himself, with Bobby's close friend Ajay Devgn as the freedom fighter), this film too flopped like all the others.

Finally, in 2003, Dharmendra as well as Sunny Deol made guest appearances in mentor Arjun Hingorani's last film, *Kaise Kahoon Ke Pyar Hai*, in which Hingorani tried to make a star out of his son Amit Hingorani. But that film also did not work.

And all this while, loving sons Sunny Deol and Bobby Deol were determined that their dad should get out of his rut and return to movies and roles in an A-grade set-up worthy of his calibre and status. They were even looking for a suitable script for him. After all, something and someone had to end this very bleak phase in the career of one of Hindi cinema's most versatile and durable actors.

Chapter Ten

2004–18: Renaissance of an Actor

Aaj raat chandni hai / Aur tum mere paas ho

It was a concerted family decision: Dharmendra could not continue going on the B-grade path. Apart from the fact that he was worthy of better assignments, he had lost a good chunk of his fan base, although his unparalleled chimera was immaculate. His contemporaries, who were still working, had different and better stories to tell, career-wise, vis-a-vis this all-timer, and had graduated to mature roles by sticking to A-grade films.

For example, apart from the infinitely unusual story of triumph scripted for himself by Amitabh Bachchan (by pragmatically asking for work and then proving that he still had it in him), a junior like Rishi Kapoor too was doing a good class of films with author-backed roles, even if unsuccessful until then.

Sunil Dutt made a triumphant exit to his career with *Munna Bhai M.B.B.S.,* Vinod Khanna was coming back with author-backed roles (so what if the films did not work?) and Shatrughan Sinha was doing a film or two as well. By 2003, Feroz Khan had released another ambitious production, *Janasheen*, a tepid success, and was also open to select roles.

Manoj Kumar, Shashi Kapoor, Jeetendra and even Randhir

Kapoor had called it a day, while Rajesh Khanna was the only star stuck in the B-grade film rut due to his own issues.

And Dharmendra could not possibly go the Rajesh Khanna way!

The search was on for the right script, and meanwhile Dharmendra, the timeless lover, had signed a film with the sensational Mallika Sherawat of the twenty-three kisses (the moderate 2003 success *Khwahish*) fame—*Kis Kis Ki Kismat*. He had also done a cameo in *Hum Kaun Hai?* featuring Dimple Kapadia and Moushumi Chatterjee, with Amitabh Bachchan in a special appearance.

While the latter was a fairly ambitious but slightly delayed horror genre film rehashed from the Hollywood horror film *The Others*, it did not have a significant role for the actor. However, *Kis Kis Ki Kismat* (2004), though a dud at the box-office and panned by critics as well, had a meaty and reasonably comic role for the veteran. Dharmendra was a delight in this film, but, unfortunately for him, it did not work, one add-on reason being that just a few months earlier, Sherawat had consolidated her image as an erotic femme fatale in that year's biggest hit, *Murder*. Dharmendra's loyal fans stayed away, piqued that their idol and icon was doing 'sex comedies', which is how the film was branded.

From this point, almost for three years, Garam Dharam took a break. He knew he had to tread with caution. And then—voila! The right script was found, and director Anil Sharma, always someone who the Deols were very fond of, was entrusted with the responsibility of giving him a solid comeback in the family drama *Apne* (2007), unofficially a home production of the Deols. It was also the first film in which Dharmendra co-starred with both his sons in roles corresponding to real life—of a father and two sons. And it was a casting that was not just a gimmick. Kirron Kher, Shilpa Shetty and Katrina Kaif were their respective co-stars.

Sharma recalled, 'My script was very high on family values and feelings, and during the narration Dharamji would repeatedly excuse himself and go to the washroom.' Sharma went on, 'Soon, I realized that he was going there just to weep because the script had moved him so much, and he could not cry in front of me. He is such a tender person. When I finished my narration, he called Prakashji (Dharmendra's wife) and told her, "*Meri picture ho gayi* (my film has been finalized)!" He had an expression on his face that I can never forget!'

And as we all know, when fortune smiles, to mix metaphors, it never rains but pours. Along came two more film-makers, each brilliant—Anurag Basu, who cast him in a fabulous role in *Life In A... Metro*, a film in which three stories came to a confluence of sorts; and Sriram Raghavan, who gave the actor a small but very important role in *Johnny Gaddaar*. All three were released within weeks of each other in 2007. *Apne* proved to be a hit, *Life In A... Metro* did average business but was critically acclaimed, and *Johnny Gaddaar*, though a flop, soon emerged as a cult classic thriller. Thus in different ways and to varied extents, they were all winners.

Even more important: Dharmendra was loved in all three films, and this is what prompted Santoshi's remark (in the previous chapter) that good directors still took out good work from him. In fact, a legion of his fans were now angered (again!) by the fact that Dharmendra did not win any of the Best Acting awards that year, because there was no better-nuanced male lead performance than his work in *Apne* in 2007.

And as *...Metro* film-maker Basu put it, 'My character for Dharamji had to romance at 50-plus with a woman (Nafisa Ali Sodhi) who was shown to be 60-plus! The romance had to look cute, not repulsive. Dharmendra was my first and last choice and I was lucky that he was greedy enough for good scripts. He accepted my film when I nervously went to him and gave him a narration!'

Sriram Raghavan, who made *Johnny Gaddaar*, had told Rediff. com, 'When I was scripting, I knew I needed somebody like

Dharmendra to essay one of those key roles. I was certainly wary of casting an actor of his stature, more so because he did not know me and neither had he watched my debut directorial, *Ek Haseena Thi*. But when we met and interacted, he showed keen interest in the film. In fact, he used to interrupt me with small but good inputs. He came up with his own ideas, which made the character much more than what it was on paper.' And this is what the actor had been doing all along during his long peak phase!

Clearly, this was renaissance time in Dharmendra's mindset and persona—and due to that, in his career. The sun was shining brightly again on this timeless icon, and this time, Dharmendra steered away from previous mistakes. The crucial point that Dharmendra finally had realized was that his fans still loved him—even more than before! His single-point agenda now was that he should not betray them and what they felt for him even after almost five decades. And so was born *Yamla Pagla Deewana*.

'My fans were upset that I made them cry in *Apne*,' smiled the actor. 'They wanted to laugh again in a film with me. And so we decided that we will make a comedy. We had to find the correct story for that.'

Things fell into place when Jaswinder Singh Bath, a young writer who had won a story competition organized by a top music company, offered them the story of two conmen—a father and son duo—and the other son, who is separated from them. Samir Karnik, who was close to the Deols, was assigned the direction, but the Deols could not find a producer for this project despite the success of *Apne*.

Bollywood Box-Office India's blog reports that a broker was trying to get a producer on board. When the broker approached several top producers and production houses with the story of *Yamla Pagla Deewana* with the Deols finalized as lead players, they all found the project 'unviable'. They argued with the broker that producing this film with all the Deols—Dharmendra, Sunny and Bobby—was a mistake, and one producer even said, 'Don't take this project to any other producer. This film can kill him.'

To quote the blog, 'After receiving negative response from producers, including Shree Ashtavinayak Cine Vision Limited, Babloo Pachisia, Bharat Shah, Balaji Motion Pictures, UTV Motion Pictures, Gordhan Tanwani, Shemaroo and Smita Thackeray, the crestfallen broker decided to call up Nitin Manmohan, producer of such movies as *Insaaf, Bol Radha Bol, Laadla* and others.'

Nitin Manmohan (son of veteran character artiste Manmohan), who had not produced any film for a good while after *Chal Mere Bhai* starring Salman Khan and Sanjay Dutt in 2000, immediately came on board. The film was made at an economic budget of ₹24 crore, and even before release, Manmohan and (now co-producer) Samir Karnik had made ₹41 crore through the theatrical rights (₹25 crore) and the satellite rights (₹16 crore). The film was released on 14 January 2011 after a tumultuous response to the trailer alone.

In the theatres alone, in terms of footfall, the film was a superhit (it made at least thrice the investment in it by distributors). Dharmendra was back in the true sense at over seventy-five years of age, and for the first time, the Deols thought of a franchise.

In 2011, Dharmendra also played reel parent to daughter Esha Deol (his only other child working in films) in *Tell Me O Kkhuda*, a film produced and eventually directed (the original director was dismissed midway!) by Hema Malini, who also did a cameo in it. This was followed by another cameo, in *Singh Saab the Great* (2013) starring Sunny Deol, with Bobby Deol also in a cameo in a song.

In 2013 also came the bigger franchise film, *Yamla Pagla Deewana 2*. However, as a team, the Deols made the mistake of not making the film better but merely bigger, with shooting done in the UK, which is a strong Deol bastion in terms of fans. This time, they met with failure. And Dharmendra was again disillusioned for a while.

But he had decided by then that he was going to act only in light-hearted films. He willingly signed Subhash Ghai's comedy in Punjabi, *Double Di Trouble*, in the lead. The 2014 film, with him in his latest double role, proved a blockbuster in Dharmendra's home state. Impressed with its director, Smeep Kang, he even signed the jaded Hindi comedy, *Second Hand Husband*, that did not work.

On home production ground, Dharmendra had also presented two more films. *Socha Na Tha* (2005), then a flop but now a favorite on satellite television, was produced by Sunny Deol and introduced Dharmendra's brother Kanwar Ajit Singh's talented son Abhay Deol, along with child model-turned-actress Ayesha Takia, in a cute romance. Imtiaz Ali was introduced as a director with this film.

The other film was Kabeer Kaushik's *Chamku* (2008), an action thriller featuring Bobby Deol and Priyanka Chopra, which emerged a non-starter.

In 2016, Sunny Deol returned to direction with the crisp and very contemporary narration of *Ghayal Once Again*, a sequel to their 1990 blockbuster *Ghayal*, with him reprising the same role. Critically appreciated, the film, co-starring Soha Ali Khan and three newcomers, could not capitalize on its virtues thanks to the way Sunny Deol was perceived: Traditional Deol fans did not find him raving and ranting and showing his typical tryst with action, while younger film audiences stayed away, sure that this was another loud action marathon! Thus the film lost out both ways.

But that was the critical view. Sunny Deol commented, 'What you say could be partly true. But the main reason was that I had no corporate with me. It is a dirty battle fighting for screens and shows today, unlike the more straight dealings between producers, distributors and exhibitors in the past. From a promised 1,500 screens, they brought it down at the last moment to 500! So people assumed there was something wrong with a big film that was getting such a limited release. When people watched it later on television, they were surprised to find it so good, but by that time it was too late!'

Reflecting a sorry reality of present times, Deol added, 'I have vowed now never to go [at] it alone. Big corporate entities, headed by executives who do not know the ABC of Hindi cinema, are given preference by multiplex owners for screens and shows because they have films releasing every two months or even more often.'

However, the brothers suffered much the same experience with their bright comedy, *Poster Boyz* in 2017, another Dharmendra presentation, despite having Sony as the corporate partner.

With a never-say-die spirit, however, the Deols went full throttle into their home production *Yamla Pagla Deewana Phir Se*. Sunny Deol explained, 'Papa was disturbed and depressed when the sequel, *Yamla Pagla Deewana 2*, did not do well. But, this time, we have a terrific script.'

And putting the combined might of their moral support behind the Deols were Dharmendra's trusted friend Shatrughan Sinha and his daughter Sonakshi Sinha, Rekha, and adoring Dharmendra devotee Salman Khan, who all made cameos in a medley of old songs, including the iconic 'Rafta Raftaa Dekho Aankh Meri Ladi Hai' from the 1973 *Kahani Kismat Ki*, which Dharmendra and Rekha enacted again forty-five years later. Interestingly, this would also be the first time that the Sinha father-daughter duo came together on screen.

Kriti Kharbanda, the film's leading lady, said in mock anger, 'I was so angry when I signed the film because I thought, "S**t, *yaar*! I am not cast with Dharamji!" He's so-o-o-o-o handsome! But I have a song dance with all of them, so I am so happy! And Dharam uncle is the best dancer among all of them! On the sets, he once told me, "Producers give royal treatment to us heroes and pay us big money, but the real heroes are the fans, because if they don't come to watch your film, the producer will lose all his money!"'

PART 2:

The MAN BEHIND
The HE-MAN

Chapter Eleven

The Mammoth Movies that Never Took Off

Insaan hanse ya roye / Jo hona hai so hoye / Kya hona hai kab hona hai likhnewala jaane kahani / Kahani kismet ki

*D*harmendra's filmography would have been adorned by many more big films if a plethora of mega-projects, all announced, had seen the light of day, or more properly, the darkness of the theatres. Here is a list that is by no means comprehensive and focuses on the more important movies.

Aaghaaz Aur Anjaam

The film was announced in 1973 as the debut movie of Sudarshan Kumar, Mohan Kumar's brother, as producer. A Mohan Kumar presentation, it was to be directed by Shammi Kapoor after his directorial debut with *Manoranjan*. The co-stars were to be Shashi Kapoor and Zeenat Aman. The music was to be composed by Laxmikant-Pyarelal.

After some issues with Kapoor, Mohan Kumar stepped in as director, but then, the film was never made.

Aasmaan

Premji was to produce this film. Mohan Kumar was to direct his first outside assignment in almost two decades. Amitabh Bachchan, Hema Malini and Rekha were announced as part of the cast and Waheeda Rehman was supposed to be in the film as well. Laxmikant-Pyarelal were to compose the music.

Bhagini

Ram Mukerji, actress Rani Mukerji's father, was to direct Dharmendra, Hema Malini, Reena Roy and Amjad Khan in Family Film Club's production. Laxmikant-Pyarelal were to do the music.

Bicchoo

Dharmendra was to make his official debut as a producer with this comedy directed by Sai Paranjpye. Shabana Azmi was to be the leading lady of this film that was announced in 1983. Shankar (of Shankar-Jaikishan), was to score the music.

Chanakya Aur Chandragupta

A producer named S.S. Broca, a business tycoon, had announced this Dilip Kumar-Dharmendra film to be directed by B.R. Chopra. Hema Malini and Parveen Babi were to play the female leads. Naushad was the composer and a song by Lata Mangeshkar was even recorded. Chopra fixture Sahir Ludhianvi turned down the assignment as it was a deeply rooted Hindu subject and recommended Indeevar, who had helped him out by checking his lyrics in a similar deeply Hindu subject a decade earlier in *Chitralekha*. But this film never took off either. Incidentally, a few bars from this song had been available online.

Dagdar Babu

Writer Nabendu Ghosh was always close to Dharmendra, and launched this middle-of-the-road story as director with Jaya Bachchan as the leading lady. R.D. Burman was the composer. There are claims that the film was complete and even released in some centres.

Devdas

This was a Dharmendra-Sharmila Tagore-Hema Malini film written and directed by Gulzar as his interpretation of the Sarat Chandra classic. The film was scuttled midway by producer Kailash Chopra, brother of Prem Chopra. R.D. Burman tuned lyrics by Gulzar.

Ek Do Teen Char

Vijay Anand launched this overambitious 70 mm film in the late '70s as a production of I.K. Bahl, who was Hema Malini's then secretary and was the co-producer of her *Dream Girl*. Dev Anand, Shashi Kapoor, Rishi Kapoor, Raakhee, Parveen Babi and Tina Munim were to be in the cast, apart from Hema Malini. R.D. Burman was to score the music.

Ghazab

On the heels of the super-success of *Dharam-Veer*, producer Subhash Desai announced the 70 mm *Ghazab* directed by his brother Manmohan Desai with music by Laxmikant-Pyarelal and lyrics by Anand Bakshi in the Diwali *Screen* issue of 1977. The Desais blended the full-cast of their hit (Dharmendra, Jeetendra, Zeenat Aman and Neetu Singh) with a part of the team of *Amar Akbar Anthony*— Amitabh Bachchan, Rishi Kapoor, Parveen Babi and Neetu Singh.

As co-writer Prayag Raj stated, 'No one came forward to finance the film.' So the film did not proceed beyond this announcement. It had nothing to do with Dharmendra's 1982 double-role drama with the same title, which was a South remake produced by N.N. Sippy and directed by C.P. Dixit.

Har Pall

Art cinema man Jahnu Barua (of *Maine Gandhi Ko Nahin Mara* fame) was directing this film that also starred Preity Zinta, Shiney Ahuja and Isha Koppikar. Dharmendra appeared in a supporting role as Zinta's father. Pritam was the composer. Incidentally, Dharmendra had stepped into a role for which Amitabh Bachchan was signed first. The film was reportedly stuck at an advanced stage.

Kanoon

Producer-director Narendra Bedi left this film incomplete after six reels. It starred Dharmendra, Jeetendra and Hema Malini. Mostly, it was to star Reena Roy as well. The music was by Laxmikant-Pyarelal.

Mahaguru

A crime thriller was announced after *Loafer* by producer R.C. Kumar. Zeenat Aman was to be the female lead, with Laxmikant-Pyarelal and Anand Bakshi being repeated for the music. We do not recollect the director, but it was either Brij or Shakti Samanta. Samanta ended up never working with the actor.

Paapi Devta

This film had nothing to do with the 1996 dud of the same name, in which Dharmendra featured. Zeenat Aman was to play the lead, with Hema Malini in a cameo, in this Madan Mohla production, announced with music by Laxmikant-Pyarelal and lyrics by Anand Bakshi. Dulal Guha was to direct the movie.

Papi Pet Ka Sawaal Hai

Before finally making it with Rajesh Khanna, Shatrughan Sinha and

Kanwaljeet as a 1984 flop, the film was announced by film-maker Sohanlal Kanwar ambitiously in the 1970s with Dev Anand, Manoj Kumar and Dharmendra! The music was to be by Shankar-Jaikishan.

Samson and Delilah

The 70 mm extravaganza on the classic love fable was to be filmed by O.P. Ralhan for the producers of *Chacha Bhatija* with Dharmendra and—who else?—Hema Malini. Laxmikant-Pyarelal and Anand Bakshi were to be repeated from the 1977 hit by producers M.M. Malhotra and Baldev Pushkarna.

Sipahi

Rajan Sippy's *Sipahi* (1989) was to bring together Dharmendra, Jeetendra and Shatrughan Sinha. It was to be directed by Raj Sippy as a rework of his shelved Amitabh Bachchan film *Patthar Ke Log*.

Tanaav

As late as in 1999, Dharmendra, Naseeruddin Shah, Moushumi Chatterjee and Deepti Bhatnagar were to star in *Tanaav* directed by Vijay Reddy. Jatin-Lalit were signed for the music.

Time Bomb

Pramod Chakravorty was to direct this film starring his favourite couple—Dharmendra and Hema Malini. The music was by Laxmikant-Pyarelal, the canvas 70 mm. Later, the title was changed for some reason to *Lajawab*. But nothing happened beyond that.

Yogeshwar Krishna

This was probably among the most ambitious of the multiple epics announced in the '70s. To be directed by Ramanand Sagar, its impossible cast had Rajendra Kumar, Shashi Kapoor, Rishi Kapoor, Hema Malini, Sulkashana Pandit and starlet Tamanna. The story of the *Mahabharata*, it was to have music by Laxmikant-Pyarelal and was planned in 70 mm.

Zabardast

Dilip Kumar, Dharmendra, Rishi Kapoor, Tariq and Zeenat Aman— this was to be the star-roster of Mushir-Riaz's mammoth action drama directed by Nasir Hussain with music by R.D. Burman. It seemed to be reworked on a humbler footing later with Sunny Deol as the leading man in place of his father and different actors.

And last but not the least…as a director:

Cowboy

Yes, Dharmendra was to *direct* this film for his home banner of Vijayta Films way back in 1980. However, nothing went beyond the announcement.

Chapter Twelve

The Team Player

Humsafar mere humsafar / Pankh tum parvaaz hum /
Zindagi ke geet ho tum / Geet ka andaz hum

*I*f there is one thing that beats all other qualities of Dharmendra as a professional, it is that he is the definition of the all-too-rare entity called the 'Team Player'. When a producer signed Dharmendra, he got someone for whom the film would be everything as long as it was being made. It was never just an assignment that was undertaken to be completed for a specific remuneration, career growth or future rewards.

Veteran film-maker J. Om Prakash, who produced three films with Dharmendra—*Ayee Milan Ki Bela, Aaye Din Bahaar Ke* and *Aaya Sawan Jhoom Ke,* each a silver jubilee hit, and later directed him in his home production *Aas Paas* (1981) is extremely grateful for the actor's unforgettable gesture in their peak days.

Dharmendra had come to know that Omji (as he was known) was planning to buy a bungalow in Mumbai's Juhu-Vile Parle Development Scheme (JVPD) but was a shade short on money. Only one installment of the actor's remuneration for *Aaya Sawan Jhoom Ke* was remaining. Dharmendra refused to accept the money then, telling the producer to go ahead and buy the property instead and pay him later.

Mahesh Bhatt recounts a telling incident that spotlighted what Dharmendra was—a true-blue *mitti ka aadmi* or son of the soil.

Bhatt was assisting Padmanabh on *Do Chor* (1972), and the director wanted a particular sequence shot at the crack of dawn at one of the beaches in Goa. Dharmendra and Tanuja were shown to be on the run from the police and needed to be disguised as a truck driver and a truck cleaner respectively. Due to some confusion, Dharmendra's costume was forgotten at the hotel where the unit was parked, and the distance between location and hotel ensured that it could not be brought in time. If the shoot could not be done at the magic hour, it would incur heavy expenses as the unit would need an extra day in Goa.

Bhatt walked up to Dharmendra and took the blame for the dressman's mistake. He told him, 'Sir, I have a problem.' The actor looked at the young assistant he had known since the making of *Mera Gaon Mera Desh* and asked, '*Beta, kya hai* (What is it, son)?' When Bhatt recounted how the dressman had forgotten the actor's costume because of his lack of specific instructions, the actor, in Bhatt's own words, 'looked at the entire problem with great empathy from my perspective as a human failure.'

Dharmendra simply got up, looked around at the crew and then went to a truck driver and told him to remove his olive-green kurta and turban. And he wore them and solved the problem! Bhatt looks at this an act of tremendous generosity. 'He covered up for the lapse of a dressman, and used his imagination. By Dharam's standards, the kurta et al was obviously not clean. But only a man of the soil could have done this!' said the director.

J.P. Dutta, who directed him in multiple films between 1985 and 1993 (*Ghulami, Hathyar, Batwara* and *Kshatriya*, and had also directed Dharmendra's home production *Yateem* with Sunny Deol) makes no bones about the fact that he would have had to struggle for years more to make his first film had it not been for Dharmendra.

Expounding at length about the actor's role in his career, Dutta stated, 'My first film as an assistant was *Jwar Bhata* (1973), and the first clap I gave in my capacity as assistant was of Dharamji in a close-up. Later, when we came to know each other, he told me that the first film shooting he watched in Mumbai was of a film directed by my father, O.P. Dutta, *Aangan* (1959). He told me, "The first time I saw a director was your father, and now I am being directed by his son!"'

Dutta recalls walking to Dharmendra's bungalow a decade later when he wanted him to do *Ghulami*. The industry knew that he had even done a muhurat for the film with his friend Vinod Khanna, who was also to be the hero of his first film, *Sarhad*, which never took off. Then Vinod Khanna suddenly left for the USA for his guru Acharya Rajneesh. The only other option Dutta had was Dharmendra.

We have mentioned earlier (in chapter eight) how excited Dharmendra was when he heard the script and signed up. But at an early stage of production, producer Habib Nadiadwala had financial problems when his father Abdul Karim Nadiadwala passed away. Dutta and he discussed how to take the project forward as finances were drying up. Habib told Dutta that he had only ₹3 lakh to spare for the Rajasthan schedule. If they managed the schedule, they could show the film to a distributor and sell it.

This was the only option left and could be pulled off only if the long shoot could be done without paying the actors! Dutta took the call to do that and explained the position to Dharmendra. The actor had gauged the director's calibre after a week's shooting in Mumbai, of a jail sequence. And he immediately agreed to forgo his remuneration until money flowed in.

The grateful Dutta concludes, 'When he as the biggest star agreed, the others—Smita Patil, Naseeruddin Shah, Mithun Chakraborty,

Reena Roy and Anita Raj—naturally had to fall in line. So Dharamji should be credited for my being where I am today. Instead, he credits me for reviving his career.'

Producer, writer and director Anil Sharma, another Dharmendra devotee, even speaks of a 'karmic' connection with the actor. Having directed the actor in *Hukumat,* the biggest hit of 1987, successes like *Elaan-E-Jung* (1989) and *Tehelka* (1992) and the hit *Apne* (2007), besides in *Farishtay* (1993) and in a cameo in *Singh Saab the Great,* Sharma reveals that the first film he ever watched near his hometown was *Ganga Ki Lehren* as a kid.

'I was struck by this good-looking man doing noble things on screen, and later, I become an assistant to B.R. Chopra saab and Ravi Chopra saab on *The Burning Train,*' says the director. 'Even before that, as a schoolkid, I remember my teacher telling me to do a crisp Army haircut like Dharmendra rather than follow the long-haired other heroes Rajesh Khanna and Jeetendra!'

Sharma recalled how, on the first day of the Chopra epic's shoot at RK Studios, Dharmendra was expected to come from the *Razia Sultan* shoot. 'He was given Raj Kapoor's room for make-up. I was setting his clothes in the last room on the first floor, when I heard a commotion that seemed to echo even there. I ran down. Not less than 200 to 300 people were silently waiting for his van to come! But they were respectfully waiting some 25 feet away.'

Dharmendra and Hema Malini got out and B.R. Chopra went to meet them. The actor said that he was tired, and asked if he could shoot the next day. Chopra agreed, and when the van began to move, Sharma, as part of his duties, ran after the van. 'There were printed call-sheets, a new feature in Hindi films due to so many foreigners involved with this film,' said Sharma. 'Luckily for me, the van slowed down at the RK Studios gates and when I knocked, he looked at me and said, "*Ki hai* (what is it?)" I told him I had brought the call-sheet.'

Dharmendra asked him, '*Ae ki hondi hain* (what is that)?' Sharma smiled and told him that director Ravi Chopra had asked him to give the actor the sheets. He said that he had in any case wanted to meet and see him for the first time. The actor said softly, 'You barely look seventeen or eighteen'. And Sharma replied, 'Yes, sir. I am doing my Bachelors in Science'.

But the crux came on the last day of the New Delhi shoot of the Chopra film. It was Sharma's duty to get all stars on location at the correct time. On this day, everyone was needed and he had to ensure that the stars left the Hotel Maurya Sheraton at 2.30 p.m. for the location shoot because it was winter and the sun would set shortly after 5 p.m. Parveen Babi requested Sharma to let her go and do some personal work that she said would take just fifteen minutes. And at any shoot, that much time was always needed for setting up cameras and taking care of other technical aspects.

Sharma firmly disallowed her from leaving more than four times, not knowing that Dharmendra was within earshot. But Parveen decided to do her own thing—and finally, due to her driver not knowing the way, made it an hour later than others to the location. A furious B.R. Chopra reprimanded Sharma severely, and suddenly, Dharmendra appeared and told him, 'What else could he have done? He told her so many times that she could not go off like this'.

It was at that moment, recollects Sharma, when he came close to tears. 'I was so pleasantly shocked that a big star like him was defending a small technician, under the age of twenty years, that too from a big-name producer'. Mentally, he saluted his childhood idol, realizing his worth as a human being.

However, another scary moment that again highlighted Dharmendra's team player attitude was when, on the first day of *Hukumat*'s shooting in 1986, a dog with which Dharmendra had worked on some films like *Jhutha Sach*, landed on his foot and injured him. Angrily, the actor walked away in a huff and Sharma, now the film's director, was convinced that his first film with his idol was doomed.

After all, when the mixing of *Betaab* was going on at Rajkamal Studios in Mumbai, Sharma was working on his second film, *Bandhan Kachche Dhaagon Ka,* and he had got the opportunity to first meet him as a director some three or four years later. Sharma had gone to meet him with his brother Anuj (who became a producer later) and a broker named Mathuradas.

He was only twenty-five years old then, but Dharmendra had watched his debut film *Shraddhanjali* and had loved it. The director recalled, 'I was getting a chance to meet him when I wanted to work with him. On the spot, in those fifteen minutes I [had] got, I made up and narrated a story idea that became *Hukumat,* and he approved it immediately. After that, I had worked for a year and now this had happened!'

The director decided to visit him at home, and found that his foot was bandaged and that he had taken a dose of vaccination. He gently told the young man, 'Anil, I had warned you that the dog might do this!' and the director mustered up courage. 'How could I have imagined this would happen, Dharamji?' he managed to ask. 'The dog had worked with you in some films earlier.'

In a normal tone, Dharmendra replied, '*Accha, accha! Kal kitne baje aana hai* (Alright! So what time do I have to come tomorrow)?' And Sharma heaved a massive sigh of relief!

Anil recalls also a Nainital shoot for one of their films. Dharmendra would willingly stay in a guest house rather than in a five-star hotel if it was close to the venue. The crowd that came to watch him was so phenomenal that the actor needed a different room each day! But he was unfussy enough to eat his food in the open with thousands of people who had come to visit him or watch the shoot around him. He specially loved to do this in the rural ambience of Ranikhet.

'I have never seen such a craze!' noted Sharma. 'The chopper in which he landed was surrounded. And he managed to meet everyone too!' There was also another occasion when Dharmendra agreed to willingly change the shooting venue. 'Congress minister N.D. Tewari was to hold a meeting around that place and his people requested us not to shoot there that day, as no one would have gone to listen to the politician! And when we had to shoot *Tehelka's* scenes at 4 a.m. on location some years later, Dharmendra thought nothing of it!' raved Sharma.

Rajkumar Santoshi, who made his debut as writer-director with *Ghayal*, recalled that Dharmendra did not interfere at all in the way the film was made. 'He was a shade worried because Sunny's films were not doing well, but as Sunny stood by me and my convictions, and Dharamji had also loved the script, he did not get involved. This says a lot, because a big star could have easily bullied a new film-maker who was making a different kind of film.'

When *Ghayal* won the National Award for Dharmendra as a producer, the overwhelmed actor told the Delhi press, 'This is totally Santoshi's film, and it is because of him that I am here to get a National Award.' The director said that it was the greatness of the man to acknowledge and accept his work. 'Even when the film was being made, he would come to watch the trials and would only praise me,' said Santoshi.

Comedian Birbal declared, 'Dharam was repeated frequently by his film-makers. And why was that? It was simply because he understands a producer's problems. He is so decent—*insaniyat unn mein kut-kut kar bhari hai* (he is overflowing with humanity). If a film flopped, he would even forfeit the balance of the money due to him, but would tell the producer, "I am there with you, why worry? Let's make another film. We will adjust your losses."'

Prem Chopra recalled how Dharmendra refused to have a duplicate when, as a villain, Chopra had to tie him to a speeding jeep and pull him. 'I am sorry I do not recollect the name of the film,' said Chopra. 'But when I asked him why he was not leaving that sequence to a duplicate or stuntman, he winked and said, "Because in the next sequence, I have to tie you up and pull you!"'

Chopra affectionately said that Dharmendra was a team player like no other, and pointed this out in *Raja Jani's* song 'Kitna Mazaa Aa Raha Hai'. 'It was a clichéd situation. I am the bad man and Hema Malini dances with me to make him jealous. I started dancing during the song, and it was he who encouraged me, even though director Mohan Segal and choreographer P.L. Raj were not in favour of that.' At the premiere of the film in New Delhi, a happy Dharam told him that like he had predicted, Chopra '*Chha gaya*' (had shone in the song).

Sanjay Khan, film-maker, actor and Dharmendra's co-star in *Haqeeqat*, also has fond memories, 'What many people do not know is that the first shot of my life was for Chetan Anand saab's *Haqeeqat* and not for my first release *Dosti*. The situation in the film was that the Army was badly beaten and I had lost my best friend and associate. It's cold, I am exhausted and I burst out crying.'

Khan recollected how he had no formal training in acting. 'I managed it by thinking of the saddest moments of my life. I kept crying even after the shot was over and Chetan saab had cut the shot. And Dharmendra, who was standing next to him, came over and embraced me, saying "*Kya shot diya hai! Kya zabardast personality hai* (What a shot you have given! What a solid personality you have)!" That's how we became friends.'

Pehlaj Nihalani, who produced Dharmendra's 1987 hit *Aag Hi Aag*, recollected how Dharmendra never cancelled a single day's shoot when the industry suddenly declared a strike—the unit was in Bangalore. 'We had a twenty-five-day schedule and he made sure he completed it,' recalled the film-maker. On another occasion, when everything on set was ready and his son Sunny Deol, who was working with him in *Paap Aur Punya*, had to have an emergency surgery, Dharamji came personally to the far-off Chandivali Studios in Mumbai to inform him of the situation.

Co-star Sharmila Tagore is grateful even today to the actor for facilitating her easy departure for a West Indies Test match featuring her future husband Mansoor Ali Khan, the Nawab of Pataudi. 'I had shot for my film *Dil Aur Mohabbat* from 7 a.m. to 2 p.m. and after that, Dharam and I were to shoot for the song 'Chhalkaaye Jaam' from *Mere Humdum Mere Dost*,' said Tagore. 'We had a 2 p.m. to 10 p.m. shift and had already shot for the song for three days but had not finished it. We were at Kardar Studios and I requested him to finish the song.'

Tagore explained that her make-up took a long while as cameraman K. Vaikunth was very particular about it. 'But he used long shots that made things easier. And Dharam waited until 2 a.m. to complete the song so that I could fly on time. It's another matter that we lost the match to West Indies!' she smilingly told me.

Summing Dharmendra up, she said, 'He valued relationships. He never let anyone down, which is a quality that did not work in politics for him.'

Dharmendra had told me that he was on good terms with almost the entire industry, but that he considered Manoj Kumar, Shatrughan Sinha and Danny Denzongpa as his 'best friends' from the film world.

One of his later directors, Anurag Basu, narrated: 'Dharamji contributes so much to a character. When I first met him for *Life In A... Metro*, it was a fan moment and I was very nervous. But he made up his mind to do my film. "I am doing it, so tell me the story," he said. He was fun on the sets, narrating endless anecdotes from his career, and most of us were around him, greedy for them, and it would be a laugh-riot!'

When the unit was shooting a sequence at Mumbai's crowded Sion suburban station, they chose the last platform as it was closed.

'We wanted to hide him, but people saw him and in no time, a mob descended to watch him! He even waved his hand at all of them, and then guided me [on] how to make a space there to take the shot.'

Gulzar remembered how he needed another artiste for a brief cameo in his film *Kinara*. Many names were being thrown up, and finally, during a discussion at a shoot with the leading lady Hema Malini, she asked in ungrammatical English, 'Why my friend cannot do it?' Gulzar smiled and said that he would be his first choice if he agreed, but also told her that he was avoiding his name as their affair was on, but was supposed to be a secret.

During the lunch break at the shoot, Gulzar called up the actor and told him that he would be required for a small outdoor sequence. Dharmendra agreed on the phone itself and Gulzar told Hema Malini about it and she asked, 'He agreed without listening to the story?'

Gulzar said, 'Yes, he has faith in me!' Dharmendra had told him, 'You will never waste me!' but also complained later that he had never given him a lead role, only a guest appearance! 'I will give you a film you will love,' replied the writer-director. However, that ill-fated film, *Devdas*, was never to be completed.

Neil Nitin Mukesh, who made his debut in *Johnny Gaddaar*, recalled Dharmendra putting him at his ease in a sequence in which he goofed up his line with a nervous pause as he was surrounded by seasoned actors on the first day of shoot. The senior actor put his hand on him as a reassuring gesture to comfort him. On another occasion, he hugged Neil tight and asked, 'Are you okay? Now you should be okay!'

Dharmendra helped Neil in general throughout the film. 'He got so emotional when he once slapped me hard by mistake for a shot!' recalled the actor. 'And like family, he would wait until all my takes were done. He told me how my grandfather (the legendary singer Mukesh) and he had had a long association. He had walked a long distance once in rain for his own film's recording to meet the singer, but had found that the rain had led to the recording being cancelled.'

'You are like my grandchild!' Dharmendra would say.

Neil raved, 'He bridged the gap between us with his anecdotes of my grandfather. I somehow felt the same love and affection that my grandfather would have given me.'

(For the record, Mukesh sang for Dharmendra in his debut film *Dil Bhi Tera Hum Bhi Tere*, his first home production *Satyakam*, and some more films, while Nitin Mukesh, Neil's father, sang playback for him in his home production *Dillagi*.)

Neil remembers the interesting fact that the senior actor would take his lines and write them all in Urdu. 'He would sit on each scene and cut the grammatical errors so that the lines sounded much better!' remembered the actor. 'He told me that I should read Hindi newspapers aloud so that my diction and vocabulary would improve. It helped my confidence level. When I did *Wazir* (2016), I went back to his teachings. Ten years and twenty films later, I realized that he gave me a foundation, a base. We all get carried away with adulation, but he would sit casually with all of us, not in the least behaving like the huge star that he was.'

Randhir Kapoor recalls his magnanimity on the sets of their only film together, the Manmohan Desai bumper hit *Chacha Bhatija*. 'Let Dabboo (Kapoor's pet name in family and the industry) speak his lines first!' he would tell Desai if he felt that way about any sequence. 'Imagine, I was junior to him by a decade!' said Kapoor. 'I had worked with other heroes by then but never seen such a selfless attitude. His humility was exemplary and he had a good word for all, from big stars to junior artistes.'

Concurred Raj N. Sippy, 'He was always there for everyone, even the spot boys, light men and other workers. He may not have always solved their problems, but he would try his best to help out. And that's why he loved doing *Guddi*. Dharamji wanted to give due credit to those who actually did all the things for which stars got accolades. For example, what a viewer sees is the hero smashing a glass window, but here the truth was shown, and Dharam loved being a part of the process. Which other star would openly show that it was the duplicate artistes who would actually take all the risks and do all the dirty work for which heroes got acclaim?'

Chapter Thirteen

The Unrewarded Actor

Ya dil ki suno duniyawalon / Ya mujhko abhi chup rehne do / Main gham ko khushi kaise keh doon / Jo kehte hain unnko kehne do

*J*f there was anything left out in Dharmendra's spectacular saga of sustained and superlative success, it was the fact that his natural acting did not garner sufficient critical appreciation in the environs of mainstream Indian cinema, which has always equated theatrics, mannerisms and over-the-top melodrama with great acting.

Dharmendra's constant grudge, if we can ever consider him capable of harbouring such a negative emotion, is that he was never appreciated for his acting abilities. There is an asterisked 'conditions apply' here: Many in the industry, a deluge of his fans and all the unbiased and neutral observers, do consider him a good to great performer, and condemn the dismissal of this completely original, natural and spontaneous acting talent as a non-actor, mediocre talent or ordinary performer.

Dharmendra once told me wryly, 'I would keep getting suits stitched to be ready for an award, but ended up never winning anything. I only got Lifetime Achievement awards. But I will continue working! Films are my life!'

The crystal-clear conclusion here was that Dharmendra must have refused to lobby for any award, even when he was nominated. It is an open secret that awards are almost always manipulated and the straight-as-a-rod Dharam never believed in such practices that were resorted to by so many.

In a different context, he had once told me, '*Main apni khubiyon mein bhi khamiyaan dhoondta hoon* (I search for shortcomings even in my good qualities). This is the biggest plus point of my life— that I am not satisfied with whatever I have done, or am doing. I do not believe in shouting from the rooftops. I came here with simple dreams, and the power above has given me things beyond my expectations.'

Dharmendra has *always* lost out in self-promotion. 'How could I hype myself saying "I am this!" and "I am that!" or call myself "the star of the millennium" or whatever?' he laughed when I had posed the question to him during our very first meeting in 2011. 'I am still very weak at promoting myself. Over fifty of my films ran for 25, 50 or even 100 weeks but I could not extract any juice from that fact either! *Par isska mujhe koi dukh nahin,* because people loved me a lot and they still do. This is a field in which people forget what you have done. Within five years, the slate is wiped clean. But after fifty years, I still have the people with me.'

That fifty has grown to fifty-eight now!

Dharmendra's favourite among his own films is Hrishikesh Mukherjee's *Satyakam,* especially because of the climax. He reminisced, 'My character was suffering from cancer and had lost his ability to talk. I had to convey Satyapriya's anguish wordlessly, through my eyes only. At some point, my grandfather and spiritual guru, portrayed by Dadamoni (Ashok Kumar) walks into my room and tells me, "Now I can berate you to my heart's content without any retaliation from you." The words are bitter but they convey his love for me. I had to express I understood what my guru was saying, and that it was out of sheer love [that] he was admonishing me.'

He went on, 'Next [in the film], my wife, Sharmila Tagore, who has been a silent witness to my uncompromising life, walks into the room with incriminating papers for me to sign that could relieve my family of poverty. For the sake of my wife and son, I agree to sign the papers. But before I can actually do it, Sharmila snatches the papers out of my hand and tears them. My character had to convey his deep, undying love and gratitude for the woman who has stood by his side, through thick and thin. It was a very tough scene to do. I thank Hrishida for the faith he reposed in me.'

About his own favourite performances, apart from *Satyakam*, Dharam said, '*Main badi baat nahin karna chahta* (I don't want to talk big), but I loved my performance in *Seeta Aur Geeta*—it was a small role but [it] had soul, and there were interesting nuances, like the way I light my cigarette. I loved my work in *Hathyar* and *Ghazab* too.' In later interviews, he added *Pratiggya* to the list as well.

At the same time, the discrimination hurt. It was not just popularity that was the index here. As Abrar Alvi had told Guru Dutt, 'The boy is an original, he does not copy anybody'—and this virtue was just the starting-point. 'I never copied any star,' Dharmendra admitted. 'I changed my personality to the character, but no script was changed for me. If I had to weep, I would go back to the memory of a childhood tragedy. When it flashed before me, I would cry without glycerine.'

Thus, the malleable (as Alvi had predicted) Dharmendra could fit into any role, and had a natural penchant for comedy and romance, besides action and drama. Though his dancing skills were never great, he would serve the purpose in the few dance numbers that he did in his career. Emotions were his mainstay.

In a sense, he became and remained a complete actor.

Ironically, indeed, Dharmendra, as we have mentioned before, was only appreciated for 'underplaying' his roles, beginning with his early films *Bandini* and *Anupama* and even later in *Satyakam, Naya Zamana, Dost* and a few others. But when we observe his mind-boggling variety in comedy in films like *Seeta Aur Geeta, Sholay, Pratiggya, Chupke Chupke, Ghazab* and *Yamla Pagla Deewana* and the intensity of his work in *Ayee Milan Ki Bela, Phool Aur Patthar, Jeevan Mrityu, Mera Gaon Mera Desh, Samadhi, Loafer, Yaadon Ki Baaraat, Aas Paas, Krodhi, Ghulami, Hathyar, Apne* and others, we are indeed flummoxed that a man with such a range and capacity was never considered worthy of being among the elite acting league of Hindi film personalities.

'Obviously his connect with audience was his greatest strength!' J.P. Dutta told me. 'He had this animal presence. You see, it's very simple. It's all about a presence you cannot explain.'

Dutta explains the actor's dedication. 'He was a natural actor, and because I could mould him the way I wanted, there was a comfort level. Dharam *understood* what he had to do, what he had to become! He reminded me of the legendary veteran actor Kanhaiyalal (Chaturvedi). If a producer went to him, he would be succinct after being told what his character would be. How much would he be paid, Kanhaiyalalji would ask. Of course, in this matter Dharam was the opposite, but you get the point: He was not interested in a detailed narration, as long as he knew that he was going to play, like say, the heroine's father. Then Kanhaiyala would say, "*Bas aur nahin sunna, ladki ka baap hoon na* (I am the girl's father, right? That's all I want to know)!"'

And Dutta explained, 'Do you understand the psyche? *Main kar kya rahaa hoon* (what am I doing in the story) was the most important. He would internalize, even for a character with which he was not familiar. We are all products of our experiences and he would draw from the experiences of his life. We can only throw out what we have gone through and taken in.'

Concluded Dutta, 'Dharamji has never been given his due. And I blame the media for that! They even made fun of him—come on, there is much more to him. What an innings he has had. What a body of work. It is very special—*he* is very special!'

The director also narrated an interesting anecdote, '*Ghulami* remains one of the best outdoors of my life. For forty-five days, we lived in tents at Fatehpur Shekhawati. After the unit returned to Mumbai, I met Dharamji again for the patchwork that frequently has to be done. When we met, he just began to laugh. When I asked him why he was amused, he asked me in Punjabi, "*Arey yaar, tere naal kinne din shooting kitti* (How long did we shoot together)?"'

When Dutta replied, 'Forty-five days', the actor explained, 'Every night I would think, *charpai change karni hai, tanga baahar padti hai* (I have to change this cot. It is so short that my feet hang out)!

'Dharmendra was so involved and keyed into his character every morning that he would keep forgetting to ask someone to change the bed—for *forty-five* days. He was always so deeply into what we were shooting, that for a month and a half he slept on an uncomfortable cot!' the director said. 'I could not believe such *total* dedication.'

Dutta also recalled how the actor wanted some extra time to prepare for a scene with Paresh Rawal for *Hathyar*. It was his first sequence with the then lesser-known actor, but Dutta says that Dharmendra recognized Paresh's calibre instantly during the rehearsal itself. 'There was honesty in his work. We did a rehearsal and he called me. He asked me to give him the scene after that and requested, "*Mainu paanch minute de* (Give me five minutes)!" He went into his make-up room and when I later asked him why, he simply said that the rehearsal had made him realize he was up against a powerful actor.'

And the director stressed, 'The game was not to overshadow Paresh. It was just to ensure that he did not come off so inferior to a great actor that my scene would suffer!'

When I told him about this, Rawal simply folded his hands, looked heavenwards and commented, 'This is just the greatness of such people.'

Dharmendra's close friend, comic actor Birbal, also stated at a separate meeting, 'Dharam would go deep into his story and character, and was extremely dedicated to his work. He would discuss his character to the depths with his director and was very serious at work. Formerly, heroes looked like heroes. Today, if you can fight and dance, you can be a big star, even if you are a zero as an actor.'

Birbal found it highly unfair that Dharmendra has received only Lifetime Achievement awards. 'Sadly, Dharam's He-Man image was so dominant that it led to wrong thinking. He is a very strong actor. I would say that he is no less than anyone else who is considered a better actor than him. And as a star, he was unique. We all would chase girls, but girls would chase *him*! In short, the world knows that his good looks overshadowed his work.'

Birbal's words seem to be corroborated by Dharmendra himself. When I had asked him how he interpreted his characters, like a doctor in *Bandini*, a ghost in *Ghazab* or the botany professor in *Chupke Chupke*, he just smiled and replied, 'I hardly prepare, but when I read the script or the scene, I immerse myself deeply into it.' And what came across after all this, especially in his better roles, is nothing short of acting genius.

When asked if he did lose some stardom because of his versatility that defied all branding, Dharmendra immediately answered, 'I don't think so. Acting for me was a gift from Nature and I was not a method actor. Yes, I was a little uncomfortable dancing to songs.' Nevertheless, his style of dancing has become iconic and a rage among his fans and audiences.

He had concluded, 'I have never received an award, however hard I worked. And I'm grateful for that, because the constant striving for perfection polished my work. It's good that I did not receive any award throughout my career for Best Actor!' And no, that was not a 'sour grapes' statement, but a heartfelt admission in retrospect, though his fans from within the industry as well as outside would scoff at it.

Like director Raj N. Sippy raved, 'He is a terrific actor. When he was not nominated for *Satyakam*, *Chupke Chupke* and even in 2007 for *Apne*, I refused to believe that it was possible that fair forces were at work. I then began to think that awards are just a make-believe act. I recall watching him accept his first Lifetime Achievement Award from Dilip Kumar and Saira Banu and confessing how he had got a suit stitched every time he was nominated.'

Asha Parekh, however, had an individualistic view and opined, 'He was a good but not a great actor. But he was *excellent* at comedies.' And she knew what she was talking about. In the song 'Sona Laija Re Chandi Laija Re' from *Mera Gaon Mera Desh*, it was her co-star who had enhanced the scene with some individual touches done with director Raj Khosla's permission—like the lines: '*Sona? Yaani man ka chain khona!* (Gold? That means you lose your peace of mind).'

'He came from a school of acting that does not look like you are acting,' declared Anurag Basu. 'He was thus the most underrated actor who did not seem to act. He signed films emotionally, but was not cautious or selective about them and went with the flow. This is where he lost out on getting due recognition.'

Bharathi S. Pradhan, senior journalist and editor, assesses him as someone who, for most of his career, was a close number two to other heroes—from Shammi Kapoor to Amitabh Bachchan. 'But he saw superstars come and go and stayed there!' she points out. 'Yes, there was a phase when he was the biggest star.'

It is perhaps Rajkumar Santoshi, fan and later protégé, who is most vehement about Dharmendra's acting skills. He considers Dharmendra to be one of the finest, most versatile and sensitive actors. He said, 'See the range of that man! *Bandini, Anupama, Phool*

Aur Patthar, Satyakam, Yaadon Ki Baaraat, Pratiggya, Chupke Chupke, Sholay. He was realistic, natural, open, and above all, original.'

Santoshi feels that most actors are inspired by Dilip Kumar, and that some admit it and others do not. 'As an actor's director, I can analyse,' said the director. 'Every line is said with so much conviction without going overboard. That is why he was the favourite of a man like Hrishikesh Mukherjee. Take it from me— Dharamji is so gifted and talented that Sunny and Bobby are no match for him. Dharmendra's improvisations alone make that clear.'

As a longtime fan, Santoshi pointed out how Dharmendra was the natural and obvious choice for big action dramas. Who else, he asks, could have carried off the costume of *Dharam-Veer* and done action too? A fortnight later, the same director (Manmohan Desai)'s next film *Chacha Bhatija* saw him in a completely different avatar. He added, 'In fact, Dharamji may even do well in a completely negative role, but for his viewers, it will be difficult to digest that he will do something wrong. In their psyche, he is too much of a good and noble man!'

Santoshi rues that Hindi films never did justice to his talent. 'I was and am keen to do a film with him as an actor. That is one regret I have, but it can still happen. I have not arrived at a subject, but when I do, I will grab the chance!' he stated.

'He emerged as a versatile actor,' noted Salim Khan of the Salim-Javed duo. 'For many years, including at our peak, he was the only big action hero. But I always thought that he was best at comedy, whose elements we integrated in almost all the films we wrote with him. He had the ability and capability to maintain himself, and his pictures did well.'

As film-maker Shyam Benegal, high-priest of art cinema, who never worked with him, once opined in a purely objective manner, 'Dharmendra has a very sensitive face, which is an asset to depict complex psychological situations.'

Speaking at length on his special penchant for comedy during my interview at the time of *Second-Hand Husband*, Dharmendra revealed some secrets of his impeccable genius at making people laugh. 'I enjoy doing comedy, and it is much more difficult than doing romantic scenes,' he admitted candidly. 'Timing is all-important in comedy, and so is spontaneity. I love adding my own lines and my touches to the script and to the director's inputs, often at the last moment.'

He further explained, 'Comedy always works on the element of surprise. I did a lot of films starting with *Neela Akash* all the way to *Jugnu* with Mehmood, and he was a master at improvisation, so I had to learn to be one too. I would often tell him to at least tell me the last word, just so I could get a cue to start my lines, but he would change his lines and actions so spontaneously that I had to just react! Mehmood was blacklisted by many other heroes because it was felt that he overshadowed them, but that's a myth, you know, because no actor ever overshadows any other actor. It's the character, the situations and the lines that project one actor more than the other!'

Dharmendra narrates how in *Sholay* Salim-Javed had not written that special inflection on 'ji' in the famous dialogue '*Main aa rahaa hoon, mausiji!*' 'But that spontaneous addition of mine was what made it famous!' he says. 'Similarly, in *Mera Gaon Mera Desh*, when I come dressed as a sadhu to my heroine Asha Parekh and say, "*Sona, yaane man ka chain khona*", it was my line, and the bathroom sequence in *Naukar Biwi Ka* with the dice was also my improvisation. A good director and a good actor can work wonders together.'

Was he always aware of this comic ability, or did some director help him discover it? 'As a youngster in my village in Punjab, I was always a *maha-chaloo* (mischievous and shrewd) guy! I was witty, naughty as well as paradoxically shy because of my rustic roots. I would blush at any kind of praise about my looks or anything else and yet would make people laugh instantly with my humour.

Good directors sense these qualities and help you discover your true potential. But emotions *must* come into comedy for a greater connect,' he stressed.

The industry that always adored him as a person and needed him as a star, ironically never honoured him for what he always was and still remains—an actor par excellence.

Chapter Fourteen

Coexisting with Sunny Deol

Zindagi ittefaq hai / Kal bhi ittefaq thi / Aaj bhi ittefaq hai

This has happened just once in Hindi cinema—that a father, Dharmendra, and a son, Sunny Deol, were coexisting as top stars. Amitabh Bachchan and Abhishek Bachchan did co-exist in the industry after the senior Bachchan's comeback, and Rishi Kapoor did have more films in hand for a while than son Ranbir Kapoor, but in both these cases, the fathers played roles suitable to their ages, while only the sons were the 'regular' heroes.

And, very obviously but for one-off rare instances, like Raj Kapoor and Randhir Kapoor sharing Hema Malini as romantic co-star six years apart (*Sapnon Ka Saudagar* and *Haath Ki Safai*) or Akshaye Khanna romancing father Vinod Khanna's frequent co-star Dimple Kapadia in *Dil Chahta Hai*, fathers and sons never shared heroines. It was again left to Dharmendra to not only manage six common romantic co-stars but also work with four of them *after* Sunny had had done so!

The story began with Dharmendra's own discovery, Amrita Singh, his choice for Sunny's debut film *Betaab* (1983). After this, Singh played romantic roles opposite Dharmendra on-screen more often (*Sachai Ki Taaqat, Paap Ki Aandhi, Veeru Dada*) than with his son (*Sunny, Kroadh*). All her films with Dharmendra were released between 1989 and 1991.

Sunny Deol first worked with Sridevi in 1986 in *Sultanat*, followed by many more films, but Dharmendra worked with her only once as a romantic hero—in the 1990 success, *Naaka Bandi*.

Dimple Kapadia began her innings with Sunny Deol with *Arjun* in 1985. But she also became a frequent co-star to Dharmendra, beginning with *Batwara* in 1989.

Kimi Katkar, Sunny Deol's love interest in *Vardi* (1989), was also cast opposite Dharmendra in *Humlaa* (1992).

Yes, there were two leading ladies who worked with the father first. Poonam Dhillon, who did Sunny Deol's third release, *Sohni Mahiwal* (1984) and more, was Dharmendra's romantic co-star in many films later, but they first worked together in *Qayamat* in 1983.

Jaya Prada was Sunny Deol's leading lady in *Zabardast* (1986), and was one of Dharmendra's most frequent leading ladies right to the B-graders he did in the 1990s, beginning with, again, *Qayamat* in 1983.

And after Sunny's successful debut in 1983, Dharmendra continued to be among the top names well into the early 1990s. And in 1987, the father had a record eleven big-ticket releases, with seven being super hits, hits or successes.

Here was a father who was competing with his son as a frontline hero, not as a character artiste.

Chapter Fifteen

Melody with Muscle:
The Dharmendra Song

Aaj gaa lo mooskura lo / Mehfilein sajaa lo

A staggering 150 songs of Dharmendra became popular, hits or outright chartbusters. This was an amazing score for someone who did not much enjoy doing songs, or dancing, and yet them made them visually alluring and, in so many cases, iconic.

And above all, this achievement places him right in the forefront of our most musical stars!

Think back to the heydays of Dharmendra and the inevitable first thought will be of musclemen like Dara Singh, people you would not possibly associate with a soft, romantic image, let alone music to match. Think music, on the other hand, and we would inevitably think of all the musical stars, mostly with soft images like Dev Anand, Raj Kapoor, Shammi Kapoor or Rajesh Khanna.

No one, thus, would expect the rugged hunk of *Phool Aur Patthar* or the macho espionage agent of *Ankhen* to inspire legendary composers to come up with great music for a Jat hero who, at least during most of the fruitful phase of his career, had an action image.

Also note the fact that these two films in particular, among many others all through his career, had no lip-synched song by him.

But strangely enough, the music of Dharmendra had immense 'muscle'—a hefty melodic vigour and lyrics whose intrinsic strength matched his tough sinews.

The actor has openly expressed his love for the late Mohammed Rafi, who got the lion's share of his best songs. Nevertheless, Kishore Kumar, Mahendra Kapoor and Mukesh, in probably that order, all had great innings with him.

Go rare, and you will find that Manna Dey and Hemant Kumar had also sang rare terrific gems for this hero. Go younger, and we had an assortment of voices that worked on the actor, from Bhupinder Singh in a small part of 'Naam Gum Jaayega' (*Kinara*) down to Sonu Nigam in the title track of *Apne* a full thirty years later, followed by the 'Main Jat Yamla Pagla Deewana' re-creation in *Yamla Pagla Deewana*.

Later, Punjabi superstar Diljit Dosanjh and Javed Ali also sang for him in parts for the *Yamla Pagla Deewana* franchise's songs, but these were not full-fledged Dharmendra numbers. In fact, the actor himself recited a few lines in one of the *YPD 2* songs with Dosanjh, 'Main Taan Aidaa Hi Nachna'. Like these, there might have been some more anonymous voices too in his smaller and regional films.

The Rafi clones—Anwar, Shabbir Kumar and Mohammed Aziz, Kishore's and Mukesh's sons Amit Kumar and Nitin Mukesh respectively, Suresh Wadkar, Vinod Rathod, '90s toppers Kumar Sanu and Abhijeet, South stalwarts P.B. Srinivas, Yesudas and S.P. Balasubrahmanyam and qawwal Aziz Nazan—have all sung for Dharmendra over the years—of course with varied results, in terms of vocal compatibility and impact. A rare name was Kabban Mirza in *Razia Sultan*, but despite Kamal Amrohi shortlisting him for Dharmendra's character of the dark-skinned slave, the visual match simply was not there.

It is an axiom in Hindi cinema that when a new actor makes his appearance, it takes a while for his persona to be understood musically. The kind of films and roles he chooses and the successes and branding or image that he gets, vis-à-vis the existing top names in singers and film composers, decide the outcome of his career.

The actor's first film *Dil Bhi Tera Hum Bhi Tere* had music by Kalyanji-Anandji. The duo chose Mukesh as his voice in his duet 'Yeh Vaada Kare Jahan Bhi Rahe' (with Lata Mangeshkar singing for Kum Kum) as well as the poignant song that remains the actor's first perennial, hit, 'Mujhko Iss Raat Ki Tanhai Mein Awaaz Na Do'.

As Anandji of the music duo told me, 'It was a new experiment. We gave the ghazal—which was how the lyrics of "Mujhko Iss Raat Ki Tanhai Mein" were structured—a twist with the kind of composition we made. Till then, ghazal-based songs had a different feel in our film music.'

Thus, for the record, Mukesh became Dharmendra's first voice (as was also the case with Raj Kapoor, Sanjeev Kumar, Dharam's good friends Manoj Kumar and Shashi Kapoor, and later Jeetendra, Rajesh Khanna and Rishi Kapoor!). Also, Dharam's first lyrics were written, respectively, by K.L. Pardesi and Shamim Jaipuri.

That Special Voice—Mohammed Rafi

In 1961, the Rafi-Dharmendra association was to begin with the oh-so-soothing 'Jaane Kya Dhoondti Rehti Hai' from Khayyam's *Shola Aur Shabnam*. This was also the first of the few but memorable classics Kaifi Azmi was to write for him, an innings that ended, ironically, with the songs from the actor's first home production *Satyakam* in 1969 ('Zindagi Hai Kya'). Azmi had also penned the remaining two songs of that movie that were filmed on Sharmila Tagore, 'Do Din Ki Zindagi' and 'Abhi Kya Sunoge'.

'Rafi saab would merge into my character in all films!' said

Dharmendra. Always smiling, incapable of anger, almost a brother, is how Dharmendra remembers Rafi. When he met Rafi for the first time, he said, 'It was like a dream come true. I later came to know that he was suffering from fever that day, and my first song "Jaane Kya Dhoondti Rehti Hai", which he recorded in that condition, sounded just like me!'

He admitted that for Sunny's debut film, he would have loved to have Rafi sing, but as he had passed away, he decided to look for a similar voice and found one in Shabbir Kumar. 'I was Rafi saab's fan long before I became an actor,' he said. 'As a playback singer, he would initiate me into the mood of the song—not just me, but every actor! I am speaking from the heart, that if I had my say, I would have never taken any other voice for my songs, though I liked and respected all singers!'

Even in his 1989 production *Yateem*, Shabbir Kumar and Mohammed Aziz shared the honours. And when his younger son Bobby Deol made his debut in Dharmendra's production *Barsaat* with the Kumar Sanu-obsessed Nadeem-Shravan as composers, there was still a song by Sonu Nigam, who was again someone who sang in the Rafi mould.

Years later, in *Apne*, it was Sonu Nigam who sang the title song that was also partly enacted by Dharmendra. And in the case of *Yamla Pagla Deewana*, the Deols had wanted to use Rafi's *Pratiggya* original but that was prevented due to copyright issues between the original music label (Saregama-HMV) and that of the new film (T-Series). And so Nigam came on board again to record the re-creation.

The Rafi-Dharmendra association thus became the strongest and longest-lasting face-and-voice association for the actor. If Dharmendra represented a blend of action, innocence, playfulness or romantic passion, Rafi symbolized all that was beautiful and technically perfect in melody. And of the 150 songs mentioned above, Rafi sang around half the number.

Very interestingly, the vast majority of Rafi's songs for the actor, across composers like O.P. Nayyar, Madan Mohan, Chitragupta, Roshan, Ravi, Salil Chowdhury, Shankar-Jaikishan, Kalyanji-Anandji, Sonik-Omi, S.D. Burman, R.D. Burman, Laxmikant-Pyarelal and Ravindra Jain, eschewed the Punjabi inflection otherwise so dominant in Rafi's singing, despite the actor's Punjabi origins!

The master singer instead imparted a serene, sonorous, urban and genteel touch to Dharam's 'voice', best noticed in Madan Mohan's 'Ek Haseen Sham Ko' (*Dulhan Ek Raat Ki*), Sonik-Omi's 'Main Suraj Hoon Tu Meri Kiran' (*Dil Ne Phir Yaad Kiya*), Shankar-Jaikishan's 'Gar Tum Bhula Na Doge' (*Yakeen*) and Laxmikant-Pyarelal's 'Aaj Mausam Beimaan Hai Bada' (*Loafer*).

Only in sporadic songs like 'Main Jat Yamla Pagla Deewana' and 'Uth Neend Se Mirziyaa Jag Jaa' from the actor's Laxmikant-Pyarelal-composed home production *Pratiggya,* and occasional other numbers like 'Badraa Chhaye Ke Mele', which was the title track of *Aya Sawan Jhoom Ke*, was the Punjabi tenor brought in.

Laxmikant-Pyarelal were Dharam's favourite and most repeated composers, who did over fifty films in three decades with him from *Aaye Din Bahaar Ke* in 1966 to *Paappi Devataa* in 1996. As Pyarelal put it, 'Dharmendra's songs were mostly filmed in outdoor sequences. Laxmi (Laxmikant) and I would keep in mind Punjabi folk for him, but also modernize the songs. We needed "open" or full-throated singing for him, not the closed and introspective one that suited some other actors.'

And together the Dharmendra-Rafi combination thus represented a whopper dose of this muscle in melody, for their best songs together were chunky objets d'art, and were no less than Rafi's sparklers for his higher profile associations like with Dilip Kumar and Shammi Kapoor.

And Rafi was the only singer who gave that infinitely vital 'Dharmendra'-esque nuance to the actor's songs, regardless of the song being breezy, sad, passionate or playful. Especially with Laxmikant-Pyarelal, the songs could not be mistaken for songs performed by other actors.

Not just the songs mentioned above, but even others like 'Kya Miliye Aise Logon Se' (*Izzat*), 'Hui Sham Unka Khayaal Aa Gaya' and 'Chhalkaaye Jaam' (*Mere Humdum Mere Dost*), 'Jhilmil Sitaron Ka Aangan Hoga' (*Jeevan Mrityu*) and Rafi's last recording 'Sheher Mein Charcha Hai' (*Aas Paas*) were all unmistakable Dharmendra tracks.

This magic remained consistent in the songs made by other composers, be it 'Mehbooba Teri Tasveer' (S.D. Burman/*Ishq Par Zor Nahin*), 'Mujhe Dard-E-Dil Ka Pataa Na Tha' (Chitragupta/*Akash Deep*), 'Aapke Haseen Rukh Pe' (O.P. Nayyar/*Baharen Phir Bhi Aayengi*), 'Main Kahin Kavi Na Ban Jaaoo'(Shankar-Jaikishan/*Pyar Hi Pyar*), 'Dil To Dil Hai' (Kalyanji-Anandji/*Kab? Kyoon? Aur Kahan?*), and many others.

Kishore Kumar

Kishore Kumar, once he broke onto the scene in the early 1970s as a big-name playback singer, also had his share of triumphs with the actor. Strangely enough, he opened his account for Dharmendra not under the Burmans who loved him but with Shankar-Jaikishan, who till then, had almost exclusively used Mohammed Rafi for Dharmendra.

But with their fun song 'Munne Ki Amma Yeh To Bataa' in *Tum Haseen Main Jawan* (1970), Kishore's voice came to roost on Dharmendra as the major alternative to Rafi. The vocal deal, so to speak, was clinched with the lovely S.D. Burman litany, 'Duniya O Duniya Tera Jawaab Nahin' (*Naya Zamana*) and R.D. Burman hits from *Do Chor* (led by 'Kaali Palak Teri Gori') and *Samadhi* (the most popular being 'Maine Dekha Ek Sapna').

With *Blackmail*'s 'Pal Pal Dil Ke Paas' and 'Mile Mile Do Badan', and *Kahani Kismat Ki*'s 'Raftaa Raftaa', Kalyanji-Anandji also looked at Dharmendra through Kishore Kumar's resonant vocals. Laxmikant-Pyarelal followed suit with playful or fun numbers like 'Daal Roti Khaao' (*Jwar Bhata*) and 'Kal Ki Haseen Mulaqaat Ke Liye' (*Charas*), besides the now-cult 'Kisi Shaayar Ki Ghazal' (*Dream Girl*).

By that time, R.D. Burman had scored *Sholay*'s iconic 'Yeh Dosti Hum Nahin Todenge', and Shankar-Jaikishan had created 'Chamka Paseena Banke Nagina' (*Resham Ki Dori*). And Bappi Lahiri also latched on to Kishore as his favourite Dharmendra voice.

Mukesh

Dharmendra was also a fan of Mukesh, who was his first playback singer, and was also his voice in the Mukesh-Mahendra Kapoor-Kishore Kumar song, 'Zindagi Hai Kya' in his home production *Satyakam*. As a singer, Mukesh sang very few songs for him, but they included standout evergreens like 'Hamsafar Mere Humsafar' and 'Tumhein Zindagi Ke Ujale Mubarak' from *Purnima*, 'Baharon Ne Mera Chaman Loot Kar' and 'Aaya Hai Mujhe Phir Yaad' from *Devar*, and the lesser-known 'Kisi Ne Jaadoo Kiya' from *Chand Aur Suraj*. Laxmikant-Pyarelal, Roshan, Kalyanji-Anandji and Salil Chowdhury were composers who used this silken voice for Dharmendra. The last gem came from S.D. Burman—with 'Baaghon Mein Kaise', in *Chupke Chupke*.

Mahendra Kapoor

Mahendra Kapoor sang sporadically for the actor, but across an array of composers that included Ravi ('Zindagi Ittefaq Hai' from *Aadmi Aur Insaan*), O.P. Nayyar ('Badal Jaaye Agar Maali' from *Baharen Phir*

Bhi Aayengi), Chitragupta ('Koi Aanewala Hai' from *Mera Qusoor Kya Hai*), Madan Mohan ('Ari O Shokh Kaliyon' from *Jab Yaad Kisi Ki Aati Hai*), Laxmikant-Pyarelal ('Yeh Kali Jab Talak Phool Banke Khile' from *Aaye Din Bahaar Ke*) and even Shankar-Jaikishan ('Mere Sarkar Meri Aahon Ka Asar' from *Shikar*). These led a list of some more songs all the way to the 1980s.

List of Popular Songs by Playback Singers for Dharmendra:

Manna Dey: 'Abhi To Haath Mein Jaam Hai' (*Seeta Aur Geeta*)

Hemant Kumar: 'Ya Dil Ki Suno' (*Anupama*)

Hemant Kumar: 'Tum Pukar Lo' (*Khamoshi*)

P.B. Srinivas: 'Chanda Se Hoga Woh Pyaara' (*Main Bhi Ladki Hoon*)

Yesudas: 'Jaaneman Jaaneman' (*Chhoti Si Baat*) in part of the song

Bhupinder Singh: 'Naam Gum Jaayega' (*Kinara*) in part of the song

Nitin Mukesh: 'Prem Hai Prem Hai' (*Dillagi*)

Amit Kumar: 'Jaan-E-Man Jaan-E-Jigar' (*Ghazab*)

Kumar Sanu: 'Aaj Raat Chandni Hai' (*Kal Ki Awaz*)

Sonu Nigam: 'Baaqi Sab Sapne Hote Hai' (*Apne*)

Dharmendra's Voices:

Here is the comprehensive list of singers who lip-synched for the megastar in his films.
1. Abhijeet
2. Amit Kumar
3. Anwar

4. Aziz Nazan
5. Bhupinder Singh
6. Dharmendra himself (In *Yamla Pagla Deewana 2*)
7. Diljit Dosanjh
8. Hemant Kumar
9. Javed Ali
10. Kabban Mirza
11. Kishore Kumar
12. Kumar Sanu
13. Mahendra Kapoor
14. Manna Dey
15. Master Saleem
16. Mika Singh
17. Mohammed Aziz
18. Mohammed Rafi
19. Mukesh
20. Nitin Mukesh
21. P.B. Srinivas
22. Rahul B. Seth
23. S.P. Balasubrahmanyam
24. Shabbir Kumar
25. Sonu Nigam
26. Suresh Wadkar
27. Vinod Rathod
28. Yesudas

Dharmendra's Juke Box: 20 Most Iconic Songs

1. 'Mujhko Iss Raat Ki Tanhai Mein'—*Dil Bhi Tera Hum Bhi Tere*
2. 'Jaane Kya Dhoondti Rehti Hai'—*Shola Aur Shabnam*
3. 'Baharon Ne Mera Chaman Loot Kar'—*Devar*

4. 'Aap Ke Haseen Rukh'—*Baharen Phir Bhi Aayengi*
5. 'Ya Dil Ki Suno'—*Anupama*
6. 'Chhalkaaye Jaam'—*Mere Haumdam Mere Dost*
7. 'Yeh Dil Tum Bin'—*Izzat*
8. 'O Manjhi Chal'—*Aaya Sawan Jhoom Ke*
9. 'Gar Tum Bhula Na Doge'—*Yakeen*
10. 'Main Kahin Kavi Na Ban Jaaoon'—*Pyar Hi Pyar*
11. 'Tum Pukar Lo'—*Khamoshi*
12. 'Jhilmil Sitaron Ka Aangan Hoga'—*Jeevan Mrityu*
13. 'Kuch Kehta Hai Yeh Saawan'—*Mera Gaon Mera Desh*
14. 'Aaj Mausam Bada Beimaan Hai'—*Loafer*
15. 'Pal Pal Dil Ke Paas'—*Blackmail*
16. 'Rafta Rafta Dekho'—*Kahani Kismat Ki*
17. 'Main Jat Yamla'—*Pratiggya*
18. 'Yeh Dosti'—*Sholay*
19. 'O Meri Mehbooba'—*Dharam-Veer*
20. 'Kisi Shaayar Ki Ghazal'—*Dream Girl*

PART 3

Ye JAT YAMLA, PAGLA, DEEWANA

Chapter Sixteen

Within the Star: A Man of the Soil

Main Jat yamla pagla deewana / Ho rabba

'*I have admired him as an actor, but I admire him much more as a
human being. He is the one actor I have met who is all human.*'

—Actress Rekha's statement encapsulates
Dharmendra perfectly.

*M*ost down-to-earth celebrities are human conundrums,
but Dharmendra is a conundrum in a different sense.
The simplicity and openness of his nature blew away
fans and colleagues alike, so much so that we wondered how such
a successful man could remain so basic, so rooted and so humble.
In fact he did not even want a biography written about him. He
would rather, he told me once, come out with a coffee-table book
of pictures of his multitude of heroines—including the top names
from Vyjayanthimala and Meena Kumari to Sridevi as well as other
names from Bengal, the South and other actresses that included
Tarla Mehta and Mallika Sherawat. And with Garam Dharam, *this*
is the real conundrum.

Asha Parekh tried to put this quality in a nutshell. As his

romantic co-star in five hit films, she described Dharmendra as a human being who 'Kept the village atmosphere intact within him, and did not change much over the decades of success and fame.'

When he first became a star, the man even talked to his photograph, saying, almost disbelievingly, '*Wakayee tu actor ban gaya hai* (You have actually become an actor)!' For a BBC interview, he once declared, 'Had I not become an actor, I would be driving a tractor in Punjab. But I *still* drive a tractor at my farm in Lonavala and enjoy it!'

'He was known to be caring and careful with co-stars in crowds, and yet, he would always be conscious about his looks and image,' Parekh said. The actress recalled an amusing incident on the sets of *Mera Gaon Mera Desh*, when she had teased him one day with the words, 'Hello, Uncle Dharam!' Parekh laughingly said that he was so upset that he went and told director Raj Khosla, 'Tell her not to call me "uncle"!' When she received this communication from Khosla, she went up to Dharmendra and quipped, 'But if you call me aunty, it's perfectly okay!'

Dharam's shyness took on a new dimension when he was just a few years into the industry, at a picnic with Asha Parekh, Sadhana, Tanuja and some other actresses. They were playing the game 'Spin the Bottle', where he had to kiss the heroine at whom it pointed when the bottle came to rest. But Dharmendra actually ran away from the game!

The actor was, in fact, quite known for his shyness. His close associate, film-maker Anil Sharma, also laughingly recalled how he had once found a magazine carefully hidden under the sofa cushions in Dharmendra's own drawing room, which mentioned on the cover that the actor had been declared one among the world's ten most handsome men! Said Sharma, 'I was compelled to ask Dharamji, "Sir, *aap jaante bhi hai aap kya hain* (Do you even know what you are)?"'

Sanjay Khan, actor and film-maker, said, 'He is a simpleton, warm, unassuming and self-effacing, almost as if he does not know his own worth! When he embraces you, it's clear that there is genuine love, not any vested interest.' Khan can never forget how Dharmendra wept like a baby when he saw him in hospital after his accident—Khan had suffered terrible burns and had been critical for weeks from a grave mishap on the sets of one of his television serials. Dharmendra kept telling him, '*Main tere saath hoon*! (I am with you)!' and Khan recalls that he was 'strangely fortified' by the sincere remark.

Khan recalled Dharmendra's lasting ties with people who belonged to his village and surrounding areas. During the outdoor shoot of *Haqeeqat*, on one occasion Dharmendra and he ventured out one day from the elite Officers' Mess which they were sharing with Chetan Anand, Vijay Anand and Balraj Sahni. They wanted to have a drink with the unit. But on returning late, they were asked for the password, which they had forgotten! 'An officer had been shot dead for that reason!' said Khan. 'We were so scared and I was sweating despite the cold! We said, "*Hum log film wale hain* (We are from the film unit)!" And there was no response! So Dharmendra said loudly, "*Main Dharminder hoon* (I am Dharmendra)." A light flashed on us, and a Sardar from the Army hollered out his own introduction, abused and hugged him, and they started beating each other in delight. They knew each other!'

Putul Guha recollected the time when his father was with Dharmendra and Hrishikesh Mukherjee in the former's hotel room in Kolkata, as the silver jubilee of *Anupama* was being celebrated. 'Dharmendra was expecting two or three Jat friends from Punjab. There were loud knocks on the door. A six foot-plus Jat in turban and lungi stepped in, and Dharamji and he hugged, kicked each other, fell on the bed abusing and laughing and boxing each other! Hrishida looked at my father and suggested they move to his room to eat!'

Dharmendra's comeback film of sorts, *Apne*, also highlighted the man within him. All he craved from it, ambition-wise, was shown in his statement to me, 'I still want to see my posters everywhere!'

'*Ek aura, ek era ka naam hai Dharmendra* (Dharmendra is an aura and an era by himself)!' thundered good friend, colleague and co-star of many films, Shatrughan Sinha. 'I have never seen such charisma in anyone else. He knew that I had declined the role of Veeru in *Sholay*, so he recommended Amitabh Bachchan.'

A trait Sinha found completely endearing was that the good-natured Dharam never used Punjabi expletives and abuses when he was around. 'I had told him a true story of how I had been immensely traumatized when I had witnessed the late Prithviraj Kapoor, for whom I have monumental respect, abuse someone once,' Sinha remarked.

'After that, whenever I was in the vicinity and he felt the need to express himself freely, he would look around and ask, "*Yeh Shatrughan to nahin hai kahin? Uss ke saamne main aisi galla bhi aur gaali bhi nahin de sakta* (I hope Shatrughan isn't here. I can neither abuse nor speak freely with him around)!" Dharam is always so simple, so child-like!'

Bharathi S. Pradhan, journalist and editor, added her own funny story about the actor being always conscious about his dazzling looks and image. Bharathi once wrote in her column for a popular film fortnightly *Star & Style* that at a film function, the actor seemed tired, as if he was in need of rest. How she came to know that the statement had really upset the star was when he called her up and said, 'Why did you have to *write* that? Please, darling, next time, just call up and tell me!'

'He was so nice and conveyed it so well,' Pradhan said. 'I was used to writing what I felt about anything or anyone, but I realized that he was very hurt and for the first time in my career, I felt bad. His birthday came up soon, and I sent him flowers. And that really melted him! For years, he sweetly kept reminding me how nice he had felt when he had got "such beautiful flowers" from me! Now, *that* is Dharam!'

Bharathi narrated another incident which happened with her colleague Ingrid, who worked with *Stardust*. She had relatives visiting from out of town who wanted to meet Dharmendra. As she knew him very well, Ingrid called him and asked where she could bring them to meet him. Pradhan added, 'You know what he did? He asked for her address, said he would be passing by the place where she stayed on the way to a shoot, and actually dropped in to meet them.'

'When people came to Mumbai with dreams, Dharam paaji would offer them love and a place to stay!' added close friend and actor Gurbachan Singh emotionally. 'I was a known wrestler from Gurdaspur wanting to be an actor, and struggling for years. My father knew Dharam paaji's brother Kanwar Ajit Singh, who was serving in the railways in Gurdaspur until 1965. He also had given me letters to other friends. No one helped.'

The actor reminisced, 'When I went to visit Dharam paaji, I was broken—he was my last hope. All he said was that I could stay with him as long as I wanted, and asked me to bring my luggage, which I had kept at (eminent wrestler) Dara Singhji's house. Dharam's house is a dharamshala (a charitable rest-house for travellers)! If Dharamji had not given me a roof over my head, I would have left Mumbai!'

Singh has even written a heartfelt couplet in Dharmendra's honour:

Jab jab meri guzri kahaani yaad aati hai
Kisi meherbaan ki meherbaani yaad aati hai

Whenever I look back at my story,
I remember the kindness of someone so kind

Dharmendra, said Singh, has a habit of caringly enquiring about his well-being periodically. '*Kisi cheez ki kami to nahin* (Do you need anything)?' was a question asked not only of Singh but of so many others, said the actor. 'He is so large-hearted! People get swollen egos after one film or one hit. Dharam paaji remains grounded even now.'

A special memory of their association, which has always been more personal than professional, is of Singh buying the legendary actor's Volkswagen in 1975. 'It was a specially fitted car, and I only paid for it by 1979,' recalled the actor.

Leena Chandavarkar, co-star in *Rakhwala* and *Ek Mahal Ho Sapno Ka*, got sentimental as she remembered her co-actor. An unforgettable incident for Chandavarkar was Dharmendra's role in saving her husband Siddharth Bandodkar's life after the accident he had with his gun. Her husband was admitted in a hospital and the actress was at her wit's end when the medicine needed urgently to save her husband's life was not available anywhere.

Chandavarkar remembered the actor calling up to enquire about Siddharth, and when she wept and told him her problem, Dharmendra actually managed to get the medicine for her. She said, 'He saved Siddharth's life! Later, when another medicine was needed that could only be found in London in those days, I called Dharam again. He actually contacted his friends in London and within a day or two, got it flown to Mumbai through a captain he knew in the airlines.'

Dharmendra actually went to the airport to get the medicine and brought it to the downtown hospital in his jeep. 'It was pouring as it was the rainy season, and Dharam was driving his open jeep himself. I came to know of this because he gave it to someone at the entrance to the hospital and went away,' she recalled.

Later, when her brother went to the Deol residence with ₹20,000 (the cost of that drug), Dharmendra was very angry. He showed her brother his clenched fist and said, '*Yeh do kilo ka haath dekhte ho* (Do you see this huge hand of mine)? I will beat you with it! How can you offer me money? Wouldn't you do the same for me?'

On Diwali that year, Chandavarkar and her husband visited the Deols with gifts. 'His mother would call me bahu (daughter-in-law) and said that I was like a grihalaxmi. I touched her feet, and she told me that Siddharth was like her third son.'

Selflessness could well be the middle name for this megastar. His secretary Dinanath Shastri wanted to make a Bhojpuri film with Dulal Guha after Guha had worked with Dharmendra in *Chand Aur Suraj*. Recalled Putul Guha, 'Dinanathji had this subject of three brothers and one stepbrother. They went to make Dharamji listen to the story. He loved the story so much that he told them both that they should make a Hindi film instead, and that the well-written characters for Kanhaiyalal and Durga Khote could speak in a Bihari dialect, so that the film would appeal there as well.'

The result was *Dharti Kahe Pukar Ke*, starring Jeetendra and Sanjeev Kumar with Nanda, which was Guha's first hit! Later, his then-secretary Iqbal Singh produced *Kaalia* (1981) with Amitabh Bachchan, which was also a hit. Even his brother-in-law Ranjit Virk, made his debut as a producer with Amitabh Bachchan in *Benaam*, a decent success in 1974.

As director Anurag Basu explained, 'This soft-spoken man was so transparent that he did not have to do much to get into people's hearts. He did it naturally, effortlessly.'

On the other hand, this shy gentleman's naughtiness and sense of humour were well-known as well. 'I remember Dharamji as a very naughty man on the sets,' said Aruna Irani, who did several films with him and played his sister in *Charas*. 'He was always laughing and joking, and we would enjoy his jokes. He was a very hospitable man and would share his food with me. For me, he is like a badmaash paaji (naughty big brother)!'

Irani stresses on the fact that Dharmendra was 'As khubsoorat (beautiful) inside' as he was in looks. 'He is an emotional man too, especially with women, and he would joke with me, "Don't tell anyone that I am a flirt!"' she laughed.

Also endorsing Dharmendra's naughtiness is comedian Birbal, the megastar's close friend and associate of many years, who recalled in particular one hilarious incident. 'Though I do not remember the film, we were shooting at Vijaya-Vauhini Studios in Chennai,' said the comedian. One evening saw both of them and other team members gathered over drinks. 'All of us were a bit high when Dharam told me, "Birbal, call up Omji (character artiste Om Prakash) and speak to him in *his* voice!"' said Birbal, who was a good mimic. 'I was drunk, but I said, "*Joote khaane hai kya* (He will beat me up)!" But Dharam asked me, "*Itna bhi kehna nahin maanega* (You won't listen even to this small request)?" And so I called Omji, but he did not pick up the phone.'

Birbal explained that Om Prakash was used to staying at the Hotel Ashoka there for decades, and had instructed the hotel management that he should not be disturbed after 9.30 at night. 'When I remembered that, I called up the hotel reception, stating that I was D.I. Shetty from Vauhini and had very important work.'

Birbal asked them to connect to Om Prakash's room as it was urgent. The conversation went something like this:

Birbal: 'Omji, this is Somji speaking.'

Om Prakash: '*Tu kahaan se bol rahaa hain* (From where are you speaking)?!'

Birbal: '*Ji, main apne munh se bol rahaa hoon* (I am speaking from my mouth, sir)!'

Om Prakash: '*Tu hai kaun! Main teri aisi-taisi kar doonga, meri neend ko disturb kiya* (Who are you to disturb my sleep? I will teach you a lesson)!'

Birbal: 'I am making a film called *Barbaad Jawani* (Ruined Youth).'

Om Prakash: '*Main tujhe barbaad kar doonga* (I will ruin you)!'

Birbal then told him that he wanted to cast the actor as a hero with Lalita Pawar (the 1930s siren who had graduated to negative character roles by then, especially as an evil mother or mother-in-law!) opposite him. He told the senior actor that he was a huge fan and wanted to sign him. A furious Om Prakash heaped invectives and threats on Birbal and hung up!

The next morning, on the set, the team could barely conceal their laughter as they listened to Om Prakash's angry recount of what had happened the previous night. He looked narrowly at Birbal's comedian colleagues B.B. Bhalla and Mohan Choti and demanded to know whether they had mimicked him. Dharmendra exasperated Om Prakash further by stating that he too had received a similar call from someone speaking in his own voice!

'It was none of us!' Dharmendra then told the senior actor with a straight face. Birbal was the only remaining member of the group, and Om Prakash gave him one disdainful look and remarked, 'He does not even come out with his own voice properly! How can he imitate me?'

After a few days, Dharmendra did tell the veteran the truth, and Birbal was duly and severely rebuked! 'Even on sets, Dharam would always sit and chat with us. He always thought of all of us as equals,' Birbal added. 'I enjoyed working with him more than any other star.'

In Dharmendra's own words, 'When Shashi Kapoor was in hospital, Manoj (Kumar) and I decided to visit him on the following morning. *Apna yaar hai* (he is our close friend), we thought. The next day, we saw a newspaper item, with a photograph of one of our top stars exiting the hospital. My film was on release, and I called up Manoj and said, "Let's not go. We are going to meet our friend, not to get publicity. People will think I want publicity for my film!" Manoj agreed.' Happily for both of them, Kapoor came back from the hospital and lived for a few years more!

But Dharmendra also added, 'I cannot believe that Dev Anand is no more and that Dilip Kumar saab is inactive. They were my idols! At that time, I never thought that they would age one day, or that Dev saab and Raj saab would go. You like to think of your idols as those who have drunk the elixir of eternal youth! I miss them a lot!'

Showbiz, he told me six years ago, is 'show off biz' now. 'But it is still bigger than the biggest business and also the best. I remember tears in a fan's eyes when we finished a brief conversation at an airport abroad. What can be the name you can give to such a relationship? But that warmth has gone within the industry, like the time when I could call up colleagues if I was upset about something.'

Subhash Ghai put it succinctly, 'The difference between him and other stars is that Dharamji is not a political but a simple soul! Veteran actor Om Prakash had introduced me to him, and had predicted that he would be a great star—both Dharamji and I were strugglers then. Dharamji shook hands—his hand was huge!—with me, but the warmth in his eyes showed a beautiful and original soul. Besides, the handshake was enough for me to read him. Other stars had the "Keep away from me" demeanour. But Dharamji was so warm, he attracted people to him.'

'With Dharmendra, what you see is what you get,' declared his *Ali Baba Aur Chalis Chor* director Umesh Mehra. 'I don't think there is a negative bone in that man's body! He is completely upfront, has a pure heart, and there is no manipulation.'

Dilip Kumar, the man who inspired Dharmendra to take up this profession and co-starred with him, too, in *Paari* and *Anokha Milan*, echoed Sippy's statement. When asked in a 1981 interview about which younger actors he liked, he had said, 'All the young actors are good. *Par ek aadmi aisa hai, uss aadmi ka naam hai Dharmendra, jiske dil mein jo hai wohi zubaan pe hai* (But there is one man named Dharmendra with whom what you see is what you get)!'

The emotions were completely reciprocated. Dharmendra only kept Dilip Kumar's photograph in his house besides those of his parents and sons. He even admitted that he never copied him as an actor (when everyone else did so openly or covertly) 'because he did not dare to do so!' Molding his life instead along Dilip Kumar's personal and professional approach, he took serious heed of his advice when stardom came his way—like Kumar's warning to not get swayed by sycophants. He even told Kumar's wife Saira Banu jovially that she had competition because he too loved 'Yusuf saab (Kumar's real name)!'

Even about his own spectacular success, Dharmendra has a grounded opinion. He just smiles and says, 'I am what I am today because of my mother's blessings and the love of the people. My parents told me that if you are intrinsically good, God bestows his choicest blessings on you. I was on great terms with all my film-makers, co-stars and even the other heroes, though not all were emotional bonds. If some of them did something to me that they should not have, I never bothered. *Khudi se jeeyo zindagi sudhar jaayegi* (Live life your own way, you will never regret it!),' added the actor poetically.

This also explains the trashy films he was a part of for a long while. 'Dad was amazing,' said Bobby Deol. 'His family was the most precious of all to him, and he always wanted them to have the best. This is why dad always worked like a busy bee. He isn't proud of many of his films, but very happy and self-satisfied that he worked so much only for his family.'

This simple man of the soil does not thus care for smoke-filled restaurants and sophisticated company, but till date, enjoys wayside cafés and local dhaabas (roadside food stalls). He loves travelling on highways with trucks around and likes to go off on solo picnics., After moving to Mumbai, and even after becoming a successful actor, he had a weakness for airports, and for many months, he would go there in the evenings whenever he could. He simply sat outside in his turquoise-coloured Fiat, and sipped hot coffee from a thermos.

As he always likes to reiterate, Dharmendra was a part of the industry and yet did not conform to the ways of most of the fraternity. 'I first met Dharamji after *Bandini*,' recalled Pahlaj Nihalani, who was a child then, but came from a family of distributors. 'Whenever, as a fan, I would write to him on a postcard, he would, in response, send a photograph of his! One day, as a kid, I went to meet him and he opened the door himself, he called me in, gave me tea and also some photographs. The general impression I got in his house was as if I was in Punjab.'

When the actor's home production *Satyakam* flopped, Nihalani recalled that he had called all the distributors who had suffered losses and given them ₹22 lakh. Hardly anyone did that then, recalled the producer, who finally worked with him in 1987 in *Aag Hi Aag*. On the other hand, Nihalani's family earned a mega-fortune from *Phool Aur Patthar*, which they had distributed in some territories. Nihalani goes to the extent of saying that 'Dharamji is the best person in the country!'

Fans also meant everything for him. Sunny Deol recollected a huge crowd outside his hotel when Dharmendra was shooting. Instead of being holed up in his room, the actor came out on the balcony of his room, greeted them and threw several pieces of paper to all his fans, each having his autograph! 'My father is an emotional person, and his fans reciprocate emotionally!'

Gen Y actress Kriti Kharbanda, who worked with all the three Deols in *Yamla Pagla Deewana Phir Se*, revealed, 'Dharam paaji even now respects his fans, and would pose with each one of hundreds who came to watch our shoot in Hyderabad, some coming all the way from Punjab. Many in the unit told Dharam uncle that he could meet all of them while being seated on a chair and even take group photographs that way, but he refused, saying that every one of them was important! Later, he told me that stars are *nothing* without these people, and the producers always had a misconception that stars made fortunes for them, whereas it was these people who bought tickets and made them rich!'

It is Asha Parekh again who decisively sums up Dharmendra in a nutshell: 'To me, he represents manhood. How many of our heroes can match him in that?'

Chapter Seventeen

The Meena Kumari Phase

Nigahen kyoon bhatakti hai / Kadam kyoon dagmaate hain / Tumhi tak hai har ek manzil / Chale aao chale aao

The first unfortunate involvement that happened in Dharmendra's life was that with Meena Kumari.

Most of the industry believes—and perhaps, rightly so—that it was the star-crossed actress, bereft of enough love and affection in real life, who took a fancy to the strapping young man she had come to know since the time they began shooting for *Purnima*. This film was followed rapidly by *Main Bhi Ladki Hoon* (which was released first), *Kaajal* (not opposite each other) and *Phool Aur Patthar*, with which Dharmendra, on a quick ascent, zoomed into the top echelons. Three more films followed—*Chandan Ka Palna*, *Majhli Didi* and *Baharon Ki Manzil*, but all of those bombed.

As mentioned, it was *Purnima* that was launched first, and like with so many top heroines whom he worked with for the first time, the new young actor asked a friend, 'What is she like?' Meena Kumari's biographer states that Dharmendra was 'petrified at the prospect of facing her in front of the camera.'[1]

---

[1]Mehta, Vinod, *Meena Kumari: The Classic Biography*, HarperCollins, 2013.

The actor was quite intimidated by the man's reply that she could outclass him with a mere glance, a twitch of the lips or a 'dialogue'. The friend advised him to touch her feet when they first met.

As a result, the biography goes on, Dharmendra approached her with the utmost respect, humility and willingness to learn. The young actor had claimed to be her ardent fan and worshipper. He would watch her movies and dream that if he became an actor he would do a film with her.

When they were introduced at Chandivali Studios, Dharmendra was 'thrilled, happy and gratified' that she was warm, friendly and encouraging towards him. The touching her feet part has no confirmation, but the book insists that she did say, 'The boy will rise. He is not a routine entry.'

And that's when we come to the relevant part: At that point in time she needed a stable and devoted man to care for her. And young Dharmendra was the right man in the right place at the right time.

We would rather not, thus, give credence to the theory that Dharmendra used Kumari to move up the starry ladder and then discarded her. Let us examine things step by step: Firstly, none of their films, but for *Main Bhi Ladki Hoon* produced by AVM Productions, was a big film-maker's project. O.P. Ralhan (*Phool Aur Patthar*) had given hits but was no mighty film-maker. Hrishikesh Mukherjee, who directed *Majhli Didi*, arguably the pair's biggest flop, was no one to take casting suggestions from any star, senior (like Meena Kumari) or junior (like Dharmendra).

Dharmendra, as we have seen, had a very promising box-office track record (best described as 'upwardly mobile' in contemporary lexicon) that had already given him an edge over contemporaries and some seniors, so we must say that the idea that Dharmendra used Meena Kumari for career advancement does not hold water. As for their coincidental biggest hit together, *Phool Aur Patthar*, it was Dharmendra's work and physique (strictly in that order) that zoomed his status way up when the film was loved. Meena Kumari's star position, at worst, was unaffected, and at best, it helped her get her last few films as a leading lady before shifting to character roles in 1968.

An anonymous source has stated that initially the relationship was only about work, but with an extra contribution from Kumari's side. She would instill confidence in Dharmendra by correcting him, making him practice his shots, explaining things so that he could understand his work better and overcome his weaknesses—and all this especially in her spare time, even for films in which she was not his heroine.

It is said that by 'grooming and correcting weak points,' the actress, deprived of love, wanted to engage his attention, as she was too much of a reputed name to make a pass openly. This way, she would get to spend time with him, without making her real intentions known to anyone, including him. Almost a daily visitor at her house at Juhu's Janki Kutir, they would open a bottle and spend hours together.

But, contrary to popular perception, Dharmendra managed to restrict her alcohol consumption when he was there with her. He was everything she needed and wanted—loving, honest and caringly reliable. But when he would leave, she would go berserk with the bottle.

At parties and premieres, Meena openly showered affection towards Dharam. Sometimes she would even take his hand and the next day it would be in print. On one occasion, mischievously almost, she recited a love couplet from Ghalib, which left no doubt in the audience's mind about Dharmendra's position in her heart.

Once, returning from Delhi after the premiere of *Kaajal*, when he arrived at the airport, the authorities noticed his inebriated state and refused to let him in the plane. 'But I must get back to Bombay. I must, Meena is waiting for me,' he is said to have told them. This statement and incident were faithfully reported in the papers the following day.

Kumari's biographer also notes how she had once gone on a picnic with many friends including Dharmendra. When he was somehow placed in a different car while returning, the actress became hysterical. She wanted to know why he was not sitting beside her, whether he had run away, or if something had possibly happened to him. Despite all assurances, she stopped the car, went out and actually sat down cross-legged in the middle of the road, and began repeating, 'Where is my Dharam?'

Other rumours, of drinking incidents and fights, also abounded in this phase.

Kumari's biographer admits that Dharmendra was among the very few men who were genuinely good to her. Each time he went to see her, he would come out of her room crying. 'I can't help it,' would be his honest reply when asked the reason by Kumari's sister. Though the popular view is that Dharam and the actress had been intimate for three years, industry insiders say that it was no more than six months. A much younger and married Dharmendra had nothing to offer in terms of the love and security Kumari craved.

Suffice to say then that at that point in time, both Dharmendra and Meena Kumari benefitted, albeit in different ways, from each other's companionship. In his case, it was more of a qualitative gain as an actor, and for her, he was perhaps the solace she needed through that traumatic phase of her life.

The actress, even after she stopped seeing Dharmendra, thus had great regard for him: As he was her protégé and pupil. She had helped him, and she took legitimate pride when he finally made it. Dharam himself has openly accepted the debt he owes to her for making him what he is today.

Chapter Eighteen

The Family Man

Baaqi sab sapne hote hain / Apne to apne hote hain

The mukhda of Sameer's title-song for Dharmendra's A-grade comeback film *Apne* exhibited a rare truism—everything else in life can be a dream or an illusion, but one's own family is where one truly belongs. To a man who had always harboured dreams of making it big in a world he barely knew of, Dharmendra's family provided the classic support—from parents to spouse and kids.

Of course, I could never meet his parents Kewal Kishen Singh Deol and Satwant Kaur, or his brother Ajit Singh Deol, who later came to be known as actor Kanwar Ajit (mainly in Punjabi films) and also as a producer and eventually as Abhay Deol's father, as said earlier.

It was Manoj Kumar who spoke of the relationship their respective fathers, who had finally come down to settle in Mumbai, enjoyed with each other. 'His father was very fond of me, and my father was very fond of Dharmu. The best thing was that every morning they both would meet for walks along with the fathers of film-makers Madan Mohla and Lekh Tandon. It was so wonderful to see them spend two hours laughing and joking with each other.'

And as Leena Chandavarkar had said, Dharmendra's mother considered her like her third bahu (daughter-in-law). That was how welcoming Dharmendra's family was to his friends from the industry.

The Family Anchor

Of all my interactions with Dharmendra, one meeting has somehow remained as a special memory for a reason that may appear to be extremely trivial. We were sitting together exchanging notes and Dharmendra was also showing me some old photographs stored on his mobile phone, and I requested him to mail some of them to me. When it was time to leave, he escorted me via a different route, as some work was going on in the compound. We thus passed his bungalow lawns where two ladies were sitting, engrossed in their conversation.

Dharmendra introduced me to one of them as '*Mera dost* (my friend)' and, for the first time in years of our acquaintance, I was meeting Mrs Prakash Deol—a woman who looked radiantly handsome and content. After all, she was the sheet anchor of the Deol family, the woman who had seen it all, the bad times and the uber-good times, and weathered them as no bulwark could have done.

We exchanged greetings, and I ruminated on how this superhuman woman must have looked after and cared for all, from in-laws to their four children, the families of her children, especially of sons Sunny and Bobby, and all those who lived with them—from close and distant relatives to others from their village, and everyone else.

Here was this woman in person, the wife who patiently stayed back in Punjab—with a baby son—while her husband was struggling (without any certainty whatsoever of future prospects) in the Hindi film industry, going through his initial heartbreaks and then taking all the steps towards ultimate stardom. Her silent moral and (after stardom) actual support counted hugely.

Those few seconds of interaction gave me the instant feel of an extraordinary homemaker, who had allowed Dharmendra every peace, progress and support by being a solid pillar in his life. I recollected Asha Parekh speaking about Prakash Kaur and her daughters coming on vacation on the sets of *Shikar* and I contemplated yet again on the time-tested proverb that behind every successful man is a woman. There was something in those eyes that had met mine for just a few seconds, which showed so transparently that she was a woman of such substance that the term itself took on an infinite new dimension.

I do not have the faintest idea if I will ever get to meet Dharmendra's and Prakash's two daughters Vijayta and Ajeeta, because Dharmendra has never let them appear in public after they grew up, but if this wonder woman had any role to play in their upbringing, they must be beautiful women from the inside, and complete people in every way.

And however improbable it may seem to the layman, it is *absolutely* believable that Dharmendra had once told me, 'Prakash is also looking for a suitable groom for Esha (Deol).'

Bharathi Pradhan recollected the times when the media was limited, there was easy access to the celebrities, and so there were a lot of personal interactions. 'It was very easy to talk to Dharam, and the best time to catch him at home was early morning. Most big stars had a PRO or a secretary, and we would all try and get the separate bedroom number from a star, in case their staff acted difficult.'

One interview Pradhan remembers was taken over many mornings at his house. 'At that point Dharam was off drinks and he was sitting at his nice bar upstairs drinking lassi!' she recalls. 'Dharam was very hospitable, and yet there was a subtle Lakshmanrekha. We could not get close to his wife or daughters. We never crossed borders, we accepted them, however nice and friendly he was. Once, I saw her sitting at the airport, and when I smiled at her, she smiled back. When I came back, she had disappeared, and he said, "Oh, she was wary because you are there!"'

Prakash was always there, Pradhan revealed, when there would be photo-sessions, and Pradhan remembered Prakash being the queen of the house and said, 'Anything and everything was "*Prakash ko bolo na* (Tell Prakash),"—he was very much dependent on her.' And he still is, as we have Bobby Deol's affectionate tweet of his dad and mom celebrating a candlelit Valentine's Day 2018 dinner with each other and calling them 'My forever Valentines.'

Pradhan also talked of the time when she had met Dharmendra after Sunny Deol's launch. She had asked him, 'I am sure that your second son (Bobby) will also join films. What about your daughters?' (Vijayta Films, his banner, is named after one of them). The man did not lose his temper but in his trademark style, ever so sweetly, told her, 'Please, darling, don't ever write that you asked me this question!'

Sunny Deol and Bobby Deol

The bright spots in Dharmendra's future generations were both launched with a lot of personal involvement: Sunny Deol in the blockbuster *Betaab* in 1983 and Bobby Deol in the successful *Barsaat* in 1995. The gap of approximately twelve years in their respective launch pads was roughly the same as between their ages, as Sunny was born on 19 October 1956 and Bobby on 27 January 1969.

My first exposure to the love between the two brothers, as something very different from what we see of 'filmi' siblings and nearer to that between lay people, was when I was interviewing Bobby for the first time in 1999 in his vanity van. We were in the campus of Mumbai's Don Bosco High School. The brothers were shooting for *Dillagi*, and Sunny was both his co-star and director.

A unit hand came and informed Bobby of the status of the shooting (when his next shot would be) and went off, and Bobby told me that he would have to go in about ten or fifteen minutes. But within ten minutes, there was a knock on the door and Sunny peeped in. I had never met him until then, and the way they conversed with each other in Punjabi was just like a loving, concerned parent enquiring after and speaking to a child, who answered with due respect.

What struck me then, as with their mother years later, was the expression of undiluted affection in the elder brother's eyes. If anything, it reflected upon the way the brothers had been brought up. Bobby was like the youngest child in any house, pampered, looked after in that extra-loving manner, and at the same time, protected.

Even today in their family, the youngsters touch their elders' feet, do not cross the parent-child boundary beyond a certain permissible freedom entailed by their profession, and sit down to eat together when all are around.

Sunny and Bobby live under the same roof with their parents as a joint family, with their respective wives Pooja and Tanya, Sunny's children Karan and Rajvir, and Bobby's kids Aryaman and Dharam respectively. The sanskaar and values their parents have imbibed in them are still intact, even after the former have lived for almost six decades in the 'big, bad city of Mumbai' and the supposedly amoral Indian film industry.

Expressing pride towards his sons for the upbringing they have acquired and continue to propagate, Dharmendra once said, 'We are all still learning about life every day. We are all becoming better human beings!' His voice turned soft as he dwelled on his grandson, Sunny's son Karan Deol, soon to take his first steps in acting. '*Uss mein mera khoon hai*—he will become something,' he said.

He continued proudly, 'I see kids today getting so much freedom from their parents. Then, of course, there are computers, from which both good and bad things have come up. The sabhyata (decorum) and tehzeeb (cultural etiquette) for which we Indians were known have also gone. But I am very proud of my sons, who continue to show and propagate the sanskaar my wife Prakash and I have given them.'

The Deols are emotional people, prone to oblige relatives and friends as well as colleagues and sweet talkers. They are not manipulative but have always tended to get manipulated by others. This is probably one of the key reasons why Sunny, despite mega-hit films like *Betaab, Tridev, Ghayal, Darr* and above all *Gadar: Ek Prem Katha*, is not exactly considered an A-list star circa 2018. The same is true of Bobby, whose hits include *Soldier, Gupt, Ajnabee* and *Humraaz*, besides having accomplished performances in films like *Dillagi, 23 March 1931: Shaheed* and *Naqaab*.

Their bungalow in Juhu remains an open house for relatives, friends and even the media. Dharmendra has even launched many of his kith and kin as producers over the years, and nephew Abhay Deol (Ajit Singh's son) as an actor with *Socha Na Tha*. Interviews with the Deols have always tended to be long, comfortable and intimate conversations rather than formal and hurried media interactions.

On screen, Dharmendra and Sunny appeared together for the first time in the 1986 *Sultanat* (*Saveray Waali Gaadi* with Dharmendra in a cameo released earlier that year; in the 1982 *Sunny*, they never appeared together in a frame). Sunny recalled an action sequence wherein the two were fighting each other. Sunny hit his father's knee with his sword by mistake. 'I was so scared that I froze. Dad realized that I was paranoid, so he pretended that he wasn't hurt at all. He never even mentioned it,' he stated.

Over the years, Sunny has been talking to him more and more often. He told *The Telegraph*, 'I love dad and 24/7 I keep wondering what I can do to make him happy. That's the way I am. Dad wants us to be friends, but I think it is difficult to be friends with your parents, because there will always be boundaries. And a friend can never take a parent's place. I can never be his friend.'

Sunny also remembered his dad trying to take up his homework when he was very young. 'I would hide the books under the bed! I was a very naughty child and dad was very strict then,' he said.

It was Sunny, along with Bobby, who decided to revive his father's status, make him stop signing B-grade movies to merely earn money and gave him the author-backed *Apne* (2007) in which all the three Deols came together for the first time.

From the mid-2000s, the Deols have learnt a valuable lesson: To form a solid bond even on screen. Doggedly pursuing a dream ('There was a time when no producer wanted to touch *Yamla Pagla Deewana!*' recalled Sunny), they repeated their real-life relationships after the serious *Apne* (2007) in this mirthquake of action—and hit pay dirt.

The mad 2011 caper that made a huge impact overseas and netted over ₹75 crore in India proved that the Deols did not just have their loyal fan base, but could also win newer addicts. Sunny Deol's famous '*dhaai kilo ka haath*' (a hand weighing 2.5 kilos) mixed with his tender smile and nature was the perfect foil for the two father-and-son rogues portrayed by Dharmendra and Bobby in this lost-and-found caper.

Talking about the film, Sunny said, 'We took eighteen months to lock the script. After *Apne*, it was important to make something totally different from the serious emotional family drama for the three of us to come together again. An action comedy with a lost-and-found angle, but with a difference, was ideal. The original concept was mine, about two brothers. It was called *Double Trouble*, but my father heard the idea and asked, "Why not *Triple Trouble* with me in it too?" So, I thought of bringing in the third character. He played our father.'

Would he take the liberties Bobby's and his character take with their father in that film? 'No way!' Sunny grinned. 'We are scared of him too, and we respect him too much to be like our screen characters. On screen, our characters are like friends who jokingly abuse one another, but off the camera, we don't even sit near dad, unless he wants to talk to us. When we face the camera, we forget our relationships and become our characters.'

Through this, and despite the *Yamla Pagla Deewana 2* debacle that happened in mid-2013, their relationship remains rock-solid as always.

In an interview to *Mid-Day*, Sunny categorically stated, 'I still cannot look my father in the eye. Even now, if I am doing anything wrong, the thought of dad getting to know about it scares me. I still feel like a child in front of him,' as he equated a father to shelter and a mother to cuddles.

He also let on that his son, Karan Deol, is similarly shy with him. 'When Karan told me that he wanted to become an actor, I told him, "*Tujhe jo banna hai tujhe banna hai, main kuch nahin kar sakta* (Whatever you want to become, you have to, I cannot do anything to influence you). He is trained abroad but still shares our value systems. While shooting in the United Kingdom on my birthday, he wrote such a wonderful poem for me that I had tears in my eyes, and so did dad."

'But even if I want to, Karan and I can't be friends,' emphasized the actor. 'Friendship takes away the element of parenthood. One cannot be too lenient with the child because then there will be no fear in them, and they won't value anything you give them. Karan shares his secrets with me, but maintains a distance. You can call it his reservation or respect towards me, despite being the new generation boy,' Sunny continued with a hint of pride. And Sunny is also proud of the fact that his younger son, Rajvir, is also interested in joining films.

Bobby has said, 'My father is my inspiration. Whenever I go to take any tips or advice, he simply tells me, *"jo bhi karo dil se karo"* (Whatever you do, make sure you do it from the heart). And, I always keep this guru mantra in mind.'

He stressed that while his father is like a friend, 'I still get nervous when he walks into the room. We lead simple lives that are not at all "filmi" or ostentatious. My family is my religion. My mother, a small-town lady who got married early by today's standards, is my emotional anchor.'

Agreeing with his elder brother's views on his father not being strict with them, Bobby remembers only one incident when Dharmendra had lightly rapped him because he had refused to go for a preliminary exam. 'Daddy was very lenient, but mom was very strict. She would beat us a lot, especially me, because I was the notorious one,' confessed the younger brother.

The Deols not only love each other but always love people—and people love them.

The goodwill that the Deols enjoy is remarkable—through names like Amitabh Bachchan, Salman Khan, Aamir Khan, Shah Rukh Khan, Akshay Kumar, Ajay Devgn, Hrithik Roshan, Rekha, Aishwarya Rai Bachchan and Sonakshi Sinha, all ready to oblige them with appearances in their films or at events.

Sunny, like his father, has steadfastly maintained that the Deols have always looked to the audience for their due. 'More than going up on stage to receive awards, we think the love and affection that we get from the audience is important. The industry is like a mandi (marketplace). We just make our films here. *Gadar: Ek Prem Katha* never won any award, but millions of people watched it, and *that's* more important. I would much rather have people showering us with blessings than display trophies at home.'

He had also added later, in the context of current cinema culture, 'I would rather be a good human being and be known as one rather than as a sweet talker and manipulator. Dad has taught us to be emotional and warm to people.'

And so, in keeping with the changing times and their father's growing fans even among today's film-makers, co-stars, technicians and Gen Y in general, the Deols have persuaded their father to join Twitter.

Here is a family that clearly believes in 'love and let love.'

Abhay Deol

Abhay Deol is in a completely different space from his uncle and cousins, a space that he has carefully devised to harness his strengths and conceal his weak points and also look at films he likes to feature in, different from the mainstream approach of the Deols.

As per the Deol tradition, he was introduced in a home production, *Socha Na Tha,* a film that flopped but has grown to become a cult film now. Here is the boy who was brought up in the same joint family with common rules and treatment, but stands out today. 'Sunny Deol was almost like a parent for me, besides Dharam taaya and my father,' he has said.

Very interestingly, Abhay calls his uncle 'pappa' and his real father, Ajit Singh, as 'uncle'.

Asked recently—at the press meet of his newest film *Nanu Ki Jaanu*—about whether he would not like to co-star with Dharmendra or his cousins, he said that he respected his uncle so much that he would not be able to say anything bad to him (his uncle's character, that is) if the script required it!

'I also do not know if I can act normally if he is there!' he admitted. 'I would love to work with them, and before that I would be extra diligent about the script that stars us together, because I would want it to be that much perfect.'

The actor, known for his quirky choices of roles and films, says,

'My one fix is, I wouldn't know how to be anybody else other than who I am in front of my brothers and pappa (Dharmendra). It's so difficult for me to imagine acting like someone else in front of them! If I have to be rude to pappa, I don't even know if I'll have the courage to perform in front of him. That's my own personal fear!' he said.

Abhay added, 'The one thing that I have inherited from the Deol family is the whole emotional aspect. We are more emotional than most people are. We are very shy of the media or public at large. We like being private and we are all slightly hot-headed.'

In turn, the other Deols are truly proud of the individualistic Abhay. Dharmendra had stated in our first interview, 'Oh, Abhay is doing a great job! Like Bobby, Abhay too is a gifted and natural performer. They speak a lot with their eyes. Bobby and Abhay underplay well when they receive right scripts and imaginative directors. And Sunny has matured a lot as a director as well and gave his best to *Ghayal Once Again*. Sunny, Bobby and Abhay have kept the family tradition alive and glorious.'

The Deols clearly know how to value their own in their private space. As Abhay put it, 'When we're all together under one roof, we never discuss cinema. There is so much else to talk about.'

Chapter Nineteen

The Second Deol Family

Kisi shaayar ki ghazal / Dream girl /
Kisi jheel ka kanwal / Dream girl

With Dharmendra having an alternative family (after he married Hema Malini in 1980 and they had two daughters, Esha and Ahana), the actor feels blessed by the fact that he could balance both his households and keep them happy and grounded.

And in 2011, when Esha's re-launch was planned by her mother, Dharmendra put in his bit with an important cameo, playing Esha's father and Hema Malini's husband, in the film, *Tell Me O Kkhuda*—also produced and directed by Hema Malini. 'Dharam saab was very ill at that time, but he did everything to ensure that his work in the film was completed,' recalled co-star Rishi Kapoor. He further said, 'It reminded me of how my grandfather (the late Prithviraj Kapoor) had done everything he could when doing my brother's debut film *Kal Aaj Aur Kal*.'

Among the multiple films Dharmendra and Hema have done together, there was *Dream Girl*, his then girlfriend and future wife's home production, officially produced by Jaya Chakravarthy, Hema Malini's mother, and I.K. Bahl, her secretary. Chakravarthy also produced *Swami* the same year, in which Dharam-Hema lent their commercial clout in cameos, and which incidentally did better business than *Dream Girl*.

In the early 1980s, R. Renuka, the actress' aunt, produced *Do Dishayen*, which starred Hema Malini in a double role opposite Dharmendra, but unfortunately the film bombed. Of course, the hit pair also did Dharam's home productions, *Pratiggya* and *Dillagi*. And they were again cast in cameos when Ajit Singh produced, co-wrote and co-directed *Meherbaani*.

How It All Began

The Dharmendra-Hema Malini love story took off with their first few films. When *Sharafat, Tum Haseen Main Jawan* and *Naya Zamana* were consecutive blockbusters within twelve calendar months, it was the birth of not just a hot reel pair but a real pair of lovebirds, although Hema, initially, only liked him and was not in love with him as she knew he was married. Dharmendra, however, fell madly in love.

But their first meeting had been years before that. 'I had been invited to the premiere of K.A. Abbas' film *Aasmaan Mahal*,' Hema smiled at the memory. 'I had signed my first film *Sapnon Ka Saudagar* and word had spread. I had gone with my mommy. Shashi Kapoor and Dharamji were standing together, and when they saw me, they exchanged comments in Punjabi—"*Kudi vaddi changi hai!*"—that I was a nice-looking girl!'

She was introduced to them as Raj Kapoor's 'Dream Girl' (a term devised by publicist Bunny Reuben), and while she recalled them both as handsome and sweet and exchanged polite greetings, she regrets, even today, that the photographs taken of them together and printed in *Screen* have never come into her possession.

'I remember that he was always very loving, soft-spoken and

affectionate. I was working with so many heroes, but looked forward to working with Dharamji. And the way he would hold my hand was so tender and affectionate,' recollected Hema Malini. 'Slowly, he became a little more persistent, but I never bothered—initially.'

By 1975, with both of them shooting together for so many films and all releases proving to be hits and even superhits, Dharmendra was besotted with his lady-love. He would, for their scenes together, keep doing retakes and had taken the light boys into confidence! He had a code for them: If he touched his nose, it would mean he wanted a retake; when he pulled his ear, it would mean that the shot was okay and they need not pretend that one more take was needed!

Obviously the light boys had to mess up by some technical means (as they controlled the trolleys and reflectors) and would get a tip of a princely hundred rupees—per gaffe! On good days, recalls Hema in her biography, the retakes would make them richer by a few thousand rupees.[1]

Dharmendra ensured that the dubbing for his film *Dost* was done in Bangalore, and a *Dharam-Veer* set also erected there, as *Sholay* was being shot near the city. The Sippys, G.P. and son Ramesh, had no choice but to play cupid. Dharmendra would find excuses to come to the shoots with Hema, even when he was not needed, and would reportedly beseech the younger Sippy to tell her only good things about him. Putul Guha also recalled Dharmendra complaining to his father, director Dulal Guha, about how Hema would pay little heed to his romantic overtures. 'They were cast in two films my father was making then—*Dost* as well as in Dharamji's home production *Pratiggya*,' he stated.

By the time they were shooting for *Charas*, that too in far-off Malta, Hema's father, who otherwise got along extraordinarily well

---

[1]Mukherjee, Ram Kamal, *Hema Malini: Beyond the Dream Girl*, HarperCollins, 2017.

with Dharmendra, insisted on accompanying them to keep them
away from each other when not shooting. In her biography, Hema
laughingly recollects how Dharmendra would manage to sit in-
between them in cars or buses on some pretext or the other.

A Love Story Begins

A true love story begins when reciprocation commences. The
number of films they were doing together kept increasing. And
with time, the actress began to feel differently. After all, she had
envisioned her future husband to be someone just like Dharmendra,
only, unmarried!

Hema Malini told me, 'As time passed, it became more and more
impossible to describe what I felt for him, or better still, define the
relationship. I looked forward to working with him. To be honest,
I never thought of marrying him. My only argument is that I didn't
fall in love consciously. It was destiny and my fortune.'

There was this time when Hema was irritated at her parents'
obsession with finding a suitable boy, for which they were already
looking at not just businessmen and doctors but even co-stars! (The
Jeetendra chapter happened then). When this pressure increased
because of the disapproval towards their growing relationship, she
says, 'I told them, "Find somebody, fine!" But I think now that if
they had found someone, I would have probably turned him down!'

Dharmendra was persistent, and finally Hema said, 'Okay!
Okay!' She knew her parents would not like it ('No parent would!')
but it seemed so right, that it was difficult to decide anything else.
One day, she called him and said, 'Marry me, now.'

In her recently released biography, Hema Malini tells it all. 'The
truth was that I didn't know what I wanted. I knew that I was attracted
to him, but the relationship had no future. In the beginning, we were
just good friends. I enjoyed his company. We were paired opposite

each other in so many films...there came a time when we were shooting together not just for days or weeks but for months. Soon, it became a habit to be with each other all the time.'

The Secret Wedding

Dharmendra and Hema Malini have always denied the allegation that they had converted to Islam to get married, and have reiterated that it was a political ploy against the two as Members of Parliament in the Bharatiya Janata Party. As for the actual wedding, it was an Iyengar affair, and became the reason for the biggest scoop of the 1980s. And we got the details, so to speak, straight from the horse's mouth.

Bharathi S. Pradhan was the one who got hold of this gigascoop— through pure luck. Her colleague Jayanthi from *Star & Style*, an Iyengar herself like Hema, was visited in Mumbai by their family vadhyar (priest), and he casually mentioned that he had come to Mumbai just a week earlier for conducting the wedding ceremony of Dharmendra and Hema Malini.

Jayanthi confided in Pradhan one momentous Monday morning. Pradhan, as luck would have it, was going to Madras (as Chennai was then called) to cover the shoot of a Jeetendra film. 'It was pure coincidence!' she recalls. 'There was not even a whisper of any such news! My initial reaction was scepticism, as Dharam was already married, but after thinking it over, I decided to find out for myself.'

Pradhan went armed with the name of the vadhyar and the temple to which he was affiliated. Though sharing a room with a rival magazine's scribe, she took Gopal Pandey, the PRO who had taken the media contingent there, into confidence. Early next morning, Pradhan and Pandey took a rickshaw to the temple's location. 'You can imagine the distance when, in those days, the fare was ₹60,' smiled Pradhan. Pandey stayed at a short distance with the tape recorder on, while Pradhan, as she could speak Tamil, connected with the priest.

The man requested them to meet the same evening to an address closer to the main city, and there he told Pradhan *everything*. 'I got the date, time, venue (Hema's brother's residence!), how the wedding rites were conducted, who attended (from Dharam's side, it was only his father) and what they were all wearing. Clearly, with Dharam wearing a veshti (a South Indian garment), the ceremony was conducted in the Iyengar tradition,' recalled Pradhan. The day of the wedding was 2 May 1980.

It was crystal clear that the priest had no inkling that he was giving out a scoop. He had never been sworn to secrecy because Hema's family had not, in their wildest imaginations, thought anyone from the media could reach him.

When Pradhan broke the news, complete with a 'Stop Press' for that *Star & Style* issue, with a four-page center-spread and two lines added on the cover, there was practically an earthquake in filmland. 'Even that was an understatement!' smiled Pradhan. 'The issue was even discussed in [the] Parliament!'

'Before that, I had also rung up Jayaji, Hema's mother, who confirmed all the details, and admitted that she was upset because Dharmendra was closer to her age than Hema's,' Pradhan went on. The actress herself was livid, glared at Pradhan when they next met at a studio, and walked off. She even gave an interview to one of the pulp film magazines that existed then, denying each and every word of the story, but some months later, when she was pregnant, she herself gave all the details Pradhan had mentioned to *Filmfare*!

The magazine added that Dharmendra gave Hema two diamond rings, while his father gave her a saree. Hema gave Dharmendra a ring and so did her mother. Hema even said, 'I had mentally married him a long time ago, and the ceremony was just to please our families!'

Dharmendra also gave her an Iyengar mangalsutra (the symbol of marriage).

But how did Dharmendra react to Pradhan's scoop?

'I met him a long time after!' she answered. And the true sport that he is, the actor's prime reaction was incredulousness and admiration for her intrepidity! Though embarrassed, he never pulled Pradhan up, but just said, 'I cannot believe you actually went to Madras. What a story!' And this wonderment was repeated in quite a few encounters with Pradhan since, with the actor exclaiming each time, 'How did you get that story?'

A delightful footnote of sorts to this love story was added by Rishi Kapoor. 'Those were the days when there was no mobiles, no social media, nothing!' remembered Rishi Kapoor, who, with his newlywed wife Neetu, was staying for a while in Bangalore's Ashok Hotel when they heard the buzz about Dharmendra's marriage. 'We were to both shoot for *Kaatilon Ke Kaatil*. When someone told me the news on the phone, I told him, "Don't be silly. He is a married man!" There was a rooftop restaurant in the hotel and Neetu and I were the only guests there that same night. And we saw Dharmendra and Hema Malini walk in.'

Kapoor added, 'We formed a foursome on the table. Neetu was pregnant, and Dharmendra looked at my wife and gestured to Hema, as if to say, "*Ab yeh bhi hona hai apna* (now this will be our situation too)."'

The two couples then took to the dance floor together. 'It was very cute watching both of them together, and Dharam saab was also embarrassed and blushed as he told us that they had indeed got married!' smiled Kapoor.

Settling Down

Hema Malini, in a joint television interview given along with her daughters Esha and Ahana, said, 'I never competed with the other family. When in love, you give, and only give, you do not demand. Dharam was already married. How could I torture a person I loved?'

Dharmendra, for years, would share a meal with Hema and, later, their daughters Esha and Ahana. If, rarely, he would sleep in that house at night, they would be concerned that he was unwell! He was always there for his daughters and Hema, and never interfered in her personal or professional life. And the children never minded when they came to know the truth about their parents at different ages and stages. As Esha says in the book, 'Had my mother married an Iyengar, she would have been just a housewife today.'

There were a few things Dharmendra insisted on, though. Both Esha and Ahana were to wear salwar-kameez, and jeans were forbidden, as were shorts or sleeveless dresses. He was set about certain things, a classic possessive Punjabi father; but thanks to the independent Hema, he slowly began to evolve.

Dharmendra had never attended any of Hema's classical dance recitals, despite hearing so much about them. After attending one, he told her, 'You look completely different, as if you do not belong to me.' And he did not wish to see any more of her performances on stage!

Initially, he was also against his daughters performing at Hema's dance recitals and would say, '*Bacchon ko mat sikhana* (Don't teach dance to the girls)!' but changed his mind after watching them. As Hema stated, 'It was not his fault that he thought along those lines. The North Indian definition of "naach" usually refers to crass dances. When he saw the sublime and pure nature of what I did, he changed his stance to "Dance, okay; films, NO!" And he would also add, "*Mummy ke jaise karo dance.*"'

When Esha did make her debut as an actress in 2002 with *Koi Mere Dil Se Pooche*, her father did not speak to her for six long months! But slowly, that too changed. 'Not only did he let Esha

Deol come into films, but at one point, even Ahana's screen debut had been planned,' reveals Pradhan. 'Of course, Esha was completely like Hema, who wanted to make it in films, if necessary, without any help or encouragement.'

'The Dharmendra of today is a very different Dharmendra!' observed Pradhan. 'And of course part of the credit also goes to Hema Malini. In 2011, he not only played the key role of Esha's father (and Hema's husband) in Hema's home production *Tell Me O Kkhuda*, but was also sitting in, listening to a story and vetting it when Ahana's on-screen debut (which never happened) was being planned.'

The film in question was to be directed by Shoojit Sircar, of *Vicky Donor* and *Piku* fame. Again, Pradhan was let into this secret, and this time the informant was Esha Deol! Ahana remains reclusive, prone to spend time with husband Vaibhav and son Darien at Dharmendra's farm in Lonavala. Nevertheless, there are film-making ambitions latent within her that can erupt anytime.

Directing Dharmendra!

Hema Malini directed her husband in *Tell Me O Kkhuda* along with daughter Esha Deol, calling him (in her capacity as his director) a 'highly involved actor who gets so much into the skin of the character that it becomes difficult to put cinematic reigns on him.' As she put it, 'I had stalwarts like Rishi Kapoor, Vinod Khanna and Farooq Sheikh in my film, but directing Dharmendra was a challenge for me. Before giving the shot, he used to ask so many questions that I had to prepare myself beforehand. He is an involved actor and sometimes his involvement in the scene was so tremendous that you couldn't even call off the shots,' she said.

In the film, Hema managed to give Dharmendra the look of a Goan don, sporting a black tuxedo, with sideburns and tattoos on his arms. Esha had conceived this look for her father that was way different from his normal appearance.

How the Two Families Got Along

It was not just about Prakash Deol looking for a boy for Esha—there was an easy bond between the two families. Ajit Singh's son, Abhay Deol, has always been a buddy to Esha and Ahana Deol; and Esha has always admired the kind of quirky films he chooses to do.

Abhay introduced himself to Esha in school, saying, 'I am your elder cousin brother, your Ji-chacha's son.' He later similarly introduced himself to Ahana Deol on a Juhu street! He also actively participated in Esha's wedding, is very fond of her husband Bharat, and still talks to her every other day.

Sunny Deol is best described by the sisters to be more like their father, and Hema also shares the same views. They first broke the ice in 1992, when Dimple Kapadia was cast in Hema's maiden film as producer-director, *Dil Aashna Hai*. At one point, she was scared of doing a specific sequence, and sent her good friend Sunny Deol to 'speak to her'. Hema not only reassured him, but they got talking, ending the twelve-year phase of no contact. When Hema Malini met with an accident a few years ago, it was Sunny who first reached her when she was flown to Mumbai, and also supervised her medical treatment.

The festival of Raksha Bandhan has also been a special day for the junior Deols. Hema's biography revealed that the two sisters always tie rakhis to all their brothers. And the forthcoming debut of Karan Deol is also something to which they are looking forward.

It's all (with)in the family.

Chapter Twenty

The Poet Within

Main kahin kavi na ban jaaoon / Tere pyar mein ae kavita

Dharmendra did become a poet, and to tweak the meaning of his 1969 *Pyar Hi Pyar* hit song 'Main Kahin Kavi Na Ban Jaaoon/Tere Pyar Mein Ae Kavita' a bit, it did happen for the love of 'Kavita' (poetry), not Kavita—the heroine's name in that film! The actor always had a yen for poetry and good words, did write some verse occasionally like most of us do, but it required a catalytic circumstance for the hidden poet within him to come out and then flower.

It was in 2007 that the He-Man and eternal charmer of Hindi cinema lay recuperating—for thirty seemingly interminable days—after his knee surgery in the USA, days after the premiere of *Apne* in Los Angeles. 'No one can share your pain, and I was scared of the loneliness, so I began writing,' said the actor, when we spoke about this tryst with poetry and his ability to deliver his deepest feelings though Urdu and Hindi verse.

This brief conversation came about during our first interview at his house. One of my questions pertained to him making his 'debut' as a film lyricist by writing a Punjabi song, 'Kadd Ke Botal', in the Deol home production *Yamla Pagla Deewana* that was then on release, with its music already out.

The song, rendered in the film by Sukhwinder Singh, Rosalie Nicholson and Harshdeep Kaur, was whimsically dismissed by the actor as nothing important, while son Sunny Deol said, 'My father has always been writing poetry. He was inspired by a situation and we all loved what he had written. But Dad is always surprising us!'

Nevertheless, when Dharmendra first revealed this then unknown facet of himself to me, all he told me was, 'I write Urdu poetry and might come out with a compilation in Urdu soon.' He said that he was only expressing his feelings as they arose within him, without any compulsion to write for the sake of writing something.

However, it was director Mahesh Bhatt who shed a deeper and more poignant light on this highly fulfilling hobby and its origins, recalling a flight in which they were seated together. 'It was a meeting decades after we worked together. I was a success, and he was no longer at the top,' said the film-maker. 'He was very happy to see me, but clearly emotionally frail. With complete candour, he told me that normally contemporary people do not duly acknowledge older artistes. He was happy I had acknowledged him.

'He told me about the time he was in that hospital room in America, all alone, and his story really touched me,' Bhatt went on, and quoted Dharmendra almost verbatim:

'"I was there all alone in a room when suddenly I heard this voice. 'Dharam? *Pehchaana mujhe? Nahin? Main teri doosri maa— tanhaai—hoon. Bachpan mein, gaon mein, dopahar mein, aur jab tu struggle kar rahaa tha tab bhi main tere saath thi! Jab tu kaamyab ho gaya, tu mujhe bhool gaya!* (Do you remember me? No? I am your second mother—loneliness! I would be there with you right from your childhood in your village, in the afternoons when no one was around, and even when you were struggling! When you achieved success, you forgot me)!'"

Mused Bhatt, 'I could not believe that these words were coming out of him. We all tend to stereotype human beings, and we knew Dharam as a man of brawn and muscle, that's all. But I realized then that this man was a son of the soil, with a sensitivity that told him that solitude *was* inescapable when a star is past his prime. Dharamji added that he pined for being on the sets, and for the aroma of the evening snacks they serve. Instead now, there was silence, except for the sound of his own breath, he said!'

Bhatt said, 'This man had flowered into a poet. Dharam held my hand throughout the flight, and his brawn and charisma was still intact. His final gem was *"Aaj ki taarikh mein log accha dikhna chahte hain, accha banna nahin chahte* (Today, people want to look good, not become good souls)!"'

The film-maker went on, 'When loneliness and the twilight zone confront such people, they have the grace and courage to face the unpalatable truth. And they evolve into fantastic people. All this moved me so much that I shared it with his son, Sunny.'

And the straight-from-his-heart quality is evident in his works as Dharmendra just rattles off his poetry even though the precious words are documented in his notebooks. To reiterate what his idol Dilip Kumar once said, 'There is one man in the industry who wears no mask. What he says is what he feels. There is only frankness and openness, no guile or deceit. And that is Dharmendra!'

We present here the few gems told to me by this sensitive soul, each one reflecting his innermost thoughts at various stages in his life, with a lot of truisms expressed in a very free and lucid fashion.

Zaati zindagi rahe poshida
Issi mein usski khushnumaai hai
Ho jaati hai nilaam chaurahe pe sar-e-aam jab jab aayi hai
Hum industry mein hain par industry ke nahin hain
Shohrat khalal ho chuki hai mere liye
Dilon mein mohabbat maangi thi

Shohrat to maangi nahin thi
Shohrat mili aur ashohrat khalal ho gayi
Meri taaseer-e-mohabbat mein itna dum hai
Maine phir ibaadat ki
Mujhe shohrat nahin mohabbat chahiye
Mohabbat ki pehli seedhi
Tu nek banda hai mera
Jahaan tak jaa sakta hain neki se mat bhataknaa
Neki tera sabse badaa auzaar hai.

The beauty of one's personal life remains in its privacy,
But over here, it is openly auctioned on the streets,
We are in the industry but do not belong here,
I had asked for the love of the people
Not for the fame that only became an obstacle to receiving love.
Though there was so much power in my own love,
I still prayed and said,
I want love, not fame.
And on the first step towards that love,
He replied, you are a good soul
Do not stray from goodness,
That is your biggest weapon.

Dharmendra also wrote the following lines to describe what he is, and these also show his attitude to life.

Mannaton ki murad duaon ki den malik ki meher ka ek vardaan
hoon main
Mahaan maa ki mamta azeem baap ki shafqat ka azeem-o-shaan
ek ehsaan hoon main
Insaniyat ka poojari chhoto ko laad-pyaar badon ka aadar-
sammaan hoon main
Duniya saari ban jaye ek kunwa

Ekta ki hasraton ka armaan hoon main
Mohabbat hai khuda
Khuda ki mohabbat ka farmaan hoon main
Neki meri shakti hai badi mujhse darti hai
Aisa uttam atamsammaan hoon main
Pyar mohabbat aap ki seenchti hai jazbaat ko mere
Issi liye aaj bhi jawaan hoon main
Khataa agar ho jaaye baksh dena yaaron
Galtiyon ka putla aakhir ek insaan hoon main

I am the blessed boon of so many prayers and vows to the Almighty
A great mother's and a great father's love have conferred the majestic favour of life on me
I am a devotee of humanity, someone who showers love on the young and respects and honors elders
The world should become one family
I desire and yearn for this unity
For love is God
And I am the mandate of God's love
Goodness is my strength
Evil fears me
I am that kind of extraordinary self-respect
Your love nurtures my innermost feelings
And that is why I am young even today
If I err, please forgive me friends,
For at the same time I am an embodiment of mistakes
After all, I am a human being!

And the man, who almost never spoke evil about anyone, beautifully expressed a small but intense thought on the negative power of criticism and harsh words.

Jaayzaa jaayaz ho naajaayaz nahin
Tanqeed tanqeed ho tanz nahin
Soch le kuch kehne se pehle
Ghaav talwar ka bhar jaata hai
Labz ka nahin.

Let my feelings be apt, not unjustified
Let my criticism be criticism, not ridicule
Think a lot before you speak
A wound from a sword heals
But not that which is inflicted by the lips.

And here is Dharmendra on his pet topic of drinking as well as romance.

Pee sharab behisaab
Na rakkha mashooqon ka hisaab
Sambhaalaa, kise nahin girne kise diya
Mujhe mila meri wafaaon ka sawaab
Wafaa karne jaan jaati hai
Wafaa nibhaane mein nasha hai.

I drank and romanced without keeping count
But I supported all, did not let anyone fall,
And I got the rewards for my faithfulness.
Being faithful has an intoxicating satisfaction
Though it is very tough to be faithful.

About when he had starry dreams in his eyes, he wrote:

Naukri karta, cycle pe aata jaata
Phir bhi posters mein apni jhalak dekhta
Raaton ko jaagta anhone khwab dekhta
Subah uth kar aaine se poochta
Main dilip kumar ban sakta hoon kya?

I was doing a job, commuting on a cycle
Even then, I would see myself on the film posters in the streets
I would stay awake at night
Or see strange dreams
And on waking up, I would ask the mirror,
Can I become like Dilip Kumar?

And probably the nearest that Dharmendra ever came to praising himself was through this reflection of how the camera perceived this man of the soil and made him what he is. Here is immodesty, Dharmendra-style!

Hasrat-e-qaid khud mein har dilkashi kar loon
Main camera hoon bechain rehta hoon
Hasrat-e-qaid hai ek din dilkashi meri
Le gayi kheton mein ek din deewangee meri
Gumsum apne kaam mein mazdoor se ek naujawan ne
Jaane kya kar diya
Main ruk gaya dekhta rahaa
Aisa dilkash bhi na tha
Par kuch tha jisse main ruk gaya tha
Kadakti dhoop mein
Tambe si rangat thi
Libaaz khaki
Khoob tha usspe jach rahaa
Dekhte hi mujhe muskura diya
Kya dekh rahe ho
Apnapan tha baaton mein usski
Anhone sapne the aankhon mein usski
Aisa lagaa koi apna hai
Main usska sapna hoon
Woh mera sapna hai
Jaane kab qaidi ho gaya

Milte hi mere iss naye qaidi ko
Har koi poochta kaun hai yeh kya naam hai isska
Ek din yeh kuch banega
Camera kehta hai dharam naam hai mere iss qaidi ka
Mamooli mechanic hai tubewell company ka.

I desire to capture everything beautiful within me
I am the camera, a crazy soul that once went into the fields
And I stopped when I saw a labourer, busy at work,
I kept looking at him, there was something special in him
Though he was not all that attractive
He was tanned in that strong sun
Dressed in khaki that suited him so well,
When he saw me, he smiled and asked, 'What are you looking at?'
There was intimacy in his talk
And strange dreams in his eyes
I felt he was someone close
I was his dream and he was mine
I cannot say when he became my prisoner
Yet everyone who met my new captive asked
Who is he? What is his name?
He will become someone someday
And I, the camera, replied that his name is Dharam,
And he is a mere mechanic in a tubewell company.

Here are some more brief reflections on life by this unique legend.
To demonstrate the difference between taarif (praise) and qadar (value), he writes:

Hoti hai taarif ahmiyat ki
Insaniyat ki magar qadar hoti hai

Important people are praised
But good human beings are valued.

Main seena taan ke chala
Par garda mein kabhi akad nahin aayi
Aur pair hamesha dharti pe teeke rahe.

I walked with my chest out
But I never let pride engulf me
And my feet were always planted firmly on the ground.

Mohabbat aap ki naa deti roshni agar mere naam ko,
Kaise banta dharam main aap ka
Pahunchta kaise iss muquaam ko

If your love had not illuminated my name
How could I have become your Dharam, and reached where
I have?

Parvaah karke dekh
Pyar hi aa jaayega
Dushmun bhi banke
Yaar aa jaayega!

Care deeply for someone
You will only get love in return
And you will see your foe
Come to you as a friend!

Chal rahe ho to bataane ki zaroorat nahin
Ruk gaye jis din poochta koi nahin
Jaante hain jo dhol woh peet-te nahin
Chalte rehte hain bas dekhte nahin.

If you are walking on, there is no need to tell anyone
The day you stop, no one will care.
So, those who keep walking do not make a noise about it
But keep moving, heeding no one.

Koi mooskurata hai main haath badhaata hoon
Koi haath badhaata hai main seene se lagaa leta hoon.

If someone smiles, I extend my hand
But if someone extends his hand, I embrace him.

Chapter Twenty-One

Straight from the Heart: Dharmendra's Friends Speak

Yeh dosti hum nahin todenge…

Shatrughan Sinha

Along with Danny Denzongpa, Shatrughan Sinha is Dharmendra's closest friend in the industry. The number of films they have done together are legion, from 1969 to the 1990s. Sinha, who turned down a cameo in a film some years ago that was starring his daughter Sonakshi Sinha as he did not want a gimmicky casting with his star daughter, was seen for the first time with her in a song cameo in a Dharmendra home production, Yamla Pagla Deewana Phir Se. Clearly, rules can be broken to oblige friends.

'There was a small scene in *Pyar Hi Pyar*, which was our first film together. Pran blackmails Vyjayanthimala and is in turn blackmailed by me. The scene required me to be tied and gagged. When the shot was over, the crew forgot to untie me, and Dharmendra noticed it. He asked them why they had left this baccha (kid) tied up!

'Who was I then? I had come from nowhere, and he was a big star. I had only a few minutes of role in the film. He certainly could not have guessed that I would become big too, but that did not matter either. The point that he had noticed someone like me was very touching.

'But this was not at all my first meeting with Dharmendra. He had come with Deven Verma, the character actor, to Pune's Film & Television Institute, to address us as students. I had watched *Anupama*, and both the hero and the song "Dheere Dheere Machal" were haunting me! He was so full of charm and magic, his hair combed back. I was a small lad from Patna, and when the time came to speak to him, I childishly asked a classic small-town question to him in Hindi, "*Aap baalon mein kaun sa tel lagaate hain* (Which oil do you apply on your hair)?" And he replied, "*Main baalon mein tel nahin lagaata* (I do not put oil on my hair)!"

'Knowing that many in the industry went to [watch] the races in Mumbai, I got in a second question in Hindi again, "Do you visit the Race Course on Sundays?" And his answer was a simple "Nahin (No)!" I felt very foolish indeed! But for me, it was love at first sight!

'I never dreamt I would become so famous and would get to work with Dharmendra in so many films. I am a great fan of Dharmendra, the late Vinod Khanna and Kabir Bedi. They would praise my voice, but I would be inspired by them, and especially with Dharam's personality in totality. His carefree and simple demeanour was so infectious that I had to pinch myself to realize that I was actually sitting next to him.

'Dharmendra would pick me up on the way to the Alibag (a small town near Mumbai) shoot for *Blackmail*, in which I was the villain. We would chat about everything. When we stayed back there, we had evening walks together. His love for me was so much that if he had any reservations about my negative character getting a sympathetic death in the film, he never expressed it.

'Dharmendra always treats me like a younger brother. People did try to create a distance between us, but he resisted. People tried to provoke him by saying that I had stolen the thunder from him in *Dost*. But all that Dharmendra said was, "He is like my younger brother." Dharmendra has love and admiration for me, but to me he is the biggest star.

'He is a man of tremendous dignity, who never interferes in the script. Though junior to him, there was a time when I almost took the same price as him! He knew this, but it never mattered to him. Manipulation of any sort was unknown to his nature. The fan in turn—me!—would tease him no end and play so many pranks on him. He loved my company and my sense of humour. Like I would say something under my breath during my death scene in *Blackmail* and he would laugh.

'The only sore spot in our relationship came when Dharmendra was the only prominent actor who never visited me during my health crisis some years ago. This time, people tried to instigate me. But then I came to know that he was upset over some personal issues and had planned to go to Canada. In the final analysis, what did it matter?

'The number of films we have done together are many, though sadly, very few have succeeded after *Dost*, like *Loha*, *Aag Hi Aag* and *Insaniyat Ke Dushman*, all in 1987. And Dharam never even knew that his brother Ajit Singh, who has always predicted a great future for me, had signed me for a small role in his home production *Dillagi*. But we loved working together.'

Danny Denzongpa

Dharmendra regards Danny Denzongpa as one of his two closest friends in the industry, as mentioned earlier. Meeting Denzongpa was not easy as he barely lives in Mumbai and is inaccessible in the interiors of Sikkim where he is away from Wi-Fi and the phone. But when we finally met,

*he came up with a really sweet picture of the legend of whom he first
became a fan, then a junior colleague and finally a close friend.*

'Dharam is like an elder brother who is very friendly with me. In
return, I could, however, be very frank with him and never thought
of him as my senior!

'My earliest recollection of Dharmendra, while in boarding
school in Nainital, where we boys smuggled in and read film books,
was through the film magazine *Picturpost*. This was a pocket-sized
monthly Hindi film magazine published in the South, in which I
first saw pictures of this man who talked then of being a fan of
Dilip Kumar. He looked handsome, like Hollywood's Gary Cooper
and like John F. Kennedy, and tough, like actors in Western movies.

'At another outing, I watched a song from *Shola Aur Shabnam*,
and instantly liked him. I then made it a point to watch all his films,
and loved him especially in *Bandini, Anpadh, Devar* and *Anupama*.
During college, which was in Darjeeling, I heard the news that his
Aaye Din Bahaar Ke was being shot there. I rushed down to the
location, which needed walking for 4 kms from the point where I
had to alight from the local bus.

'That is when I saw Dharam in person for the first time. He
was just as I had imagined him, robust and looking very fit. And
we shook hands.

'After coming out of the Film & Television Institute of India
as a trained actor, our first encounter was at the premiere of B.R.
Chopra's *Dhund* (1973), and he came up to me, praised my work
and encouraged me. I wished that someone one day would cast me
with this He-Man.

'A near-chance came when *Sholay* was offered to me, but I
had to turn it down as my dates were committed to Feroz Khan's
Dharmatma. Dharmendra was present in producer G.P. Sippy's office
when I had been called.

'Later, of course, we got to do, coincidentally, the *Dhund* film-maker B.R. Chopra's *The Burning Train* and also *Chunaoti, Jagir* (*Teen Murti* in Bengali), *Aag Hi Aag, Zalzala* and *Khule-Aam*. With the first film, we became fast friends.

'Dharam was shooting in Shimla for some film, and drove down to Delhi, where we were staying at the Maurya Sheraton hotel and shooting for *The Burning Train* near the railway station where they make the railway bogies. He reached in the evening, and when we hugged, I found him burning with fever. I told director Ravi Chopra, who was insisting on shooting, that we must cancel the shoot as Dharam was sick.

'Finally, he had to be put on a drip and was ill for five days, because it was pneumonia, with his Mumbai physician, Dr Kanubhai Shah, needing to be called. As the location was not available after his recovery, we ended up shooting our sequence later at the Qutab Minar.

'A memory I cherish is of shooting in the Bandipur forests for *Khule-Aam*. Like me, Dharam loves nature—the flowers and forests are very dear to him. As there was no gym available there, all of us—Puneet Issar, Chunky Pandey, Neelam and I—would go jogging on the rough jungle trail every evening. We were crossing by Dharam's cottage when he enquired where we were off to, and then said, "*Main bhi aata hoon* (I am coming too)!"

'We were a shade apprehensive as he was so senior—about fifty-five, I think—but he was no less than any of us. He would even do crunches and push-ups after the jogging, so I asked him how he managed all that! He then spoke about the akhada (wrestling ring) where he would wrestle in his village, and the time he would drill huge stones on his first job.

'Dharam trusts me a lot. During a shoot, Bobby Deol, his sisters and mother had come along, and the three children would be studying in his room. I suggested that since it was like a vacation for them, they should be told to swim in the pool to relax rather than be cooped up all the time like that, and he listened to me.

'During *Zalzala*, Bobby was in college, a very shy kid who had come with his mother on location. The unit was shooting in Pahalgam, and my then girlfriend, Kimi Katkar, was also in the cast of the film. When I learnt that the discotheque was not functioning, I lent them my own music set and Kimi, her friends and Bobby all danced away, after Bobby nervously told his father that he wished to dance. It was I who told Dharam, "If he does not dance now, he will dance like you do on screen! Plus, it will help him open up, as he is too shy." Again, he agreed to my suggestion.

'During the making of *Chunaoti* in Nashik, while taking a walk, I had chased a river to a dam that overflowed and found a pond, hidden from view, where one could swim and even a small picnic could be held. It was Dharmendra's birthday soon and we went to that spot to swim and have champagne in the moonlit night!

'But the gesture I cannot forget is what happened during the shoot of *Aag Hi Aag*. We were shooting at Bhalla Bungalow in Pali Hill in Mumbai. For some reason, there were no vanity vans, and since there were only two make-up rooms, Dharam and I had to share one, while the ladies got the other. Dharam was a shade drunk, and I was tense because I had to leave for a twenty-five-day outdoor [shoot] the next morning. I told him about my predicament, and he was galvanized so much that we completed our work, despite his inebriation!

'Another memory is of a difficult Bengali song we had to enact in the bilingual *Teen Murti*, whose Hindi version was called *Jagir*. I was driving the car and Dharam and Mithun Chakraborty had to sing, and to ensure that he got the lip-synch right, Dharam had managed to get the Bengali lyrics written on big cardboard placards in Urdu, placed so he could see them inside the car!

'For me, Dharmendra remains a dedicated, gifted actor with

his own approach to acting. He never performed mechanically, and was melodramatic only if the script was written that way. I was glad when he refused the Best Supporting Actor Award they wanted to give him for *Ayee Milan Ki Bela*. He has something special in him, which is why he has survived in films for so long.'

Irshad Kamil

Irshad Kamil, one of today's topmost lyricists commanding the highest price per song, hails from Punjab. Also a poet, author and littérateur, Kamil speaks with a lot of affection for a man with whom he has been barely associated professionally. And, like Anil Sharma, he professes to have a karmic connection with the legend.

'I hail from Maler Kotla, a hamlet in Punjab that is close to Dharamji's village of Sahnewal. My childhood has been spent with Dharamji being referred to as a cult figure, about whom everyone would talk.

'I was shown the mohalla (area) and the house where Dharamji resided when he worked with the Punjab State Tubal Corporation, a government organization, as a drill mechanic. The photography shop, John & Sons, where he had a friend, was still there [see Chapter 2].

'There were stories abounding about him, like some dant-katha (folklore)! We were shown the two movie halls, Moti and Kamal talkies, where he would come almost every evening to watch movies. One of my class fellows there spoke about Dharamji's old friend Mohammed Din Bhatti, who kept visiting and staying with him later in Mumbai, and of the fact that Dharamji had paid for his Haj pilgrimage. He had even given him a small role in *Pratiggya*—of a waiter in a dhaaba scene!

'In the entire state of Punjab, Dharamji remains, even today, an iconic figure. Not many know that *Socha Na Tha*, which Dharamji produced along with Sunny Deol, was the first film I signed, not knowing at all that he was to be my first producer! It is another matter that *Chameli* released a year earlier [Kamil also wrote some lyrics for it].

'I met composer Sandesh Shandilya at a recording and he liked the Punjabi touch in my songs, so he approached me when Imtiaz Ali had signed him for *Socha Na Tha*. While signing the film I got to know that Dharamji was the man behind this launch film of his nephew, Abhay Deol!

'It was at the screening of the first cut of the film, for the unit, that I actually saw and met Dharamji, at Mumbai's Ambience Studio. I reached slightly late, the show had begun, and at the end of the show, I saw Dharamji in conversation with Imtiaz, praising him for making a beautiful movie, while I stood at a distance.

'Then Dharamji happened to ask Imtiaz who had written the songs, as he had liked the lyrics, and why the lyricist had not been called. That was when Imtiaz brought him to me. He asked me how I had managed the Punjabi flavour, and I said that I hailed from Punjab, from a village called Maler Kotla. He was so thrilled that he hugged me tightly for a long time, as if he was embracing his village! He said, "*Aisi khushboo wahaan ki mitti se hi aa sakti hai* (Such a fragrance in the songs can come only from that soil)!"

'It was five years later that he called me again, and said, "*Maine suna hai tu bahut bada geetkaar ho gaya hai* (I have heard you have become a big-shot lyricist)!" He wanted a song from me, again with Sandesh, for *Yamla Pagla Deewana*. Sunny would explain the situation, he told me.

'The song was "Sau Baar Yeh Kahe Dil", and after it was recorded, I was called to his office and asked how much my remuneration would be. But working for him was like offering flowers to a deity. I can never take money for anything I do for him.

'Today, I am aware that Dharamji also writes shaayari. His thoughts and language are amazingly good. Dharamji is an icon in every sense.'

Jeetendra

The flashpoint came when it was announced in the mid-1970s that Jeetendra was to marry Hema Malini, with the blessings of their elders. Dharmendra had then rushed to Chennai to stop the wedding. Despite that episode, Jeetendra and Hema Malini continued to work together well into the 1980s; and Dharmendra and Jeetendra shared an easy and personal relationship.

'The first time I actually saw Dharmendra was when I was in college and had gone to watch a movie at Mumbai's Regal cinema. I was just sixteen or seventeen, and we friends all started shouting, "Dharminder! Dharminder!" on seeing him!

'The first film in which we worked together, *The Gold Medal*, never had a proper release, and was not well-made either. He only had a guest appearance in it. We finally worked together in Manmohan Desai's *Dharam-Veer*, that too because Shashi Kapoor, who was to do my role earlier, somehow backed out. Later, I did most of my multi-starrer films with Dharmendra rather than anyone else.

'He never carried any baggage of superstardom, of being senior, of being *someone*. The best part was that it was easy working with him. He was very honest, childlike and if he liked you even a bit, he would go all the way to make you happy, even at the cost of his [own] happiness.

'You all know about the marriage incident. But later, not even one per cent of any unpleasantness remained between Hema, Dharam, my wife Shobha and me. In fact, Shobha and he are like sister and brother. Shobha and I got married during the making of *Dharam-Veer*. And Hema and I did so many films together later as well, some of which also starred Dharam opposite her, but most had nothing to do with him.

'Dharam is a lovable and sensitive soul, but he had his clear limits. We were shooting in Srinagar once for different films, and were drinking together one evening when a lot of fans came to watch him from a distance, as always. If they came close, he would be very cordial to them. But one day, a few took liberties and got personal and he became very angry and told them all to get out! He could never tolerate misbehaviour.'

Salim Khan

Salim Khan and Dharmendra came to Mumbai at around the same period, and in that sense were fellow strugglers, as Khan too wanted to be an actor. However, destiny decreed that he became the biggest name in screenwriting as the senior half of Salim-Javed, and later wrote several blockbusters with the actor. In the 1990s, Khan also wrote a solo film for Dharmendra, Mast Kalandar, *which unfortunately flopped.*

'Dharmendra has been continuously working since 1960—a journey of an incredible fifty-eight years, and for almost thirty years of this phase, he was among the top names. He is a harmless person, *aur maal ke andar durability hai* (He was made of durable stuff)! I first knew him as a soft-spoken struggler in my own struggling times.

'He emerged as a versatile actor. For many years, including at our peak, he was the only big action hero. But I always thought that he was best at comedy, whose elements we ensured in almost all the films we wrote with him (*Seeta Aur Geeta, Sholay, Chacha Bhatija*). It was only in *Yaadon Ki Baaraat* that he was completely serious and intense. He had the ability and capability to maintain himself, and his pictures did well.

'Javed and I were very comfortable with this quiet man and had a very good working relationship with him. He never created problems with other stars. And he was the biggest and highest-paid star of *Sholay*.

'Before doing *Yaadon Ki Baaraat*, we had called him up and asked [him] why he was not accepting *Zanjeer*, because we had written it with Dharmendra in mind. But he turned it down because he had some problems during the making of his home production *Samadhi*. So, after Dilip Kumar, Dev Anand and Raaj Kumar all turned down the role, Dharmendra unintentionally created a competitor while losing that hit film—Amitabh Bachchan!'

Subhash Ghai

Ghai trained as an actor with the Film & Television Institute of India (FTII), Pune, but went on to be one of the most successful writers and film-makers. His only directorial venture with Dharmendra, Krodhi, was his first flop, and Subhash Ghai felt miserable about it. But he remains an admirer of the actor and the man, with whom he has also produced a hit Punjabi film, Double Di Trouble, in 2014.

'I was a student at the FTII when I happened to watch *Shola Aur Shabnam*. I remember discussing with other students my view that here was an actor who does not seem to act. His simplicity, clothes, walk and his smile work a lot.

'In that era of Shammi Kapoor and Rajendra Kumar, we would have debates on whether Dharmendra would become a star or not. I personally was of the opinion that would be loved by the audience as the boy-next-door. One fellow student said that he would have no future. Another stated that he would be good only for art cinema!

'He is different, I had thought. Such people, over the decades, make it, especially when initially helped by strong lyrics, like Dharam's '*Raakh ki dher mein shola hai na chingari hai* (There are neither embers nor sparks in this mound of ash)' in his song 'Jaane Kya Dhoondti Rehti Hai' from *Shola Aur Shabnam*. Or much later, Jackie Shroff in my film *Hero* sings *Apni Taqdeer To Zero Hai* ('My future is zero'), when the heroine says, *Tu mera hero hai* ('You are my hero'). Such lyrics always help new stars by creating empathy for their images. Mysteriously, these songs thus seem to create identification with the masses for such new actors!

'Dharam had much more going for him. He could be a typical Bengali boy, like in some of his early movies. The roles he got and the writer-directors decided his future. His smile was innocent, attractive, like a well-built boy. He was a stud, therefore, with innocent looks. So he appealed to all—girls, mothers and even seductresses, besides to boys and men as a role-model!

'Today, his success story is a big inspiration. Yet he remains a simple, not political soul. And I call him an unparalleled handsome star who does not know how to sing and dance—if you notice, he is always controlling his left hand with his right in his song sequences!'

Randhir Kapoor

Randhir Kapoor, who co-starred with Dharmendra in just one film, is also grateful to the senior actor—with whom he has had several joyous moments on sets and off—for the way he accommodated his father when they did a film together, and for how he always raves about his older colleague.

'Dharam Uncle is a delight, and working with him in that lovely movie *Chacha Bhatija* was sheer joy! He is a very, very good co-star and a friendly, wonderful and terrific human being. I was so much junior to him, and he was a superstar, yet he would often tell director Manmohan Desai, *"Itne lines mere ko mat do* (Don't give me so many lines to speak)! Let Daboo (me) speak them, I will stand at the back." Having worked by then with quite a few senior actors, this was the first time I was hearing somebody say this.

'And the way he treated elders was something to see! The way he interacted with Dada Moni (Ashok Kumar), Dilip (Kumar) saab, Dev (Anand) saab and my father (Raj Kapoor), the respect he showed them was extraordinary. He went out of his way to accommodate my father in every way during *Mera Naam Joker*, when he was busy and at the top. On the other hand, he also had a nice word for everybody, even if he was a junior artiste.

'There was so much to learn from Dharam Uncle, his humility, his approach to work, his sincerity—I would notice that he was very involved in his scenes, and that his dedication to his work, his profession was immense. He would be very jovial on sets, but totally serious when it came to work.

'I would also call him "chacha" (uncle) in real life. We would have great fun partying as he and I were both fond of drinking as well as eating good things! We have not met in a while, but we do keep exchanging messages every other day.

'A bad word about him is just not possible, and everybody in the industry has the same opinion about Dharam Uncle—what a guy he is! Frankly, if I did hear something bad, I would not believe it!'

Raj N. Sippy

Sippy directed Dharmendra in six films—Qayamat, Baazi, Sitamgar, Loha, Shehzaade and the unreleased Mukka, one of which was Dharmendra's home production, and he was also the executive producer in two more—Guddi and Chupke Chupke, both co-produced by his father N.C. Sippy. But more than that, they remain friends with high regards and respect for each other.

'Let me share an amusing, lesser-known fact about Dharam—he *hated* putting on beards and moustaches! I made him do it in *Shehzaade*, and he did it only out of love for me, his biba, which means younger brother.

'I was one of the very few allowed to go up to his sitting room on the terrace, and we had some lovely evenings there. He had this habit with me that I had to tell him the essence of a story in two minutes, or he would not do the film! But I always managed. There was also no question of turning down his home production when he approached me through his brother Ajit Singh to make *Sitamgar*. The film was delayed for seven years and ruined by Parveen Babi's problems then, but Dharam never interfered even a bit, though the film starred Rishi Kapoor and Poonam Dhillon as well, and it was his money at stake.

'What Dharam is within is best described by what I myself witnessed one day at his bungalow. He came to know that a Sardar had come to his gate, threatening to kidnap Bobby Deol if they did not pay up a specific amount of money. Dharam went out to see the man and gave him two tight slaps, and the man went reeling across the road and started bleeding! And Dharam himself took him to a doctor, telling him, "Next time you need any money, just tell me. I will give it to you! Why do you have to threaten us?" Can you believe that?

'On the humorous side, I would use Hema Maliniji's name, with whom I had also worked separately in *Satte Pe Satta*, as a trump card whenever he tried to drink on my [film] sets, with his man Bhanwar bringing the booze secretly. I would say, "Let me phone Hemaji!" and he would stop me and apologize.

'To say that Dharam is a good human being sums it all. If anyone in the unit had a problem, he would become a part of it and lend his helping hand, come spotboy or lightman.'

An Icon Forever

Pal pal dil ke paas tum rehti ho…

The Dharmendra saga continues—full, as it always has been, of smiles, love and everything positive. Most of his time now is spent in the idyllic surroundings of his farm in Khandala—that is where his simple soul is happiest, close to the nature that he has always been fond of, rather than living in the '*banaavati duniya* (fake world)', as he once termed the film industry. He would rather be around birds and animals—celebrating even the birth of a baby calf on Twitter!

Dharmendra is an early riser—a 'morning person' as he calls himself. He wakes up early and does pranayam and yoga. He makes it a point to take care of his health and fitness. 'I eat less, drink more milk, and what invigorates me is goodness of the soul,' he says. As perhaps the best-looking leading man ever in Indian cinema, he says, quite simply, 'It is human nature to [want to] look best and fit at any age.' Yes, his love affair with the camera also continues in full spate.

Life continues to evolve from the time he would get 2 annas (4 annas meant 25 paise) to celebrate his birthday. Every year on his birthday, a sea of fans throng to his residence from across the length and breadth of the country, and are treated to food packets, cakes and soft drinks. Inside his house, Dharmendra is busy hugging fans and visitors, shaking hands continuously, and as a close friend reveals, 'Unwrapping gifts like a child does!'

Yamla Pagla Deewana Phir Se, the third film in the Deols' pet franchise, has now come and gone, uncelebrated, disappointing his fans so much that it did not fare well even in Punjab, UK and Canada—all, traditionally, Dharmendra strongholds!

Does it mean that Dharmendra's draw is over, or is a thing of the past? *Absolutely not!* It simply means, as it did pre-2007, that his fans want him to stay relevant. After all, the film was outdated even with reference to his son Bobby Deol's era!

It is axiomatic that fans can *never* be angry with their iconic Jat favourite, though the only way they can express their acute disappointment is, obviously, by refusing to buy tickets for his movie. The Deols are an emotional lot. Dharmendra was bent on giving fans another version of *YPD* after the second one bombed, and emotional as always, he went in for a script and project he should have steered clear of in today's times.

And the contemporary and breezy entertainer that released alongside, *Stree*, which devoured the Deol-a-thon, could be a classic yardstick of what kind of cinema Deol fans might be craving for from Dharmendra in particular and the Deols in general. The Deols would do well to reflect on a proper comeback again for Dharmendra.

With 92,400 followers on Twitter circa late October 2018, and a blue-tick handle@aapkadharam, it is proof that the actor, who will soon enter his sixtieth year in cinema, is not someone who can be written off yet. Even today, he keeps tweeting about his present and past associates with love and affection. He freely appreciates sportsmen of all cadres, and also posts a lot of humorous content, such as the video he posted from London of him matching steps with a moving digital image of a young girl walking. 'Love is my vitamin!' he once told me. 'I work for love, not fame or money. And fans are my wings!'

Illustrative of his never-say-die spirit is his tweet on 4 September 2018 (*Yamla Pagla Deewana Phir Se* released on 31 August), which said, 'A DEFEAT IS A LESSON TO LEARN, A CHALLENGE TO DARE!!! Enjoying the shoot with an open mouth panther.'

Dharmendra is also looking forward now to their next production, *Pal Pal Dil Ke Paas*, that launches Karan Deol, his grandson, and is being directed by Sunny Deol. Quite recently, he surprised the team by going to their outdoor shoot quietly and watching the proceedings before revealing his presence. 'Karan is very good, but has to learn on his own,' he had told me once.

Having seen it all, Dharmendra just asserts one simple credo of his life that keeps him going: 'Why brood? Rejoice! God has plans!'

All this cheer and optimism always can only come from a person who has seen every shade of life, and taken its buffets and bouquets with equal pragmatism and grounded humility. Dharmendra once said that Salman Khan (who had cameo in his latest film) is a lot like him, and we can't help but completely agree with that. So does Khan, for at the launch of Asha Parekh's biography *The Hit Girl*, he stated openly that he would never write an autobiography saying, 'Dharam uncle would know what I mean!' A hearty laugh followed, and Dharmendra, himself present in the audience, echoed it.

The similarities between the two actors are indeed amazing. Both have been underrated talents, have faced severe crises in their careers and risen like phoenixes, and have been known to wear their hearts on their sleeves. With emotions ruling them even to the point of being betrayed, manipulated or used by numerous associates, what has brought both of them so far in their journeys is their undying love for their profession, their innate natures, and as a result, the unshakeable faith and affection of fans. So paradoxically, *both* have lived life on their own terms.

As Dharmendra once said in an NDTV interview, 'Salman reminds me of myself. I was almost like him in my early days. I like his attitude and the way he leads his life. He has a great body too.' So we need not even add that while they both represent machismo to the fairer sex, they are equally well looked upon as ideal brothers, sons and close friends by men and women of diverse ages!

We mention this here only to pinpoint the fact that when someone loves life and all its aspects so much, it is perhaps understandable that they make a few professional mistakes along the way. Salman Khan's father Salim Khan has said elsewhere in this book that Dharmendra is made of durable stuff. The same is also true of his son, with whom the senior actor shares a very deep and personal bond. 'Salman is like me, he always responds to his heart's calling,' he told me once when the topic of Khan's home production in which Dharmendra starred—*Pyaar Kiya To Darna Kya*—had come up.

As Sonakshi Sinha told me on the eve of *Yamla…* 's release, 'To be even thought of for a song by Dharamji was such a complete honour that I cancelled everything I had planned, to accommodate his shoot. I was just told by Salman Khan, "Let's do a song for Dharamji." And he added, "What's your dad doing? Call him also na!" We decided even the costumes just a day earlier!'

To sum up, if the biggest superstar of today, Salman Khan, considers Dharmendra as *his* biggest superstar and idol, it means something—something special.

As Dharmendra's own poem goes:

Chahat hi boyi hai jo ab kat rahi hai
Shohorat chali jaati hai chahat nahin.

I have sowed the seeds of love, which are now being reaped
Fame is ephemeral, but love is forever.

And Dharmendra is forever.

Bibliography

The Man Who Spoke in Pictures: Bimal Roy, Ed. by Rinki Roy Bhattacharya, Penguin Books

Bollywood Box-Office Blog

Baatein Kahi Ankahi, RJ Anmol on YouTube

Hema Malini: Beyond the Dream Girl, Ram Kamal Mukherjee, HarperCollins India

Deccan Chronicle, 2018, Reena Kapoor

Deccan Herald, Rajiv Vijayakar

Dharmendra Walks Down Memory Lane, Vimal Sumbly & Loveleen Bains, *Ludhiana Tribune*, 4 January 2002

DNA, 2011, Prachi Kadam

Filmfare—Meet the Shy Hero, 28 October 1966 and other articles by Arjun Dev Rashk, N.V. Gopalakrishnan and K.N. Subramaniam

India-West (USA), Rajiv Vijayakar

Meena Kumari: The Classic Biography, Vinod Mehta, HarperCollins India

Mid-Day, 2017, Anupriya Verma

NDTV.com, 2018, Shruti Srivastava

Rendezvous with Simi Garewal, Star Plus

Screen, Rajiv Vijayakar

Shemaroo, Courtesy: Jai Shah

Star & Style, Bharathi S. Pradhan

Ten Years with Guru Dutt: Abrar Alvi's Journey, Sathya Saran

The Hindu, 2015

The Telegraph, 2013, Karishma Upadhyay

The Times of India, 2009 & 2017

The World of Hrishikesh Mukherjee, Jai Arjun Singh, Penguin India

Yaadein, Farrukh Viqar on YouTube

Films of Dharmendra

Badal jaaye agar maali / Chaman hota nahin khaali /
Baharen phir bhi aati hain / Baharen phir bhi aayengi

1960s

Dil Bhi Tera Hum Bhi Tere (1960) – Ashok (as Dharminder)
Director: A. Hingo
Music: Kalyanji-Anandji
Opposite: Kum Kum
Co-starring: Balraj Sahni, Usha Kiron

Boy Friend (1961) – Inspector Sunil Singh (as Dharminder)
Director: Naresh Saigal
Music: Shankar-Jaikishan
Co-starring: Shammi Kapoor, Madhubala

Shola Aur Shabnam (1961)** – Bunnu
Director: Ramesh Saigal
Music: Khayyam
Opposite: Tarla Mehta
Co-starring: M. Rajan

Keys:
*Success
**Hit
***Superhit
Unmarked films were flops
Home productions have titles in **bold**

Soorat Aur Seerat (1962)
Director: Rajnish Bahl
Music: Roshan
Opposite: Nutan

Anpadh (1962)** – Deepak M. Nath
Director: Mohan Kumar
Music: Madan Mohan
Opposite: Mala Sinha
Co-starring: Balraj Sahni

Shaadi (1962)* – Ramesh R. Malhotra (as Dharmindera)
Director: Krishnan-Panju
Music: Chitragupta
Opposite: Indrani Mukherjee
Co-starring: Saira Banu, Manoj Kumar, Balraj Sahni

Bandini (1963)* – Devendra
Director: Bimal Roy
Music: S.D. Burman
Opposite: Nutan
Co-starring: Ashok Kumar

Begaana (1963)
Director: Sadashiv Row Kavi
Music: Sapan-Jagmohan
Opposite: Supriya Choudhury
Co-starring: Shailesh Kumar

Pooja Ke Phool (1964) – Balraj 'Raj'
Director: A. Bhimsingh
Music: Madan Mohan
Opposite: Mala Sinha
Co-starring: Ashok Kumar, Nimmi, Sandhya Roy

Mera Qasoor Kya Hai (1964)* – Vijay
Director: Krishnan-Panju
Music: Chitragupta
Opposite: Nanda

Haqeeqat (1964)* – Captain Bahadur Singh
Director: Chetan Anand
Music: Madan Mohan
Opposite: Priya Rajvansh
Co-starring: Balraj Sahni, Sanjay Khan, Jayant

Ganga Ki Lahren (1964) – Ashok
Director: Devi Sharma
Music: Chitragupta
Opposite: Savitri
Co-starring: Kishore Kumar, Kum Kum

Ayee Milan Ki Bela (1964)*** – Ranjit (as Dharminder)
Director: Mohan Kumar
Music: Shankar-Jaikishan
Opposite: Saira Banu
Co-starring: Rajendra Kumar

Aap Ki Parchhaiyan (1964)** – Chandramohan Chopra
Director: Mohan Kumar
Music: Madan Mohan
Opposite: Supriya Choudhury

Main Bhi Ladki Hoon (1964)* – Ram
Director: A.C. Trilokchander
Music: Chitragupta
Opposite: Meena Kumari
Co-starring: Balraj Sahni

Purnima (1965)* – Prakash
Director: Narendra Suri

Music: Kalyanji-Anandji
Opposite: Meena Kumari
Co-starring: Anita Guha

Neela Aakash (1965)** – Aakash
Director: Rajendra Bhatia
Music: Madan Mohan
Opposite: Mala Sinha

Kaajal (1965) *** – Rajesh
Director: Ram Maheswari
Music: Ravi
Opposite: Padmini
Co-starring: Raaj Kumari, Meena Kumari

Chand Aur Suraj (1965) – Surajprakash
Director: Dulal Guha
Music: Salil Chowdhury
Opposite: Tanuja
Co-starring: Ashok Kumar, Nirupa Roy

Akashdeep (1965)* – Tarun
Director: Phani Majumdar
Music: Chitragupta
Opposite: Nanda
Co-starring: Ashok Kumar, Nimmi

Phool Aur Patthar (1966)*** – Shaaka
Director: O.P. Ralhan
Music: Ravi
Opposite: Meena Kumari, Shashikala

Mohabbat Zindagi Hai (1966) – Amar
Director: Jagdish Nirula
Music: O.P. Nayyar
Opposite: Rajshree

Mamta (1966)* – Barrister Indraneel
Director: Asit Sen
Music: Roshan
Opposite: Suchitra Sen
Co-starring: Ashok Kumar

Dil Ne Phir Yaad Kiya (1966)** – Ashok
Director: C.L. Rawal
Music: Sonik-Omi
Opposite: Nutan
Co-starring: Rehman

Devar (1966)** – Shankar J. Rai
Director: Mohan Segal
Music: Roshan
Opposite: Sharmila Tagore and Shashikala
Co-starring: Deven Verma

Baharen Phir Bhi Aayengi (1966) – Jiten Gupta
Director: Shahid Lateef
Music: O.P. Nayyar
Opposite: Mala Sinha, Tanuja
Co-starring: Rehman

Anupama (1966)** – Ashok
Director: Hrishikesh Mukherjee
Music: Hemant Kumar
Opposite: Sharmila Tagore

Aaye Din Bahaar Ke (1966)*** – Ravi
Director: Raghunath Jhalani
Music: Laxmikant-Pyarelal
Opposite: Asha Parekh and Nazima

Paari (1966)** (Bengali Film) – Ghanashyam
Director: Jagannath Chaterjee

Music: Salil Choudhury
Opposite: Pranoti Bhattacharya (Ghosh)
Co-starring: Dilip Kumar, Abhi Bhattacharya

Majhli Didi (1967) – Bipinchandra
Director: Hrishikesh Mukherjee
Music: Hemant Kumar
Opposite: Meena Kumari

Jab Yaad Kisi Ki Aati Hai (1967)
Director: Naresh Saigal
Music: Madan Mohan
Opposite: Mala Sinha (double role)

Ghar Ka Chirag (1967) (guest appearance)
Director: Jagdev Bhambri
Music: Madan Mohan
Co-starring: Indrani Mukherjee, Dev Kumar, Waheeda Rehman, Biswajeet

Dulhan Ek Raat Ki (1967) – Ashok
Director: D.D. Kashyap
Music: Madan Mohan
Opposite: Nutan
Co-starring: Rehman

Chandan Ka Palna (1967) – Ajit
Director: Ismail Memon
Music: R.D. Burman
Opposite: Meena Kumari
Co-starring: Mumtaz

Shikar (1968)*** – Ajay Singh
Director: Atma Ram
Music: Shankar-Jaikishan
Opposite: Asha Parekh
Co-starring: Sanjeev Kumar

Mere Humdum Mere Dost (1968)** – Sunil
Director: Amar Kumar
Music: Laxmikant-Pyarelal
Opposite: Sharmila Tagore
Co-starring: Mumtaz

Izzat (1968)* – Shekhar/Dilip P. Singh (double role)
Director: T. Prakash Rao
Music: Laxmikant-Pyarelal
Opposite: Tanuja and Jayalalitha

Baharon Ki Manzil (1968) – Dr Rajesh Khanna
Director: Yakub Hasan Rizvi
Music: Laxmikant-Pyarelal
Opposite: Meena Kumari
Co-starring: Rehman

Baazi (1968) – Ajay
Director: Moni Bhattacharya
Music: Kalyanji-Anandji
Opposite: Waheeda Rehman

Ankhen (1968)*** – Sunil
Director: Ramanand Sagar
Music: Ravi
Opposite: Mala Sinha
Co-starring: Kum Kum

Yakeen (1969)* – Rajesh/Garson (double role)
Director: Brij
Music: Shankar-Jaikishan
Opposite: Sharmila Tagore

Satyakam (1969) – Satyapriya
Director: Hrishikesh Mukherjee
Music: Laxmikant-Pyarelal

Opposite: Sharmila Tagore
Co-starring: Ashok Kumar, Sanjeev Kumar

Pyar Hi Pyar (1969) – Vijay Pratap
Director: Bhappi Sonie
Music: Shankar-Jaikishan
Opposite: Vyjayanthimala
Co-starring: Shatrughan Sinha (cameo)

Khamoshi (1969) – Mr Dev (guest appearance)
Director: Asit Sen
Music: Hemant Kumar
Opposite: Waheeda Rehman
Co-starring: Rajesh Khanna

Aya Sawan Jhoom Ke (1969)** – Jaishankar
Director: Raghunath Jhalani
Music: Laxmikant-Pyarelal
Opposite: Asha Parekh

Aadmi Aur Insaan (1969) – Munish Mehra
Director: Yash Chopra
Music: Ravi
Opposite: Saira Banu and Mumtaz
Co-starring: Feroz Khan

1970s

Man Ki Aankhen (1970) – Rajesh Agarwal
Director: Raghunath Jhalani
Music: Laxmikant-Pyarelal
Opposite: Waheeda Rehman

Tum Haseen Main Jawaan (1970)*** – Sunil
Director: Bhappi Sonie
Music: Shankar-Jaikishan
Opposite: Hema Malini

Sharafat (1970)*** – Rajesh
Director: Asit Sen
Music: Laxmikant-Pyarelal
Opposite: Hema Malini

Mera Naam Joker (1970) – Mahender
Director: Raj Kapoor
Music: Shankar-Jaikishan
Opposite: Kseniya Ryabinkina
Co-starring: Raj Kapoor, Manoj Kumar, Rajendra Kumar, Dara Singh, Rishi
Kapoor, Padmini, Simi Garewal

Kankan De Ohle (1970/Punjabi) – Banta Singh
Director: Omi Bedi
Music: Sapan-Jagmohan
Co-starring: Ravindra Kapoor, Indira, Asha Parekh

Kab? Kyoon? Aur Kahan? (1970)** – CID Inspector Anand
Director: Arjun Hingorani
Music: Kalyanji-Anandji
Opposite: Babita

Ishq Par Zor Nahin (1970)
Director: Ramesh Saigal
Music: S.D. Burman
Opposite: Sadhana
Co-starring: Biswajeet

Jeevan Mrityu (1970) *** – Ashok Tandon/Bikram Singh
Director: Satyen Bose
Music: Laxmikant-Pyarelal
Opposite: Raakhee

Jeevitha Samaram (1971) Malayalam dubbed version of *Jeevan Mrityu*

Rakhwala (1971)* – Deepak
Director: A. Subba Rao
Music: Kalyanji-Anandji
Opposite: Leena Chandavarkar
Co-starring: Vinod Khanna

Naya Zamana (1971)*** – Anoop
Director: Pramod Chakravorty
Music: S.D. Burman
Opposite: Hema Malini

Mera Gaon Mera Desh (1971)*** – Ajit
Director: Raj Khosla
Music: Laxmikant-Pyarelal
Opposite: Asha Parekh
Co-starring: Vinod Khanna, Laxmi Chhaya

Guddi (1971)* – Dharmendra (as himself)
Director: Hrishikesh Mukherjee
Music: Vasant Desai
Opposite: Jaya Bhaduri (Jaya Bachchan)
Co-starring: Samit Bhanja, Sumita Sanyal

Seeta Aur Geeta (1972)*** – Raka
Director: Ramesh Sippy
Music: R.D. Burman
Opposite: Hema Malini
Co-starring: Sanjeev Kumar

Samadhi (1972)* – Lakhan Singh/Ajay (double role/father and son)
Director: Prakash Mehra
Music: R.D. Burman
Opposite: Asha Parekh and Jaya Bhaduri (Bachchan)

Raja Jani (1972)*** – Rajkumar Singh
Director: Mohan Segal

Music: Laxmikant-Pyarelal
Opposite: Hema Malini

Lalkar (1972) – Major Ram Kapoor
Director: Ramanand Sagar
Music: Kalyanji-Anandji
Opposite: Mala Sinha and Kum Kum
Co-starring: Rajendra Kumar

Anokha Milan (1972) – Ghanshyam
Director: Jagannath Chaterjee
Music: Salil Choudhury
Opposite: Pranoti Bhattacharya (Ghosh)
Co-starring: Dilip Kumar, Abhi Bhattacharya

Piya Ka Ghar (1972)* – (guest appearance as himself)
Director: Basu Chatterjee

Do Chor (1972)* – Tony
Director: Padmanabh
Music: R.D. Burman
Opposite: Tanuja

Loafer (1973)*** – Ranjit
Director: A. Bhimsingh
Music: Laxmikant-Pyarelal
Opposite: Mumtaz
Co-starring: Anil Dhawan

Keemat (1973)* – Mr Gopal (Agent 116)
Director: Ravee Nagaich
Music: Laxmikant-Pyarelal
Opposite: Rekha

Yaadon Ki Baaraat (1973)*** – Shankar
Director: Nasir Hussain

Music: R.D. Burman
Co-starring: Zeenat Aman, Vijay Arora, Tariq, Neetu Singh (cameo), Aamir Khan (child artiste)

Phagun (1s3) – Gopal
Director: Rajinder Singh Bedi
Music: S.D. Burman
Opposite: Waheeda Rehman
Co-starring: Vijay Arora, Jaya Bhaduri (Bachchan)

Kahani Kismat Ki (1973)*** – Ajit Sharma
Director: Arjun Hingorani
Music: Kalyanji-Anandji
Opposite: Rekha

Jugnu (1973)*** – Ashok/Jugnu
Director: Pramod Chakravorty
Music: S.D. Burman
Opposite: Hema Malini

Blackmail (1973) – Kailash Gupta
Director: Vijay Anand
Music: Kalyanji-Anandji
Opposite: Raakhee
Co-starring: Shatrughan Sinha

Jheel Ke Us Paar (1973)* – Sameer Rai
Director: Bhappi Sonie
Music: R.D. Burman
Opposite: Mumtaz and Yogeeta Bali
Co-starring: Shatrughan Sinha (cameo)

Jwar Bhata (1973)* – Balraj aka Billo
Director: A. Subba Rao
Music: Laxmikant-Pyarelal
Opposite: Saira Banu

Resham Ki Dori (1974)* – Ajit Singh
Director: Atma Ram
Music: Shankar-Jaikishan
Opposite: Saira Banu

Patthar Aur Payal (1974)** – Ranjeet Singh
Director: Harmesh Malhotra
Music: Kalyanji-Anandji
Opposite: Hema Malini
Co-starring: Vinod Khanna

Pocketmaar (1974) – Shankar
Director: Ramesh Lakhanpal
Music: Laxmikant-Pyarelal
Opposite: Saira Banu

Dukh Bhanjan Tera Naam (1974/Punjabi)** – (guest appearance)

Do Sher (1974) – (guest appearance)

Kunwara Baap (1974)** – (guest appearance)
Opposite: Hema Malini

The Gold Medal (1974) – Acharya (guest appearance)
Director: Ravee Nagaich
Music: Shankar-Jaikishan
Co-starring: Jeetendra, Shatrughan Sinha, Raakhee

Dost (1974)*** – Manav
Director: Dulal Guha
Music: Laxmikant-Pyarelal
Opposite: Hema Malini
Co-starring: Shatrughan Sinha, Amitabh Bachchan (cameo)

International Crook (1974) – Shekhar
Director: Pachhi

Music: Shankar-Jaikishan
Opposite: Saira Banu
Co-starring: Feroz Khan

Teri Meri Ik Jindri (1975) – (guest appearance)

Saazish (1975) – Jaideep
Director: Kalidas
Music: Shankar-Jaikishan
Opposite: Saira Banu

Pratiggya (1975) *** – Ajit Singh
Director: Dulal Guha
Music: Laxmikant-Pyarelal
Opposite: Hema Malini

Ek Mahal Ho Sapno Ka (1975) – Vishal
Director: Devendra Goel
Music: Ravi
Opposite: Sharmila Tagore and Leena Chandavarkar

Dhoti Lota Aur Chowpatty (1975) – (guest appearance)

Chupke Chupke (1975) ** – Dr Parimal Tripathi aka Pyare Mohan
Director: Hrishikesh Mukherjee
Music: S.D. Burman
Opposite: Sharmila Tagore
Co-starring: Amitabh Bachchan, Jaya Bhaduri (Bachchan)

Chaitali (1975) – Manish
Director: Hrishikesh Mukherjee
Music: Laxmikant-Pyarelal
Opposite: Saira Banu

Apne Dushman (1975) – Brijesh
Director: Kailash Bhandari

Music: Kalyanji-Anandji
Co-starring: Reena Roy, Sanjeev Kumar

Sholay (1975) *** – Veeru
Director: Ramesh Sippy
Music: R.D. Burman
Opposite: Hema Malini
Co-starring: Sanjeev Kumar, Amitabh Bachchan, Jaya Bhaduri (Bachchan)

Kahtey Hain Mujhko Raja (1976) – (guest appearance)
Director: Biswajeet
Music: R.D. Burman
Opposite: Hema Malini
Co-starring: Biswajeet, Rekha, Shatrughan Sinha

Santo Banto (1976/Punjabi) – (guest appearance)

Chhoti Si Baat (1976) ** – (guest appearance as himself)
Director: Basu Chatterjee
Music: Salil Choudhury
Opposite: Hema Malini

Charas (1976)** – Suraj Kumar
Director: Ramanand Sagar
Music: Laxmikant-Pyarelal
Opposite: Hema Malini

Tinku (1977) – (guest appearance)

Maa (1976) – Vijay
Director: M.A. Thirumugham
Music: Laxmikant-Pyarelal
Opposite: Hema Malini

Giddha (1976) – (guest appearance)

Barood (1976) – (guest appearance)
Opposite: Hema Malini

Swami (1977)** – (guest appearance)
Opposite: Hema Malini

Kinara (1977) – Chandan Arya (guest appearance)
Director: Gulzar
Music: R.D. Burman
Opposite: Hema Malini
Co-starring: Jeetendra

Khel Khiladi Ka (1977) – Shaki Lutera aka Raja Saab aka Ajit
Director: Arjun Hingorani
Music: Kalyanji-Anandji
Opposite: Hema Malini
Co-starring: Shabana Azmi, Dhruv

Dream Girl (1977)* – Anupam Verma
Director: Pramod Chakravorty
Music: Laxmikant-Pyarelal
Opposite: Hema Malini

Do Chehere (1977) – (guest appearance)

Dharam Veer (1977)*** – Dharam Singh
Director: Manmohan Desai
Music: Laxmikant-Pyarelal
Opposite: Zeenat Aman
Co-starring: Jeetendra, Neetu Singh

Charandas (1977) – (guest appearance)

Chala Murari Hero Banne (1977) – (guest appearance)

Chacha Bhatija (1977)*** – Shankar
Director: Manmohan Desai
Music: Laxmikant-Pyarelal
Opposite: Hema Malini
Co-starring: Randhir Kapoor, Yogeeta Bali

Shalimar/The Deadly Thief (1978/Hindi and English) – S.S. Kumar
(English version of DVD released as *Raiders of the Sacred Stone*)
Director: Krishna Shah
Music: R.D. Burman
Opposite: Zeenat Aman
Co-starring: Shammi Kapoor, Rex Harrison, John Saxon, Sylvia Miles

Phandebaaz (1978) – Rajkumar Kakkad/Rana Shantidas (double role)
Director: Samir Ganguly
Music: R.D. Burman
Opposite: Moushumi Chatterjee
Co-starring: Hema Malini (cameo as herself)

Dillagi (1978) – Swarnakamal
Director: Basu Chaterjee
Music: Rajesh Roshan
Opposite: Hema Malini
Co-starring: Mithu Mukherjee, Shatrughan Sinha

Azaad (1978)** – Ashok (Azaad)
Director: Pramod Chakravorty
Music: R.D. Burman
Opposite: Hema Malini
Co-starring: Shoma Anand

Pati Patni Aur Woh (1978)** (guest appearance)
Opposite: Hema Malini

Dil Kaa Heera (1979)* – Rajat Sharma
Director: Dulal Guha

Music: Laxmikant-Pyarelal
Opposite: Hema Malini
Co-starring: Sachin

Kartavya (1979)* – Vijay Rai
Director: Mohan Segal
Music: Laxmikant-Pyarelal
Opposite: Rekha
Co-starring: Vinod Mehra

1980s

Chunauti (1980) – Shakti Singh (guest appearance)
Director: Satpal
Music: Laxmikant-Pyarelal
Co-starring: Feroz Khan, Neetu Singh

Ram Balram (1980) – Ram
Director: Vijay Anand
Music: Laxmikant-Pyarelal
Opposite: Zeenat Aman
Co-starring: Amitabh Bachchan, Rekha

The Burning Train (1980) – Ashok Singh
Director: Ravi Chopra
Music: R.D. Burman
Opposite: Hema Malini
Co-starring: Parveen Babi, Neetu Singh, Asha Sachdev, Padmini Kapilla, Jeetendra, Vinod Khanna, Navin Nischol, Vinod Mehra

Alibaba Aur 40 Chor (1980/Hindi and Russian) * – Alibaba
Director: Umesh Mehra and Latif Faiziev Music: R.D. Burman
Opposite: Hema Malini
Co-starring: Zeenat Aman

Insaf Ka Tarazu (1980)*** – (guest appearance)

Putt Jattan De (1981) – Chaudhary Dharam Singh

Professor Pyarelal (1981) – Ram aka Professor Pyarelal
Director: Brij
Music: Kalyanji-Anandji
Opposite: Zeenat Aman
Co-starring: Shammi Kapoor, Yogeeta Bali

Krodhi (1981) – Vikramjit Singh aka Acharya Shradhanand
Director: Subhash Ghai
Music: Laxmikant-Pyarelal
Opposite: Hema Malini and Moushumi Chatterjee
Co-starring: Shashi Kapoor, Zeenat Aman, Sachin, Ranjeeta

Kaatilon Ke Kaatil (1981)* – Ajit aka Badshah
Director: Arjun Hingorani
Music: Kalyanji-Anandji
Opposite: Zeenat Aman
Co-starring: Rishi Kapoor, Tina Munim

Aas Paas (1981) – Arun Choudhury
Director: J. Om Prakash
Music: Laxmikant-Pyarelal
Opposite: Hema Malini

Naseeb (1981)*** – (guest appearance as himself)

Teesri Aankh (1982)
Director: Subodh Mukerji
Music: Laxmikant-Pyarelal
Opposite: Zeenat Aman
Co-starring: Shatrughan Sinha, Neetu Singh, Rakesh Roshan, Sarika

Samraat (1982) – Ram
Director: Mohan Segal
Music: Laxmikant-Pyarelal

Opposite: Hema Malini
Co-starring: Jeetendra, Zeenat Aman

Main Intequam Loonga (1982) – Kumar Agnihotri 'Bitto'
Director: T. Rama Rao
Music: Laxmikant-Pyarelal
Opposite: Reena Roy

*Ghazab** (1982) – Ajay Singh or Munna/Vijay Singh (double role)
Director: C.P. Dixit
Music: Laxmikant-Pyarelal
Opposite: Rekha

Do Dishayen (1982)
Director: Dulal Guha
Music: Laxmikant-Pyarelal
Opposite: Hema Malini

Baghawat (1982) – Sandeep Kumar Rohilla
Director: Ramanand Sagar
Music: Laxmikant-Pyarelal
Opposite: Hema Malini, Reena Roy

Badle Ki Aag (1982) – Sher Singh 'Shera'
Director: Rajkumar Kohli
Music: Laxmikant-Pyarelal
Opposite: Reena Roy and Smita Patil
Co-starring: Jeetendra, Sunil Dutt, Sarika

Rajput (1982) – Manu Pratap Singh
Director: Vijay Anand
Music: Laxmiknat-Pyarelal
Opposite: Hema Malini
Co-starring: Rajesh Khanna, Vinod Khanna, Ranjeeta, Tina Munim

Meherbaani (1982) – (guest appearance)
Directed by: Kanwar Ajit Singh and A. Nairang

Music: Ravindra Jain
Opposite: Hema Malini (guest appearance)
Co-starring: Mahendra Sandhu, Sarika

Betaab*** (1983) (**Only as presenter in home production**)
Director: Rahul Rawail
Music: R.D. Burman
Starring: Shammi Kapoor, Sunny Deol, Amrita Singh

Ambri (1983) – Dharam Singh (guest appearance)

Razia Sultan (1983) – Yakut Jamaluddin
Director: Kamal Amrohi
Music: Khayyam
Opposite: Hema Malini
Co-starring: Parveen Babi, Sarika

Naukar Biwi Ka*(1983) – Deepak Kumar/Raja
Director: Rajkumar Kohli
Music: Bappi Lahiri
Opposite: Reena Roy, Anita Raj
Co-starring: Raj Babbar

Jaani Dost (1983) – Raju
Director: K. Raghavendra Rao
Music: Bappi Lahiri
Opposite: Parveen Babi
Co-starring: Jeetendra, Sridevi

Andhaa Kanoon (1983)*** – (guest appearance)

Qayamat (1983) – Shyam aka Rajeshwar
Director: Raj Sippy
Music: R.D. Burman
Opposite: Jaya Prada, Poonam Dhillon
Co-starring: Shatrughan Sinha, Smita Patil

Sunny (1984) – Inderjeet (guest appearance)
Director: Raj Khosla
Music: R.D. Burman
Opposite: Waheeda Rehman and Sharmila Tagore
Co-starring: Sunny Deol, Amrita Singh

Raaj Tilak (1984) – Zohravar Singh
Director: Rajkumar Kohli
Music: Kalyanji-Anandji
Opposite: Hema Malini
Co-starring: Reena Roy, Yogeeta Bali, Sarika, Sunil Dutt, Raaj Kumar, Kamal Haasan, Vikram, Ranjeeta

Jeene Nahin Doonga (1984) – Shaka
Director: Rajkumar Kohli
Music: Laxmikant-Pyarelal
Opposite: Anita Raj
Co-starring: Roshni, Raj Babbar, Shatrughan Sinha

*Jagir/Teen Murti*** (1984/Hindi and Bengali) – Shankar
Director: Pramod Chakravorty
Music: R.D. Burman
Opposite: Zeenat Aman
Co-starring: Mithun Chakraborty, Shoma Anand

Dharam Aur Qanoon (1984) – Rahim Khan
Director: Joshi
Music: Kalyanji-Anandji and Raamlaxman
Opposite: Jaya Prada
Co-starring: Rajesh Khanna, Vinod Mehra, Asha Parekh

Baazi (1984) – Ajay
Director: Raj Sippy
Music: Laxmikant-Pyarelal
Opposite: Rekha
Co-starring: Ranjeeta, Mithun Chakraborty

Jhutha Sach (1984) – Vijay/Tiger
Director: Eesmayeel Shroff
Music: R.D. Burman
Opposite: Rekha

Ranjhan Mera Yaar (1984/Punjabi)

Karishma Kudrat Kaa (1985) – Vijay/Karan (double role)
Director: Sunil Hingorani
Music: Kalyanji-Anandji
Opposite: Anita Raj
Co-starring: Mithun Chakraborty

*Ghulami** (1985) – Ranjit Singh
Director: J.P. Dutta
Music: Laxmikant-Pyarelal
Opposite: Reena Roy, Smita Patil
Co-starring: Mithun Chakraborty, Naseeruddin Shah, Anita Raj

Sitamgar (1985) – Sonu/Shankar
Director: Raj N. Sippy
Music: R.D. Burman
Opposite: Parveen Babi, Poonam Dhillon
Co-starring: Rishi Kapoor

Saveray Wali Gaadi (1986/guest appearance)
Director: Bharathi Raja
Music: R.D. Burman
Co-starring: Sunny Deol, Poonam Dhillon

Mohabbat Ki Kasam (1986) – (guest appearance)

Main Balwaan (1986) – Inspector Chowdhury
Director: Mukul S. Anand
Music: Bappi Lahiri
Co-starring: Mithun Chakraborty, Meenakshi Seshadri

Begaana (1986) – (guest appearance) (**second film with this title after 1963**)
Director: Ambrish Sangal
Music: Anu Malik
Co-starring: Kumar Gairav, Rati Agnihotri, Raj Kiran

Sultanat (1986) – General Khalid
Director: Mukul S. Anand
Music: Kalyanji-Anandji
Opposite: Neeta Mehta
Co-starring: Sridevi, Sunny Deol, Karan Kapoor, Juhi Chawla

Watan Ke Rakhwale (1987) – Mahavir
Director: T. Rama Rao
Music: Laxmikant-Pyarelal
Co-starring: Sunil Dutt, Mithun Chakraborty, Moushumi Chatterjee. Divya Rana

Mera Karam Mera Dharam (1987) – Ajay Shankar Sharma
Director: Dulal Guha
Music: Laxmikant-Pyarelal
Opposite: Moushumi Chatterjee and Yogeeta Bali

Mard Ki Zabaan (1987) (guest appearance)
Director: K. Bapaiah
Music: Laxmiknat-Pyarelal
Co-starring: Jackie Shroff, Poonam Dhillon, Kimi Katkar

Insaaf Ki Pukar (1987) – Vijay
Director: T. Rama Rao
Music: Laxmikant-Pyarelal
Opposite: Anita Raj
Co-starring Jeetendra, Bhanupriya, Avinash Wadhawan

*Dadagiri** (1987) – Dharma (Dada)
Director: Deepak Shivdasani
Music: Anu Malik

Opposite: Rati Agnihotri
Co-starring: Padmini Kolhapure, Govinda

Aag Hi Aag (1987)** – Sher Singh
Director: Shibu Mitra
Music: Bappi Lahiri
Opposite: Moushumi Chatterjee
Co-starring: Shatrughan Sinha, Richa Sharma, Neelam, Chunky Pandey

Superman (1987) – Superman (guest appearance)
Director: B. Gupta
Music: Kamal Kant
Opposite: Ranjeeta
Co-starring: Ashok Kumar, Puneet Issar

*Insaniyat Ke Dushman*** (1987) – Inspector Shekhar Kapoor
Director: Rajkumar Kohli
Music: Anu Malik
Co-starring: Dimple Kapadia, Anita Raaj, Smita Patil, Shatrughan Sinha,
Raj Babbar, Sumeet Saigal

*Loha*** (1987) – Amar
Director: Raj N. Sippy
Music: Laxmikant-Pyarelal
Co-starring: Shatrughan Sinha, Karan Kapoor, Madhavai, Mandakini

*Hukumat**** (1987) – Arjun Singh
Director: Anil Sharma
Music: Laxmikant-Pyarelal
Opposite: Rati Agnihotri, Swapna
Co-starring: Shammi Kapoor

Jaan Hatheli Pe (1987) – Soni
Director: Raghunath Jhalani
Music: Laxmikant-Pyarelal
Opposite: Hema Malini
Co-starring: Jeetendra, Rekha, Raj Babbar

Insaaf Kaun Karega (1987)* – Veeru
Director: Sudarshan Nag
Music: Laxmikant-Pyarelal
Opposite: Jaya Prada
Co-starring: Shatrughan Sinha, Madhavi

Zalzala (1988) – Inspector Shiv Kumar
Director: Harish Shah
Music: R.D. Burman
Opposite: Rati Agnihotri and Anita Raaj
Co-starring: Shatrughan Sinha, Rajiv Kapoor, Kimi Katkar, Vijayeta Pandit

Soorma Bhopali (1988) – Mahendra Singh/Dharmendra himself (guest
appearance in a double role)

Sone Pe Suhaaga (1988) – Vikram/CBI Officer Ashwini Kumar
Director: K. Bapaiah
Music: Bappi Lahiri
Opposite: Poonam Dhillon
Co-starring: Nutan, Sridevi, Kimi Katkar, Jeetendra, Anil Kapoor

Khatron Ke Khiladi (1988) – Balwant
Director: T. Rama Rao
Music: Laxmikant-Pyarelal
Opposite: Anjana Mumtaz
Co-starring: Sanjay Dutt, Chunky Pandey, Madhuri Dixit, Neelam

Mardon Wali Baat (1988) – Yadvinder Singh
Director: Brij
Music: R.D. Burman
Opposite: Shabana Azmi
Co-starring: Sanjay Dutt, Jaya Prada

Mahaveera (1988) – Ajay Verma (guest appearance)
Director: Naresh Saigal
Music: Kalyanji-Anandji

Co-starring: Shatrughan Sinha, Raaj Kumar, Raj Babbar, Dimple Kapadia, Anita Raaj, Salma Agha, Vinod Mehra

Paap Ko Jalaa Kar Raakh Kar Doonga (1988) – Shankar
Director: K.R. Reddy
Music: Ravindra Jain
Opposite: Anita Raj
Co-starring: Govinda, Farha, Tanuja

Ganga Tere Desh Mein (1988) – Cobra/Vijay Nath
Director: Vijay Reddi
Music: Laxmikant-Pyarelal
Opposite: Jaya Prada
Co-starring: Shatrughan Sinha, Dimple Kapadia, Raj Babbar

Yateem (1989) (**Only as presenter in home production**)
Director: J.P. Dutta
Music: Laxmikant-Pyarelal
Starring: Sunny Deol, Farha, Sujata Mehta

Sachai Ki Taqat (1989) – Havaldar Ram Singh
Director: T. Rama Rao
Music: Laxmikant-Pyarelal
Opposite: Amrita Singh
Co-starring: Govinda, Sonam

Nafrat Ki Aandhi (1989) – Sonu
Director: Mehul Kumar
Music: Bappi Lahiri
Opposite: Anita Raaj
Co-starring: Madhavi, Jeetendra

Hathyar (1989) – Khushal Khan
Director: J.P. Dutta
Music: Laxmikant-Pyarelal
Co-starring: Rishi Kapoor, Sanjay Dutt, Amrita Singh, Sangeeta Bijlani, Asha Parekh

Kasam Suhaag Ki (1989)
Director: Mohan Segal
Music: Laxmikant-Pyarelal
Opposite: Rekha

*Ilaaka** (1989) – Inspector Dharam Verma (guest appearance)
Director: Aziz Sejawal
Music: Nadeem-Shravan
Opposite: Raakhee
Co-starring: Mithun Chakraborty, Sanjay Dutt, Amrita Singh,
Madhuri Dixit

Batwara (1989) – Sumer Singh
Director: J.P. Dutta
Music: Laxmikant-Pyarelal
Opposite: Dimple Kapadia
Co-starring: Amrita Singh, Poonam Dhillon, Asha Parekh,
Shammi Kapoor, Vinod Khanna, Mohsin Khan

*Elaan-E-Jung** (1989) – Thakur Sultan K. Singh
Director: Anil Sharma
Music: Laxmikant-Pyarelal
Opposite: Jaya Prada
Co-starring: Swapna

Sikka (1989) – Vijay
Director: K. Bapaiah
Music: Bappi Lahiri
Opposite: Moushumi Chatterjee
Co-starring: Jackie Shroff, Dimple Kapadia

Vardi (1989)* – Havaldar Bhagwan Singh (guest appearance)
Director: Umesh Mehra
Music: Anu Malik
Co-starring: Sunny Deol, Jackie Shroff, Vinod Mehra, Kimi Katkar,
Madhuri Dixit

Shehzaade (1989) – Subedar Zorawar Singh/Inspector Shankar Shrivastav (double role)
Director: Raj N. Sippy
Music: Laxmikant-Pyarelal
Opposite: Dimple Kapadia
Co-starring: Shatrughan Sinha, Moushumi Chatterjee, Kimi Katkar, Jaya Prada, Vinod Mehra

1990s

Ghayal (1990)*** (**Only as producer**)
Director: Rajkumar Santoshi
Music: Bappi Lahiri
Starring: Sunny Deol, Meenakshi Seshadri, Meenakshi Seshadri, Raj Babbar

Veeru Dada (1990) – Veeru Dada (Siddharth)
Director: K.R. Reddy
Music: Laxmikamt-Pyarelal
Opposite: Amrita Singh
Co-starring: Farha, Aditya Pancholi

Qurbani Jatt Di (1990) (guest appearance)

Pyar Ka Karz (1990) – Shekhar
Director: K. Bapaiah
Music: Laxmikant-Pyarelal
Opposite: Meenakshi Seshadri
Co-starring: Mithun Chakraborty, Neelam, Sonam, Vinod Mehra

*Naaka Bandi** (1990) – Veer Singh
Director: Shibu Mitra
Music: Bappi Lahiri
Opposite: Sridevi
Co-starring: Chunky Pandey, Sonam

Humse Na Takrana (1990) – Amar
Director: Deepak Bahry
Music: Laxmikant-Pyarelal
Opposite: Anita Raj
Co-starring: Kimi Katkar, Mithun Chakraborty, Shatrughan Sinha

Trinetra (1991) – Raja
Director: Harry Baweja
Music: Anand-Milind
Opposite: Deepa Sahi
Co-starring: Mithun Chakraborty, Shilpa Shirodkar

Mast Kalandar (1991)
Director: Rahul Rawail
Music: Laxmikant-Pyarelal
Opposite: Dimple Kapadia
Co-starring: Shammi Kapoor

Kohraam (1991)
Director: Kuku Kohli
Music: Bappi Lahiri
Co-starring: Sonam, Chunky Pandey, Vinod Mehra

Farishtay (1991) – Veeru
Director: Anil Sharma
Music: Bappi Lahiri
Opposite: Jaya Prada
Co-starring: Sridevi, Swapna, Rajinikanth, Vinod Khanna

Paap Ki Aandhi (1991) – Dharma/Mangal (double role)
Director: Mehul Kumar
Music: Laxmikant-Pyarelal
Opposite: Anjana Mumtaz
Co-starring: Aditya Pancholi, Farha, Amrita Singh

Dushman Devta (1991) – Shiva
Director: Anil Ganguly
Music: Bappi Lahiri
Opposite: Dimple Kapadia
Co-starring: Aditya Pancholi, Sonam

Zulm Ki Hukumat (1992) – Pitamber Kohli
Director: Bharat Rangachary
Music: Dilip Sen-Sameer Sen
Opposite: Moushumi Chatterjee
Co-starring: Govinda, Kimi Katkar

Waqt Ka Badshah (1992) – (guest appearance)

*Tahalka** (1992)
Director: Anil Sharma
Music: Anu Malik
Opposite: Sudha Chandran
Co-starring: Sonu Walia, Ektaa, Pallavi Joshi, Shammi Kapoor, Aditya
Pancholi, Naseeruddin Shah

Virodhi (1992) – Inspector Shekhar
Director: Rajkumar Kohli
Music: Anu Malik
Opposite: Anita Raj
Co-starring: Armaan Kohli, Harshaa, Sunil Dutt, Poonam Dhillon

Khule-Aam (1992) – Shiva
Director: Arun Dutt
Music: R.D. Burman
Opposite: Moushumi Chatterjee
Co-starring: Chunky Pandey, Neelam, Shammi Kapoor

Humlaa (1992) – Bhawani
Director: N. Chandra
Music: Laxmikant-Pyarelal
Opposite: Kimi Katkar

Co-starring: Anil Kapoor, Meenakshi Seshadri

Kal Ki Awaz (1992)
Director: B.R. Chopra and Ravi Chopra
Music: Nadeem-Shravan
Co-starring: Amrita Singh, Raj Babbar, Rohit, Pratibha

Aag Ka Toofan (1993) (guest appearance with top billing)
Director: Kanti Shah
Music: Bappi Lahiri
Co-starring: Ravi Kishan, Farheen

Kundan (1993)
Director: K.C. Bokadia
Music: Bappi Lahiri
Opposite: Jaya Prada
Co-starring: Farha

Kshatriya (1993) (* in some centres) – Maharaj Prithvi Singh
Director: J.P. Dutta
Music: Laxmikant-Pyarelal
Opposite: Sumalatha
Co-starring: Sunil Dutt, Vinod Khanna, Sunny Deol, Sanjay Dutt, Raakhee,
Meenakshi Seshadri, Raveenda Tandon, Divya Bharati, Nafisa Ali Sodhi

Maha Shaktishaali (1994)
Director: K. Pappu
Music: Anand-Milind
Opposite: Sonu Walia
Co-starring: Ayesha Jhulka, Avinash Wadhawan, Pankaj Berry,
Sujata Mehta

Juaari (1994) – Inspector Dharam Singh
Director: Jagdish A. Sharma
Music: Bappi Lahiri
Co-starring: Armaan Kohli, Shilpa Shirodkar

Policewala Gunda (1995) – A.C.P. Ajit Singh
Director: Pappu Verma
Music: Bappi Lahiri
Opposite: Reena Roy
Co-starring: Jay Mehta, Mamta Kulkarni

Maidan-E-Jung (1995) – Shankar
Director: K.C. Bokadia
Music: Bappi Lahiri
Opposite: Jaya Prada
Co-starring: Manoj Kumar, Akshay Kumar, Karishma Kapoor

Barsaat * (1995) (Only as producer)
Director: Rajkumar Santoshi
Music: Nadeem-Shravan
Starring: Bobby Deol, Twinkle Khanna, Raj Babbar

Aazmayish (1995) – Shanker Singh Rathod
Director: Sachin
Music: Anand-Milind
Opposite: Sripadha
Co-starring: Rohit Kumar, Anjali Jathar

Taaqat (1995) – Shakti Singh
Director: Talat Jani
Music: Anand-Milind
Co-starring: Shatrughan Sinha, Farha, Kajol, Vikas Bhalla

Hum Sab Chor Hain (1995)
Director: Ambrish Sangal
Music: Bappi Lahiri
Co-starring: Jeetendra, Kamal Sadanah, Ritu Shivpuri

Fauji (1995)
Director: Lawrence D'Souza
Music: Vishal Bhardwaj

Opposite: Sonu Walia
Co-starring: Raj Babbar, Farha

Veer (1995) – Veeru Bhaiya

Smuggler (1996)
Director: Ajay Kashyap
Music: Bappi Lahiri
Opposite: Reena Roy
Co-starring: Ayub Khan, Eva Grover

Return of Jewel Thief (1996) – Police Commissioner Surya Dev Singh
Director: Ashok Tyagi
Music: Jatin-Lalit
Co-starring: Ashok Kumar, Dev Anand, Jackie Shroff, Anu Agarwal,
Madhoo, Shilpa Shirodkar

Himmatvar (1996) – Sultan
Director: Talat Jani
Music: Nadeem-Shravan
Co-starring: Hitesh, Rubaina Khan

Aatank (1996) – Jesu
Director: Desh Mukherjee and Prem Lalwani
Music: Laxmikant-Pyarelal
Opposite: Hema Malini
Co-starring: Vinod Mehra, Nafisa Ali

Mafia (1996) – Fauji Ajit Singh
Director: Aziz Sejawal
Music: Anand-Milind
Co-starring: Somy Ali, Aditya Pancholi

Paappi Devataa (1996)
Director: Harmesh Malhotra
Music: Laxmikant-Pyarelal

Opposite: Jaya Prada
Co-star: Jeetendra, Madhuri Dixit

Loha (1997) – Shankar (**second film with this title after 1987**)
Director: Kanti Shah
Music: Tabun
Co-starring: Mithun Chakraborty, Ramya Krishnan,
Special appearance: Govinda, Manisha Koirala

Agnee Morcha (1997)
Director: Raju Chutani
Music: Shyam-Surender
Co-starring: Ravi Kissen, Simran

Jeo Shaan Se (1997) – Brahma/Vishnu/Mahesh (triple role)
Director: Talat Jani
Music: Shyam-Surender
Opposite: Reena Roy, Neena Gupta and Navneet Nishan
Co-starring: Jay Mehta, Sheeba, Monica Bedi, Vikas Bhalla, Saakshi
Shivanad, Ayub Khan

Gundagardi (1997)
Director: V. Sai Prasad
Music: Jatin-Lalit
Co-starring: Raj Babbar, Vijaya Shanthi, Simran, Ayub Khan, Aditya
Pancholi

Dharma Karma (1997) – Dharma
Director: Ravi Varma
Music: Bappi Lahiri
Co-starring: Jeetendra, Rahul Roy, Eva Grover, Rohit Kumar, Trishna

Hamaara Faisla (1998)
Director: Jitendra Johri
Co-starring: Ravi Kissen

Barsaat Ki Raat (1998) (guest appearance)

*Pyaar Kiya To Darna Kya*** (1998) – Thakur Ajay Singh
Director: Sohail Khan
Music: Jatin-Lalit, Himesh Reshammiya and Sajid-Wajid
Co-starring: Salman Khan, Arbaaz Khan, Kajol, Anjala Zaveri

Zulm-O-Sitam (1998) – Superintendent Arun
Director: K.C. Bokadia
Music: Aadesh Shrivastava and Nikhil-Vinay
Opposite: Jaya Prada
Co-starring: Shatrughan Sinha, Madhoo, Arjun Sarja

Dillagi (Only as presenter in home production)
Director: Sunny Deol
Music: Anand-Milind, Jatin-Lalit, Sukhwinder Singh and
Shankar-Ehsaan-Loy
Starring: Sunny Deol, Bobby Deol, Urmila Matondkar, Preity Zinta
(guest apprearance)

Nyaydaata (1999) – DCP Ram
Director: Vicky Ranawat
Music: Shyam-Surender
Opposite: Jaya Prada
Co-starring: Siddharth Dhawan, Ritu Shivpuri, Eva Grover

Loh Purush (1999)
Director: Hersh Kinnu
Music: Dilip Sen-Sameer Sen
Opposite: Jaya Prada
Co-starring: Rohit Kumar, Monica Bedi

Munnibai (1999)
Director: Kanti Shah
Music: Sawan Kumar Sawan
Co-starring: Sapna, Durgesh Nandini

2000s

Sultaan (2000) – Sultan Singh
Director: T.L.V. Prasad
Music: Aadesh Shrivastava
Co-starring: Mithun Chakraborty, Suvarna Mathew

Dacait (2000)
Director: Jitendra Chawda
Music: Sawan Kumar Sawan
Co-starring: Satnam Kaur, Prithvi

Meri Jung Ka Elaan (2000) – Ajit Singh
Director: Kanti Shah
Music: Sawan Kumar Sawan
Co-starring: Sapna, Satnam Kaur

Jallad No. 1 (2000) – Shankar
Director: Kanti Shah
Music: Gulam Ali
Co-starring: Ishrat Ali, Shakti Kapoor

Bhai Thakur (2000)
Directors: Willy-Raja
Music: Navin Shivram
Co-starring: Sapna, Roma Navani, Amit Pachori

Saugandh Gita Ki (2001)
Directors: Willy-Raja
Music: Willy-Raja
Co-starring: Poonam Dasgupta, Hemant Birje

Jagira (2001)
Director: Kanti Shah
Music: Sawan Kumar Sawan
Co-starring: Hemant Birje, Pinky Chinoy

Indian (2001)* (**Only as presenter in home production**)
Director: N. Maharajan
Music: Anand Raj Anand
Starring: Sunny Deol, Shilpa Shetty, Raj Babbar

23 March 1931: Shaheed (2002) (**Only as presenter in home production**)
Director: Guddu Dhanoa
Music: Anand Raj Anand
Starring: Sunny Deol, Bobby Deol, Aishwarya Rai Bachchan, Amrita Singh

Reshma Aur Sultan (2002)
Director: S. Kumar
Music: Abhi-Raj
Co-starring: Satnam Kaur, Hemant Birje

Border Kashmir (2002) – (guest appearance)

Kaise Kahoon Ke Pyaar Hai (2003) (guest appearance)
Director: Anil Kumaar Sharma
Music: Viju Shah
Opposite: Farida Jalal
Co-starring: Amit Hingorani, Sharbani Mukerji, Sunny Deol (guest appearance)

TADA (2003) – Balraj Singh Rana
Director: Shishir Annapurna
Music: Dilip Sen-Sameer Sen
Co-starring: Sharad Kapoor, Monica Bedi

Hum Kaun Hai? (2004) – Virendra (guest appearance)
Director: Ravi Sharma Shankar
Music: Sanjoy Chowdhury
Co-starring: Amitabh Bachchan, Dimple Kapadia, Moushumi Chatterjee

Kis Kis Ki Kismat (2004) – Hasmukh Mehta
Director: Govind Menon
Music: D. Imman
Opposite: Mallika Sherawat

*Life In A ... Metro** (2007) – Amol
Director: Anurag Basu
Music: Pritam
Opposite: Nafisa Ali Sodhi
Co-starring: Kangana Ranaut, Shilpa Shetty, Sharman Joshi, Irrfan Khan,
Shiney Ahuja, Konkona Sen Sharma, Kay Kay Menon

*Apne ***(2007) – Baldev Singh Chaudhary
Director: Anil Sharma
Music: Himesh Reshammiya
Opposite: Kirron Kher
Co-starring: Sunny Deol, Bobby Deol, Shilpa Shetty, Katrina Kaif

Johnny Gaddaar (2007) – Seshadri
Director: Sriram Raghavan
Music: Shankar-Ehsaan-Loy and Daniel B. George
Opposite: Sonia Rakkar
Co-starring: Neil Nitin Mukesh, Rimi Sen

*Om Shanti Om**** (2007) – (guest appearance as himself)

Chamku (2008) – (**Only as presenter in home production**)
Director: Kabeer Kaushik
Music: Monty Sharma
Starring: Bobby Deol, Priyanka Chopra

2010s

Yamla Pagla Deewana** (2011) – Dharam Singh Dhillon (the song 'Kadd
Ke Botal' was written by Dharmendra)
Director: Samir Karnik
Music: Laxmikant-Pyarelal (re-creation), Anu Malik, RDB,

Sandesh Shandilya and Nouman Javaid
Opposite: Nafisa Ali Sodhi
Co-starring: Sunny Deol, Bobby Deol, Kulraj Randhawa,
Emma Brown Garett

Tell Me O Kkhuda (2011) – Tony Costello
Director: Hema Malini
Music: Pritam and Sajid-Wajid
Opposite: Hema Malini
Co-starring: Vinod Khanna, Rishi Kapoor, Esha Deol, Arjan Bajwa,
Special appearance: Salman Khan

Yamla Pagla Deewana 2 (2013) – Dharam Singh (also as singer in 'Aidaan
Hi Nachna')
Director: Sangeeth Sivan
Music: Sharib-Toshi and Sachin Gupta
Co-starring: Sunny Deol, Bobby Deol, Neha Sharma, Kristina Akheeva

Singh Saab the Great (2013) (guest appearance)

Double Di Trouble (2014/Punjabi)** (double role)
Director: Smeep Kang
Music: Jatinder Shah
Opposite: Poonam Dhillon
Co-starring: Gippy Grewal, Minissha Lamba, Kulraj Randhawa,
Neha Dhupia

Second-Hand Husband (2015)
Director: Smeep Kang
Music: Dr Zeus, DJ Flow, Jatinder Shah and Badshah
Opposite: Rati Agnihotri and Tina Ahuja
Co-starring: Gippy Grewal, Ravi Kissen, Geeta Basra

Yamla Pagla Deewana Phir Se (2018)
Director: Navaniat Singh
Music: Kalyanji-Anandji, Laxmikant-Pyarelal and R.D. Burman (all

re-creations), Sanjeev-Darshan, Vishal Mishra, D Soldierz and Sachet-Parampara
Co-starring: Shatrughan Sinha, Sunny Deol, Bobby Deol, Kriti Kharbanda, with cameos by Rekha, Salman Khan, Sonakshi Sinha

Forthcoming Film
***Pal Pal Dil Ke Paas* (Only as presenter in home production)**
Director: Sunny Deol
Music: Sachet-Parampara
Starring: Karan Deol, Saher Bamba

Acknowledgements

An enterprise like this book should not have been tougher than it seemed, but it was. It is, therefore, mandatory that I thank those who made it simpler en route.

I must first thank my friend Vinod Mirani, renowned trade guru in films, for putting me in touch with a few people by way of phone numbers that are not commonly available in film directories. A big thank you to Bharathi S. Pradhan for telling me some very interesting aspects of the actor, and about her own scoop regarding the Dharam-Hema wedding at that time, besides other cute (that's the best way to put it!) memories of the He-Man who is so much more than just that.

Among celebrities, I must first and foremost thank Manoj Kumar, Shatrughan Sinha and Danny Denzongpa. Manojji was not exactly in the pink of health when I met him for this book, but was restricted to the bed, smiling away and telling me so many interesting anecdotes of their joint struggles and friendship. Shatrughan Sinha took time off from his frenetic schedules to provide lovely and heartfelt insights, and my friend Luv Sinha deserves complete credit for coordinating and expediting the meeting with his father.

A special challenge was Danny Denzongpa, who was at the time living mostly in his home state of Sikkim, in a zone where even phones are not accessible. His manager Dakshesh made me wait patiently, having intimated the actor, for the day would come when he would be in Mumbai, he told me.

And it did! Thanks a lot, Dakshesh bhai! I wish more celeb managers were like you! For Danny, Shatrughan Sinha and Manoj Kumar form the closest friends Dharmendra has in the film industry.

I would really thank from the bottom of my heart two more names who spoke so well and quite extensively to enhance the picture of Dharmendra the person: Asha Parekh, despite having talked about him in her autobiography, gave me over an hour even as she was tied up in her own book's promotions, to answer specific questions. The other was writer-director Anil Sharma, whose passionate narration of what Dharmendra means to him was very gratifying and intense.

My friend Shashank Jare of Filmyug, the banner that gave Dharmendra some early superhits, helped me in meeting J. Om Prakash, Hrithik Roshan's maternal grandfather, and the founder of that banner. Omji too was unwell, but did mention some lovely tidbits about his association with the actor. Thanks, Shashank, for this.

And Putul Guha, son of Dharmendra's close associate, director Dulal Guha, and assistant to his dad on many films, even called me to his home for a scrumptious lunch, over which memories of the actor's association with the Guhas was wonderfully recounted. We had never met before, though I knew his son, journalist Aniruddha Guha, and it was Putul's brother Gautam Guha, a long-time Facebook friend, who put me in touch with him. Interestingly, I met Gautam for the first time at the end of our meeting!

Who else would rank as special? Well, for one, Sharmila Tagore, who promised to talk, and after being unavailable for quite a while (maybe a couple of months!), actually called back out of the blue and asked whether we could speak. I was waiting to take a star's interview at a studio, but the fortuitous delay ensured that we could complete a detailed conversation.

There is also Rishi Kapoor, who, on the phone, told me, 'Rajiv, I may not be able to tell you anything significant!' but ended up giving tremendous inputs, especially about Dharmendra's equation with Raj Kapoor and their meeting immediately after the Dharam-Hema marriage. They don't make narrators like you often, Rishi sir!

It was wonderful speaking to Jeetendra as well, always candid and genial, and all it took was a brief chat with his son Tusshar to arrange a nice and relaxed chat with the ever-busy supremo of the Balaji empire. Gulzar saab and Irshad Kamil also wonderfully filled in the dots to complete a compelling picture of the megastar, thirty years apart in their association with him!

As for Mahesh Bhatt saab—what do I say about him? He has never even directed Dharmendra. All he did was assist the directors of two of Dharamendra's films, but the stories he recounted, after accommodating me within a day, were so vividly told and fascinating that they were among the best I ever heard of our He-Man! Thanks a ton, Bhatt sir.

My friend Umesh Mehra, a colleague at a Shammi Kapoor event organized by the Information of Ministry and Broadcasting in New Delhi in 2011, also was ever-willing to give his perspective of his star, and has the distinction of being my 'opening batsman'—the first film industry member I talked to for my book.

I must mention my dear friend Jai Shah, Deputy General Manager, Corporate Services, Shemaroo Entertainment, who gave me very useful links on their official site to delve deeper into the actor's life.

And as always, my wife Nishika, for bearing with me during the long phase of writing this book, with some of my erratic mood swings, temper tantrums and mad hours of work. Also in the line of fire, sometimes, was my daughter Rhea, and during their visits home, my elder daughter Dr Neha and her husband, Dr Dhirajkumar.

I am ever grateful to Kapish G. Mehra, Managing Director of Rupa Publications and Shambhu Sahu, the former commissioning editor at Rupa, for giving me this opportunity to write on Hindi cinema's most enduring hero; to Rudra Narayan Sharma, who took over from Shambhu after I completed the draft, to Tanima Saha for being the sweetest copy editor I have ever had (this is my third book!); and the Rupa design team for designing the magnificently creative cover for this book.

.